CW00507591

THE CAMBRIDGE CO
MARIO VARGA!

One of the major novelists in world literatui
Vargas Llosa (b. 1936) is also one of Latin America's leading public intellectuals, a
critic of art and culture, and a playwright of distinction. This *Companion*'s chapters
chart the development of Vargas Llosa's writings, from his rise to prominence in the
early 1960s to the award of the Nobel Prize in Literature in 2010. The volume traces
his literary trajectory, and the ways in which he has reinvented himself as a writer.
His vast output of narrative fiction is the main focus, but the connections between
his concerns as a creative writer and his rich career as a cultural and political figure
are also teased out in this engaging, informative book.

EFRAÍN KRISTAL is Professor and Chair in Comparative Literature at UCLA.

JOHN KING is Professor of Latin American Cultural History at the University of
Warwick.

THE CAMBRIDGE
COMPANION TO
MARIO VARGAS LLOSA

EDITED BY
EFRAÍN KRISTAL
and
JOHN KING

CAMBRIDGE
UNIVERSITY PRESS

CAMBRIDGE UNIVERSITY PRESS
Cambridge, New York, Melbourne, Madrid, Cape Town,
Singapore, São Paulo, Delhi, Tokyo, Mexico City

Cambridge University Press
The Edinburgh Building, Cambridge CB2 8RU, UK

Published in the United States of America by Cambridge University Press, New York

www.cambridge.org
Information on this title: www.cambridge.org/9780521682855

First published 2012

Printed in the United Kingdom at the University Press, Cambridge

A catalogue record for this publication is available from the British Library

Library of Congress Cataloguing in Publication data
The Cambridge companion to Mario Vargas Llosa / edited by Efraín Kristal and John King.
p. cm. – (Cambridge companions to literature)
Includes bibliographical references and index.
ISBN 978-0-521-86424-4 – ISBN 978-0-521-68285-5 (pbk.)   1. Vargas Llosa, Mario, 1936– –
Criticism and interpretation.   2. Vargas Llosa, Mario, 1936– – Political activity.   3. Vargas
Llosa, Mario, 1936– – Influence.   I. Kristal, Efraín, 1959–   II. King, John, 1950–
PQ8498.32.A65Z627   2012
863 .64–dc23
2011021718

ISBN 978-0-521-86424-4 Hardback
ISBN 978-0-521-68285-5 Paperback

For Fernando de Szyszlo

CONTENTS

CONTENTS

CONTRIBUTORS

KELLY AUSTIN is Assistant Professor of Romance Languages and Literatures at the University of Chicago. Her research interests include literature of the Americas, translation studies and poetry. She has translated the poetry of Blanca Varela and is currently working on a book on Whitman, Neruda and translation. Her recent publications include 'History of the Southern Cone Novel: Argentina, Chile, Paraguay and Uruguay' for *The Blackwell Encyclopedia of the Novel* (2010).

NICHOLAS BIRNS teaches at Eugene Lang College, The New School for Liberal Arts, New York. He is author of *Understanding Anthony Powell* (2004), *Theory After Theory* (2010) and co-editor of *Vargas Llosa and Latin American Politics* (2010).

ROY C. BOLAND is Honorary Professor of Spanish and Latin American Studies at the University of Sydney, Australia. His books include *Oedipus and the Papa State: A Study of Individual and Social Psychology in Mario Vargas Llosa's Novels of Peruvian Reality* (1988), *Culture and Customs of El Salvador* (2001), and *Una rara comedia. Visión y revisión de las novelas de Mario Vargas Llosa* (2003). He is the general editor of *Antipodas*, the Journal of Hispanic and Galician Studies of Australia and New Zealand. In 2009 he was awarded the Cross of the Order of Isabel la Católica by the King of Spain, for his contributions to Hispanism.

JUAN E. DE CASTRO is an Associate Professor at Eugene Lang College, The New School for Liberal Arts, New York. He has published *Mario Vargas Llosa: Public Intellectual in Neoliberal Latin America* (2011), *The Spaces of Latin American Literature: Tradition, Globalization and Cultural Production* (2008), and *Mestizo Nations: Race, Culture, and Conformity in Latin American Literature* (2002). With Nicholas Birns he co-edited *Vargas Llosa and Latin American Politics* (2010).

DEBORAH COHN is Associate Professor of Spanish and American Studies at Indiana University, Bloomington. She is the author of *The Latin American Literary Boom and U.S. Nationalism during the Cold War* (forthcoming) and *History and Memory in the Two Souths: Recent Southern and Spanish American Fiction* (1999). She has published widely on Spanish American and US fiction.

ALONSO CUETO has published twelve novels, several short story collections and a play. His novel *La hora azul* received the 2005 Herralde Prize. He is also a professor at the Universidad Católica del Perú and a member of the Academia Peruana de la Lengua, and was a Fellow of the Guggenheim Foundation.

EVELYN FISHBURN was recently appointed Honorary Professor at University College London, where she was Visiting Professor for many years, and holds a Professor Emeritus appointment at London Metropolitan University. Her interests include the writings of Spanish American women and the use of humour in literature. The main focus of her research, however, is the work of Jorge Luis Borges, on whom she has published widely, including *A Borges Dictionary* and *Borges and Europe Revisited*. She has co-translated two plays by Vargas Llosa for radio.

CLIVE GRIFFIN is University Lecturer in Latin American Literature at Oxford University, and Fellow in Spanish at Trinity College, Oxford. His areas of research include the history of the book in sixteenth-century Spain and its American colonies, and modern Spanish American literature. His most recent book is *Oficiales de imprenta, herejía, e Inquisición en la España del siglo XVI* (2009).

JOHN KING is Professor of Latin American Cultural History at the University of Warwick. He has authored and edited more than a dozen books on Latin American culture, including editing and translating several books of Vargas Llosa's essays. His most recent monograph is *The Role of Mexico's* Plural *in Latin American Literary and Political Culture* (2007).

EFRAÍN KRISTAL is Professor of Spanish and Comparative Literature at UCLA. He is the author of *Temptation of the Word: The Novels of Mario Vargas Llosa* (1998) and *Invisible Work: Borges and Translation* (2002). He edited *The Cambridge Companion to the Latin American Novel* (2005) and the Penguin edition of Jorge Luis Borges's *Poems of the Night* (2010).

FIONA J. MACKINTOSH is a Senior Lecturer in Latin American Literature at the University of Edinburgh. She has a particular interest in Argentinian writing and has published extensively on the work of the poet Alejandra Pizarnik. With Karl Posso, she co-edited *Arbol de Alejandra: Pizarnik Reassessed* (2007), and she is the author of *Childhood in the Works of Silvina Ocampo and Alejandra Pizarnik* (2003).

GERALD MARTIN is Andrew W. Mellon Emeritus Professor of Modern Languages at the University of Pittsburgh. He translated and edited Miguel Angel Asturias's *Hombres de maíz* (1981, prologue by Mario Vargas Llosa), wrote several chapters on literature and culture for the *Cambridge History of Latin America*, vol. III (1985), vol. IV (1986), vol. X (1995) and vol. XI (1995), and wrote *Journeys through the Labyrinth* (1989) on the Latin American novel. He published *Gabriel García Márquez: A Life* in 2008 and is currently writing a biography of Vargas Llosa.

CAROLINA SITNISKY is Visiting Assistant Professor in the Department of Romance Languages and Literatures at Pomona College, California. She has published several articles on Latin American cinema and literature and is currently co-editing a volume on Latin America's twenty-first-century cinema. Her current research focuses on twentieth-century Latin American film adaptations.

MICHAEL WOOD is Charles Barnwell Straut Class of 1923 Professor of English and Comparative Literature at Princeton University. He has written books on Vladimir Nabokov, Luis Buñuel, Franz Kafka and Gabriel García Márquez, as well as *The Road to Delphi* (2003), *America in the Movies* (1975, 1989), *Children of Silence* (1998), *Literature and the Taste of Knowledge* (2005), and *Yeats and Violence* (2010). A member of the American Philosophical Society and the American Academy of Arts and Sciences, he is a regular contributor to the *London Review of Books* and the *New York Review of Books*.

ACKNOWLEDGEMENTS

We dedicate this book to Fernando de Szyszlo. He generously gave us permission to reproduce the image of the painting that inspired a chapter of Mario Vargas Llosa's *In Praise of the Stepmother* for the cover of this volume. We decided that this was an opportunity to recognise his achievements as a towering figure of twentieth-century Latin American painting and Peruvian culture. We also want to express our special gratitude to Rosvita Rauch for her intensive work with us, editing the manuscript we submitted to the press, for translating Alonso Cueto's contribution, and for creating the index in consultation with us. Rosvita helped us create a house style for our editing, and she went over every piece with astute editorial suggestions. We would also like to thank Fernando Carvallo, who conducted an interview with the Peruvian film-maker Francisco Lombardi, which was helpful for Carolina Sitnisky's chapter on Vargas Llosa and film. Edward Chauca and Gabriela Venegas prepared preliminary versions of the chronology and further reading. Ruben Gallo assisted us in obtaining access to the Mario Vargas Llosa Archives at Princeton University, and in identifying the materials we wanted to reproduce in this volume. We also thank Rosario de Bedoya, Mario Vargas Llosa's personal assistant, and our good friend, for responding to so many of our practical queries and facilitating so many of our requests. She arranged for Juan Pablo Murrugarra to take the picture of Szyszlo's painting from a private collection in Lima, and secured Mario Vargas Llosa's permission to reproduce images from one of his working notebooks. In the final stages, Alison Tickner was instrumental: she went over the book with a fine-toothed comb, and helped us to improve it, thanks to her efficient editing and thoughtful queries. We also acknowledge the grants we received from the University of Warwick and from UCLA's Academic Senate to facilitate many of the costs involved in producing the manuscript.

CHRONOLOGY

Unpublished and untranslated works appear in roman typeface within quotation marks.

1936   Born on 28 March in Arequipa, Peru to Ernesto Vargas Maldonado and Dora Llosa Ureta. Dora is abandoned by Ernesto Vargas when five months pregnant. Oscar R. Benavides is President of Peru.

1937   Moves with maternal family to Cochabamba, Bolivia, where he attends the La Salle elementary school.

1945   José Luis Bustamante y Rivero is elected President of Peru.

1946   Moves to Piura, Peru with his maternal relatives. Attends the local La Salle elementary school.

1947   Ernesto Vargas re-establishes relationship with Dora Llosa. Moves to Lima.

1948   General Manuel Odría overthrows Bustamante y Rivero to govern Peru for eight years.

1950   Attends Leoncio Prado military academy until 1952.

1952   Returns to Piura, attends San Miguel public high school, begins writing for local newspapers, and directs his own play, 'La huida del Inca' ('The flight of the Inca') at the Variedades Theatre.

1953   Returns to Lima to study law and literature at the Universidad Nacional Mayor de San Marcos.

1955   Marries Julia Urquidi, publishes first short stories, writes for *El Comercio* newspaper, and *Turismo* and *Cultura Peruana* magazines; works as news director for radio station Panamericana.

1957   Wins short-story contest organised by the *Revue Française* with 'El desafío' ('The dare').

1958   Receives bachelor's degree in literature from the Universidad Nacional Mayor de San Marcos in Lima. Visit to Amazonian jungle provides material for *The Green House* (*La casa verde*), *La Chunga* (*La Chunga*) and *The Storyteller* (*El hablador*).

1959   Obtains Javier Prado Fellowship to pursue a doctorate at the Universidad Complutense, Madrid. Short-story collection, *Los jefes* ('The Leaders'), wins Leopoldo Alas Prize (Spain). Moves to Paris, where he teaches Spanish; works as a journalist. Cuban Revolution.

1962   Receives Biblioteca Breve Prize for his first novel, *The Time of the Hero* (*La ciudad y los perros*), based on Leoncio Prado military academy experiences. Fernando Belaúnde Terry elected President of Peru.

1963   *The Time of the Hero* published, receives Crítica Española Award. Copies of *The Time of the Hero* burned in Leoncio Prado parade ground.

1964   Returns to Peru; divorces Julia Urquidi.

1965   Travels to Havana, Cuba, to participate in the jury of the Casa de las Américas Prize. Marries Patricia Llosa in Lima. The couple return to Paris.

1966   *The Green House*. Invited to World Congress of New York PEN Club. First son, Alvaro, born in Lima. The family settles in London.

1967   Awarded the Rómulo Gallegos Prize for *The Green House*. *The Cubs* (*Los cachorros*). Second son, Gonzalo, is born.

1968   General Juan Velasco Alvarado overthrows Belaúnde Terry in Peru, establishes a military government, ushering in agrarian reform in Peru.

1969   *Conversation in The Cathedral* (*Conversación en La Catedral*) and *Carta de batalla por Tirant lo Blanc*. ('A declaration of battle in favour of Tirant lo Blanc').

1970   Moves to Barcelona.

1971   *Historia secreta de una novela* ('Secret history of a novel', on the gestation of *The Green House*) and *García Márquez. Historia de un deicidio* ('García Márquez: history of a deicide'). Involvement in the Padilla case will mark end of his good relations with the Cuban Revolution.

1973   *Captain Pantoja and the Special Service (Pantaleón y las visitadoras).*

1974   Daughter, Morgana, is born.

1975   *The Perpetual Orgy: Flaubert and* Madame Bovary (*La orgía perpetua. Flaubert y* Madame Bovary). Elected to Academia Peruana de la Lengua. Co-directs film version of *Captain Pantoja and the Special Service* in the Dominican Republic.

1976   Elected President of the International PEN Club.

1977   *Aunt Julia and the Scriptwriter (La tía Julia y el escribidor).* Takes up Simón Bolívar Chair at Cambridge University.

1981   *The War of the End of the World (La guerra del fin del mundo), The Young Lady from Tacna (La señorita de Tacna), Entre Sartre y Camus* ('Between Sartre and Camus'). Produces and directs television programme, *La Torre de Babel* ('The Tower of Babel'), in Peru.

1981   Awarded Medal of Honour by the Peruvian Congress.

1982   *Kathie and the Hippopotamus (Kathie y el hipopótamo).*

1983   Participates in the Uchuraccay Commission at request of Peruvian President Fernando Belaúnde inquiring into massacre of eight journalists.

1984   *The Real Life of Alejandro Mayta (Historia de Mayta).*

1985   Awarded Legion of Honour by French Government. *La Chunga.*

1986   *Who Killed Palomino Molero? (¿Quién mató a Palomino Molero?)* and essay collection, *Contra viento y marea* ('Against wind and tide') (vol. I: 1962–72, vol. II: 1972–83).

1987   *The Storyteller (El hablador).* Becomes leader of Movimiento Libertad; opposes nationalisation of Peruvian financial system proposed by President Alan García Pérez.

1988   *In Praise of the Stepmother* (*Elogio de la madrastra*). Founds Movimiento Libertad political party in Peru; allies with other political parties forming Frente Democrático (FREDEMO).

1989   Runs for President of Peru on the FREDEMO ticket.

1990   Publishes the third volume of *Contra viento y marea* (vol. III: 1964–88) and a collection of literary essays, *La verdad de las mentiras. Ensayos sobre la novela moderna* ('The truth of lies: essays on the modern novel'). On 10 June is defeated by presidential candidate Alberto Fujimori. Returns to London.

1991   Fellow at Wissenschaftskolleg (Institute for Advanced Study), Berlin.

1992   Alberto Fujimori suspends the Peruvian constitution with support of Peruvian military.

1993   *Death in the Andes* (*Lituma en los Andes*), *A Fish in the Water* (*El pez en el agua*) and *El loco de los balcones* ('The madman of the balconies'); wins Planeta Prize, Barcelona. Acquires Spanish citizenship while maintaining Peruvian citizenship. Awarded Order of Arts and Letters by French Government (Commander).

1994   Elected to Real Academia Española (Spanish Royal Academy). Wins Cervantes Prize, Spain.

1995   Receives Jerusalem Prize.

1996   *La utopía arcaica. José María Arguedas y las ficciones del indigenismo* ('The archaic utopia: José María Arguedas and the fictions of indigenismo'), *Making Waves* and *Ojos bonitos, cuadros feos* ('Pretty eyes, ugly paintings').

1997   *The Notebooks of Don Rigoberto* (*Los cuadernos de don Rigoberto*) and *Letters to a Young Novelist* (*Cartas a un joven novelista*).

1998   Receives the National Book Critics Circle Award for *Making Waves*.

1999   Visits Dominican Republic for research on dictator Leónidas Trujillo.

2000   *The Feast of the Goat* (*La fiesta del Chivo*).

2001   *The Language of Passion (El lenguaje de la pasión)*. Awarded Doctor Honoris Causa by the Universidad Nacional Mayor de San Marcos, his alma mater. Receives Order of 'El sol del Perú', highest distinction awarded by the Peruvian government.

2002   Elected President of International Foundation for Liberty.

2003   *The Way to Paradise (El paraíso en la otra esquina)* and *Diario de Irak* ('Iraq diary').

2004   *The Temptation of the Impossible: Victor Hugo and* Les Misérables *(La tentación de lo imposible. Víctor Hugo y* Los miserables).

2005   Receives Irving Kristol Award from American Enterprise Institute for Public Policy Research in Washington, DC.

2006   *The Bad Girl (Travesuras de la niña mala)* and *Israel/Palestina. Paz o guerra santa* ('Israel/Palestine: peace or holy war').

2007   *Touchstones. Odiseo y Penélope* ('Odysseus and Penelope')

2008   *Al pie del Támesis* ('On the banks of the Thames'), *Wellsprings* and *El viaje a la ficción. El mundo de Juan Carlos Onetti* ('The road to fiction: Juan Carlos Onetti's world').

2009   *Las mil noches y una noche* ('The thousand nights and one night').

2010   Awarded Nobel Prize in Literature 2010. *The Dream of the Celt (El sueño del celta)*.

2011   In the run-off for the Peruvian presidential election, he supports Ollanta Humala against Keiko Fujimori, the daughter of the imprisoned former president, Alberto Fujimori. Humala wins the election.

EFRAÍN KRISTAL AND JOHN KING

Introduction

Best known as one of the major novelists of the last five decades, Mario Vargas Llosa (b. 1936, Arequipa, Peru) is also one of Latin America's leading public intellectuals, a critic of art and culture, and a playwright of distinction. Vargas Llosa came to prominence in the 1960s as a talented short-story writer and a masterful practitioner of the novel. His early novels were considered innovative from a technical standpoint, and politically engaged. He was concerned with the theme of corruption and its effects on individuals and communities, and he found a literary means to express it: the crossing of spatial and temporal planes. In the 1970s he reconsidered his admiration for the Cuban Revolution and other leftist causes, and reoriented both his literary and his cultural concerns in line with anti-authoritarian democratic free market liberalism. In his novels of the period he adds humour, irony and a new kind of literary complexity to his repertoire and becomes interested in the theme of fanaticism, and his new literary technique involves alternating between a realistic register and one that is clearly imaginary, based on dreams and fantasies. After his unsuccessful bid to become president of Peru in 1990, Vargas Llosa returned to literature with a more circumspect view of political action. With *The Feast of the Goat* (2000),[1] he finds a synthesis between the theme of corruption and the theme of fanaticism, and begins to develop a new literary procedure, which informs *The Way to Paradise* (2003), *The Bad Girl* (2006) and *The Dream of the Celt* (2010): the creation of a literary register that can be read simultaneously in a realistic register or as a fantasy. This mixing of registers is a form that is appropriate to conveying his new theme: reconciliation.

In Vargas Llosa's literary world some characters make appearances in several works. Lituma, for example, appears in the early short stories, in *The Green House* (1966), in *Aunt Julia and the Scriptwriter* (1977), in *La Chunga* (1986), in *Who Killed Palomino Molero?* (1986) and in *Death in the Andes* (1993); Chispas in *The Cubs* (1967), *Conversation in The Cathedral* (1969) and *Al pie del Támesis* ('On the banks of the Thames', 2008); Fonchito in *In Praise of the Stepmother* (1988), *The Notebooks of Don Rigoberto* (1997) and the children's tale *Fonchito y la luna* ('Fonchito and the moon', 2010). Vargas

Llosa's fictional world, however, is not a seamless whole. Vargas Llosa is a writer who has reinvented himself several times during his literary trajectory, and the reappearance of characters suggests corrections and modifications more often than continuities.

This being said, there is a common thread that runs through Vargas Llosa's work. He has always wrestled with the proposition that the hopes and desires of human beings invariably surpass their ability to fulfil them. Vargas Llosa's characters experience – viscerally or intuitively – what he has eloquently spelled out in his essays: that something may be painfully wrong with society or with the world as they find it; that something might not be quite right with the way human beings are wired or equipped to cope with the challenges of life; that there are irrational, destructive forces, within us or out there, against which we may have to struggle. Although we might be able to keep these forces at bay, we will never tame them altogether when they are unleashed, at least not in the kingdom of this world. Vargas Llosa's sustained exploration of the incompatibilities between experience and the imagination may well be his most enduring contribution to literature.

Mario Vargas Llosa is both a master of modernist narrative techniques and a consummate storyteller. Unlike Gabriel García Márquez – his only rival in the history of the Spanish American novel – he does not dazzle his readers with the power of a wild imagination and an equally extraordinary mastery of narrative time, to create a sense of wonder grounded in everyday social and political realities of common and uncommon people. Instead, Vargas Llosa is a novelist able to persuade his readers, from the very first line of any of his narratives, that they are being told a story of considerable human interest. García Márquez's literary conceits involve elements of surprise in narratives that move forward according to a lived experience; or backwards to accommodate the memories of individuals or collectives, including the memories stored in the popular imagination. Plot, for García Márquez, is secondary to genealogy, or to the vicissitudes and accidents of the lives of individuals and communities. For Vargas Llosa, on the other hand, plot is fundamental, and all of his narratives take the reader on a journey with an endpoint that often requires an epilogue on the significance of the concatenation of events.[2] From a technical point of view, even his most sophisticated novels, as Gerald Martin demonstrates in his analysis of *The Green House* depend on interconnected plots: Vargas Llosa's protagonists face challenges, encounter characters who will change the course of their lives, and play out situations until the game is fully over. These stories can sometimes be grounded in the intimacy of a bourgeois home, as in the novels that Roy Boland analyses in his chapter on Vargas Llosa's erotic novels; or in the heat of revolutionary activity, as Deborah Cohn explores in her chapter on the novels set in the Andes; or across large historical canvases, as in *The War of the End of the*

World (1981). This, the only Latin American historical novel meaningfully comparable to Tolstoy's *War and Peace*, is analysed here by Juan de Castro and Nicholas Birns, with a keen awareness of the political and ideological ramifications of the time the novel was written. But whatever the setting, Vargas Llosa's novels are invariably grounded in plot, and he manages to make his stories gripping even when he uses some of the most complex narrative techniques in contemporary literature. Vargas Llosa thinks of his characters, not in terms of their lives as they unfold, but in terms of the circumstances in which situations are played out. This is probably why he preferred the dramatic plots of Joanot Martorell's chivalric romance *Tirant lo Blanc*, to the episodic nature of the Spanish picaresque novel, or even *Don Quixote*. Character in Vargas Llosa's novels is revealed in situations; and one of the most remarkable aspects of his literary craft – the one most likely to get lost in translation – is his uncanny ability to suggest nuances of the spoken voice through the written word. In his creative process, as he explains in the interview that is included as the last chapter of this volume, he likes to read his work in progress aloud: this observation offers an insight about the significance of speech in his writing.

In Vargas Llosa's literary world, unhappiness and suffering are as pervasive as the two responses with which his unsettled literary characters strive to prevail over their feelings of malaise: rebellion and fantasy. Rebellion and fantasy are also responses to the uses and abuses of power. In his chapter, Alonso Cueto explores the central themes of rebellion, fantasy and power across the spectrum of novels. In the 1960s – when Vargas Llosa was a committed socialist – he expressed his discontent with the world as he had found it with an underlying sense of optimism. He was persuaded that human dissatisfaction in Latin America was directly linked to the shortcomings of social and economic realities, to the corruption and injustices revolutionary action would remedy. As he was writing his first novels, inspired by Jean-Paul Sartre's conviction that engaged literature can contribute to the political transformation of society, Vargas Llosa harboured the strong hope that his native Peru, and the rest of Latin America, would soon follow Fidel Castro's Cuba as the flagship for true liberty and justice.

Vargas Llosa became an immediate literary sensation for his masterful depiction of the corrosive effects of political corruption on human hopes and aspirations in *The Time of the Hero* (1963), *The Green House*, and *Conversation in The Cathedral*. In these three novels – as the chapters on the early novels by Gerald Martin and Efraín Kristal reveal – the Peruvian novelist demonstrated his ability to master the techniques of James Joyce and William Faulkner with rigour, and to take these literary procedures to new heights. Vargas Llosa added layers of density to his descriptions through interior monologues, and experimented with spatial and temporal planes, creating resonances and dissonances between events and conversations taking place in different times and places. He developed an indirect form of discourse in which the voice of an impersonal narrator can readily express a character's intimate thoughts, using ambiguity and ellipses to enhance the effect. These modernist techniques appear in the novels with a heightened sense of intrigue that embraces the tropes and conceits of adventure stories, of popular culture, and even the plots of the highly sentimental and melodramatic Mexican cinema of the 1940s and 1950s, which is only one example of the formal and thematic significance of film in Vargas Llosa's novels.

The early novels were critically acclaimed and commercially successful, and Vargas Llosa was eager to lend his considerable popularity and international prestige to the Cuban Revolution. 'Literature is Fire', his 1967 acceptance speech for the prestigious Rómulo Gallegos Prize in Venezuela, was the most important literary manifesto of the new Latin American novel of the 1960s. In it, he established firm connections between the kind of novel he was writing, along with Gabriel García Márquez, Carlos Fuentes and others, and their shared political ideals. These writers had much in common, including a deep admiration for the exacting standards of Jorge Luis Borges's narrative fiction, even though they could not find any political ideas worth recommending in the writings of the Argentine master.

Vargas Llosa's own disenchantment with the Cuban Revolution, and with the Latin American left, was slow and painful, as John King highlights in his chapter on the essays. The article Vargas Llosa wrote in 1968 to express his criticism of Fidel Castro for recanting his initial condemnation of the Soviet invasion of Czechoslovakia was his first public criticism of the Cuban regime. It was followed by his denunciations of censorship and human rights violations in both Cuba and the Soviet Union. The backlash against Vargas Llosa for the views he had expressed disabused him of the idea that he had earned the right to criticise the Cuban Revolution, even though he had thought of himself as a committed ally of the regime, with the right to do so. His ostracism by his former Cuban friends made him circumspect about Castro's regime, but not about his own socialist convictions, which he held for several more years. He found himself in an awkward situation, having become a world celebrity with novels he thought were contributing to socialist causes, but considered an outcast by the Latin American left and by most professional academic specialists of Latin American literature in the 1970s, who agreed that they had overestimated the significance of Vargas Llosa's contribution to literature, or at least of Vargas Llosa as a writer who fulfilled their political expectations.

The impact of this confusing and tumultuous time on his writing was immediate. As he was distancing himself from the Cuban regime, he also began to take a step back from the sombre themes of his first novels, recasting them with humour, as Michael Wood shows, in *Captain Pantoja and the Special Service* (1973). With *Aunt Julia and the Scriptwriter* he toned down the high-pitched modernist techniques that characterised his first novels, and began developing a new literary approach to explore the gap between the hopes and aspirations of his characters by alternating between two literary registers: a realistic register in which the prosaic experiences of his characters' lives alternate with another register, which is clearly informed by their compensatory fantasies. He also began to explore the theme that would dominate his narrative literature for a decade to come: the fanatic with fixed ideas, unable to see reality for what it is. In some cases, Vargas Llosa's fanatics are willing to use violence against those they consider to be obstacles to their impossible, utopian aspirations.

By the 1980s, Vargas Llosa fully abandoned his socialist convictions and became an outspoken advocate of free market democracy. His political allegiances had now shifted from Fidel Castro to Margaret Thatcher, and his enthusiasm for Sartre faded as he embraced a line of thinking (Albert Camus, Karl Popper, Isaiah Berlin, Friedrich Von Hayek) according to which the notion of a perfect human being or a realisable utopia is not only a fantasy, but the source of unnecessary violence and strife. Even though he has always been a bitter enemy of dictators and dictatorships, his political shift away from the Latin American left in particular, and utopian thinking in general, consolidated his break with the left, as it gained him new friends among Latin American entrepreneurs and liberal intellectuals.

Vargas Llosa would no longer claim that violence was a legitimate means to achieve the kind of political change that would eliminate the fundamental causes of human discontent. In fact, he began to make the case that some of the sources of political violence and instability could be traced to the notion that social utopias are possible. His novels in the 1980s – mapped by Juan de Castro and Nicholas Birns, Fiona J. Mackintosh and Deborah Cohn – were concerned with the fragility of a society assailed by religious and military fanatics, political opportunists or well-intentioned dreamers and idealists, who encounter the human propensity to idealise violence or to cynically profit from corruption or violent situations. At the time, Vargas Llosa remained optimistic that the propensities to unrest and instability generated by unhappy individuals could be effectively diffused. He thought that the literary imagination could combine elements from the realities of their imperfect lives with their most irrational drives, to give them the illusion of a fulfilment they could never achieve in the real world. This play between fiction and reality is also at the heart of his plays written in the 1980s and later, as Evelyn Fishburn shows. Furthermore, Vargas Llosa considered that the utopian thinking of the Latin American left, together with the authoritarianism of the Latin American right and a long history of corruption, were the major impediments to the establishment of the kind of free market economy that he argued could reduce misery and generate prosperity in Latin America.

Vargas Llosa ran for the Peruvian presidency in 1990, with the expectation that he could make a difference to his nation. After his unsuccessful bid, a less optimistic vision has informed his writings – fictional and non-fictional alike – imparting a growing sense that all struggles to prevail over our intractable feelings of discomfort are doomed to failure.

When Vargas Llosa began his literary career, he would refer to the 'demons' of literary creation as a metaphor for the irrational motivations that drive writers of narrative fiction to create alternative realities, and he spoke of the writer as a deicide who sought to usurp the creation of God through the creation of an alternative reality – a reality that would challenge the 'real' world. As his socialist convictions waned, he spoke of an allegorical struggle between demons and angels, referring to the tension between the forces that undermine social existence, and the compensatory activities, such as literature and the erotic, that counterbalance the inherent insufficiencies of life. Entering a third and more pessimistic period, the demons are no longer just metaphors, but rather begin to signal the presence of intractable evil. So, while literature can still attain great heights, these heights also offer a sober indication that the world in which we live is inherently unsatisfactory. Vargas Llosa's pessimism about our abilities to overcome our demons has given rise to a more conciliatory, understanding attitude towards his former enemies and rivals in both the literary and political spheres, and his own past. In his most recent work, *The Dream of the Celt*, Vargas Llosa explores the friendship formed between a strict heterosexual guard and a gay human rights activist, to propose that love comes from the acceptance of, rather than the refusal to acknowledge, a traumatic past. Even though he has been writing novels for some fifty years, his ideas have continually developed with restless energy. Vargas Llosa's pessimism in our abilities to overcome our demons has given rise to a new outlook, which informs his most recent novels, *The Way to Paradise*, *The Bad Girl* and *The Dream of the Celt*.

The *Cambridge Companion to Mario Vargas Llosa* concentrates on his vast output of narrative fiction, but it also maps out connections between his concerns as a creative writer and his rich career as a cultural and political figure. The *Companion* opens with an introductory essay by Alonso Cueto, which offers an overview of Vargas Llosa's major literary themes in the context of his personal and intellectual biography. Cueto is a highly regarded Peruvian novelist, but he is also a university professor who has written extensively on Vargas Llosa, and has edited several books about his compatriot. His essay is scholarly, but it also offers personal aperçus into Vargas

Llosa's life and literary experiences. The next nine chapters cover all of Vargas Llosa's narrative fiction. Chapter 2, by Gerald Martin, focuses on *The Time of the Hero* and *The Green House*, the novels that secured Vargas Llosa's place as a major figure in world literature, and it also addresses the first short stories. Chapter 3, by Efraín Kristal, is devoted to *Conversation in The Cathedral*, one of the great political novels in the Latin American literary canon, and on *The Cubs*, a short novel that shares some of the characters and one of the major themes of the longer novel. In Chapter 4, Michael Wood explores two novels of a transitional period in which Vargas Llosa offered ironic, humorous takes on his previous themes, while beginning to explore new directions. Chapter 5, by Juan de Castro and Nicholas Birns, is devoted to *The War of the End of the World*, a historical novel on the grand scale set in Brazil, and arguably Vargas Llosa's most ambitious work of literature. In Chapter 6, Fiona J. Mackintosh analyses two shorter novels in which Vargas Llosa addresses his concerns about the dynamics between the indigenous and non-indigenous worlds in Latin America, and about a gruesome crime of passion that takes place near a military base. Chapter 7, by Deborah Cohn, offers an analysis of two novels set in the Andes. Both are literary explorations of political violence in revolutionary contexts. Chapter 8, by Roy Boland, groups together Vargas Llosa's two erotic novels, which both feature Don Rigoberto, a man whose private erotic life threatens the stability of his public life as a respectable businessman. In Chapter 9, Clive Griffin offers a sustained analysis of *The Feast of the Goat*, Vargas Llosa's only novel about a dictator, and his second novel set outside Peru. In Chapter 10, Efraín Kristal shows that Vargas Llosa's last three novels amount to a new direction in Vargas Llosa's literary trajectory, one in which his former critique of fanaticism and political utopias has shifted to an exploration of human reconciliation. The final four chapters move from the novels to other aspects of Vargas Llosa's literary production. Chapter 11, by John King, offers an overview of Vargas Llosa's essays, focusing on the vicissitudes of his trajectory, giving pride of place to his writings on politics, literature and the visual arts. The chapter is followed by the reproduction pages from one of Vargas Llosa's working notebooks, with his preparatory notes for a course on the Latin American novel he taught at Columbia University from October 1975 to January 1976. The document illustrates Vargas Llosa's thoughts on the Latin American novel at a crossroads in his own literary trajectory: it offers insights into the sense of his own contributions to Latin American literary history, it summarises some of the concerns of his early works and anticipates future projects to come, including his interest in *Rebellion in the Backlands* by Euclides da Cunha, the book that generated his interest in the episode of Brazilian history that inspired *The War of the End of the World*. Chapter 12, by Kelly Austin, analyses Vargas

Llosa's *A Fish in the Water* (1993), the memoir of his failed presidential campaign, focusing on the tensions between a literary and a political life, and also explores the ways in which fiction enters into Vargas Llosa's autobiographical prose. Chapter 13, by Evelyn Fishburn, offers a detailed analysis of Vargas Llosa's plays, and Chapter 14, by Carolina Sitnisky, explores the use of cinematic techniques in Vargas Llosa's work, and looks at the ways that the novels have been adapted to the screen. The volume concludes with an interview in which the editors invite Vargas Llosa to reflect on aspects of his trajectory as a creative writer, paying special attention to the novels of the last decade.

NOTES

1. Publication dates are given for the first edition of the Spanish text unless otherwise stated.
2. In a subtle and nuanced analysis, Perry Anderson shows that differences in literary style also have a bearing on the divergent ways in which Gabriel García Márquez and Mario Vargas Llosa have addressed their political convictions in their autobiographical writings. Perry Anderson. 'Tropical Recall: Gabriel García Márquez'. In Perry Anderson. *Spectrum: From Right to Left in the World of Ideas*. London: Verso, 2005, pp. 210–19.

I

ALONSO CUETO

Reality and rebellion

An overview of Mario Vargas Llosa's literary themes

A life in movement

The house where Vargas Llosa was born, on 28 March 1936, has wooden railings, a small front garden and a door flanked by white columns. Relatively close to Arequipa's Plaza de Armas, at Boulevard Parra 101, its façade looks today much as it did eight decades ago. Mario lived there with his grand-parents, Don Pedro Llosa and Doña Carmen Ureta; and his mother, Dora, went to church from that home on her wedding day.

Vargas Llosa, however, was too young to have a conscious recollection of his first home. He was only a year old when the Llosa clan, led by his maternal grandfather, moved to Cochabamba in Bolivia, where he would live for the next nine years. In 1946 he returned to Peru to study at the La Salle school in Piura, a city in the northern coastal area of Peru where he would set the brothel that gave the title to his second novel, published in 1966, *The Green House* (*La casa verde*[1]). In 1947 he would go to Lima, and become a cadet in the military academy he would immortalise in his first novel in 1963, *The Time of the Hero* (*La ciudad y los perros*[2]). He returned to Piura in 1952, and moved back to Lima the following year to begin his university studies, a period that inspired the literary world of *Conversation in The Cathedral* (*Conversación en La Catedral*[3]).

Arequipa, Cochabamba, Piura, Lima: by the time he was sixteen years old, he had moved six times and had lived in two countries and four different cities. When Vargas Llosa was eleven years old, he learned of the existence of his father, whom his family had led him to believe was dead since he was a little boy. Until then he had idealised his father from a photo in which he appeared, friendly and smiling, in a sailor's cap. The authoritarian, irascible man who came into his life was a stark contrast to Mario's fantasies of a caring father he had lost as a little boy.

The intrusion of the stern and sometimes brutal man on Mario's bitter-sweet fantasy of a loving father was the first compelling evidence, in his own life, of the chasm that can arise between a fictional world and the real one. He felt as if the outside world had come crashing into his life.

Expelled from the cosy protection of his maternal family, Vargas Llosa's life became an adventure of exile and reunion, loss and discovery. Reading novels came to be an antidote to an unacceptable reality in which his father ruled over him and his mother. Vargas Llosa's literary life began with his need to compensate for a difficult reality through fantasy. In one way or another, his attempt to recover a world of dreams through literature is also an attempt to return to a lost childhood, which was also the product of his illusions; he can only return to the idealised world of his childhood, before the arrival of his father, through the novels that he reads and those that he will write.

The wanderings of his childhood are the first indication of the itinerate life he would have to the present day. From a very young age, he has been an instinctive nomad, moving from one place to another in order to cope with life. He has lived in countless cities and, even today, the only constant in his life is travel. The other distinctive inheritance from his childhood is his ethical perception of the world. Raised in a Catholic family, and influenced by his mother, aunts and uncles, he adopts a moral vision of reality. Moral evaluation will become a natural, instinctive impulse in his own life and the lives of the protagonists of his literary works. His dictators will be morally repugnant characters, and his heroes will act according to an emotional response stirred by their moral judgements. Notions of sin and punishment are ever present in his literary world. His attachment to novels of chivalry, and identification with the codes of honour and battle that inform them, is hardly surprising.

Vargas Llosa is a novelist by nature, perhaps because the novel is a motley, mercurial genre, the one most open to diversity and porous to other genres. Yet he has written numerous and notable essays (he is one of the best prose writers in the Spanish language); occasional articles on an impressive variety of subjects (including soccer and opera); major books of literary criticism; and a significant number of plays. He also embarked on an adventure reserved for individuals susceptible to taking on a considerable amount of risk when he became a candidate for the presidency of Peru. As a journalist, he reported on the situation in Iraq in the midst of occupation, and on the plight of the Palestinian people in the occupied territories. He is interested, even fascinated, by dangerous challenges of this kind because he needs to explore and test the limits of reality. This personal propensity carries through to his literary work, in which more intense forms of danger and risk serve as touchstones that reveal the identity of his characters.

The human gallery

Vargas Llosa's characters come from different human worlds and are host to myriad emotions. He has described the uncertainties of a man facing his frailties as he looks at himself in the mirror of his bathroom; the sternness of a military leader in firm command of his soldiers; the indignities suffered by an indigenous Urakusa chief taken prisoner and tortured in the Peruvian jungle; and the satisfaction of a dictator humiliating a subordinate standing before his desk. The grandeur of life attracts him, as does its small miseries.

His formal experimentation with literary technique has been a constant feature of his literary works. He is one of the few writers in the world who is in full command of a diverse range of literary procedures, which he can draw from, contrast and fuse at will.

On several occasions he has indicated that before writing a single sentence of a novel he has already sketched out an itinerary for his characters, but he is always willing to allow the original plan to change as his creative process unfolds, and to feel surprised by the paths they may ultimately take. Minor characters in an initial conception can become protagonists, while some that appeared to be central can lose their original significance in the process of writing and rewriting. For Vargas Llosa, a novel, like life itself, is a journey with unexpected twists and turns. The novelist is both a traveller and an explorer.

For Vargas Llosa, conversation is also a rich source for his literary world. In person, he gives the impression of someone who is always eager to listen to the stories his interlocutors are willing to tell, and to tell a good story himself. He is both a great writer and a great storyteller. He does not believe in the authority of the teller, but in the power of a well-told tale. He is not a weaver of episodes, but the organiser of a self-contained literary world, with a complex structure that comes alive thanks to the pulsations of a satisfying story.

Vargas Llosa projects many realistic details into his novels, even as he ultimately transcends any reality that may have inspired him. He has a meticulous sense of setting. His novels are constructed with precise facts: smells, tastes, images, dates, names. Because of the density of his geographical references, some editions of his novels have included maps to orient the reader. His prodigious visual and spatial memory is at play in his creation of the spaces in which his characters displace themselves as their adventures unfold.

The journey of life, like that of a novel, is its own justification. Vargas Llosa is fond of the Cavafy poem that speaks of the journey to Ithaca. The important thing is not arriving in Ithaca, Vargas Llosa has often said in conversation. What counts is the journey itself.

The oppressive reality

Like Vargas Llosa himself, his characters feel their best out in the open air. Over the course of his works there are great exterior scenes: the vast plains through which the dispossessed march under the direction of the Counsellor in *The War of the End of the World* (*La guerra del fin del mundo*[4]); the jungles and mosquito-ridden rivers that Fushía navigates in *The Green House*; the June night in which a group of trigger-ready conspirators wait for Trujillo's Chevrolet to appear in *The Feast of the Goat* (*La fiesta del Chivo*[5]).

His first great novel, *The Time of the Hero*, indeed begins in a sombre interior ('in the uncertain glow which the light bulb cast through the few clean pieces of glass').[6] In that novel, interior and exterior spaces are already poised against each other: the school, the house and the city. To his characters, nevertheless, reality is as confining as a closed space.

Reality is one of the forms that the paternal figure has assumed. In his 1993 autobiography, *A Fish in the Water: A Memoir* (*El pez en el agua. Memorias*[7]), Vargas Llosa tells extensively of his father's abuses during his childhood and adolescence, and in some of his novels, including *The Time of the Hero* and *Aunt Julia and the Scriptwriter* (*La tía Julia y el escribidor*[8]), published in 1977, one can detect direct echoes of this autobiographical recollection. Given that reality under the authoritarian form of the father is unacceptable, subversion of this reality – that is to say, literature, the novel, the creation of another reality – becomes urgent and indispensable. The literary vocation is not only an act of rebellion against paternal authority, but even against the authority of reality itself. If rebellion is to have teeth, it must encompass a territory as vast as the reality against which it is rebelling. The novel, therefore, has to be a total novel.

Every act of creation, according to Vargas Llosa, is a deicide. God, the supreme Father, is the creator of reality, the great rival. In *The Rebel*, Camus cites a phrase that could have been written by Vargas Llosa, that art, whatever its end, always makes God a guilty rival.[9]

The vice of truth

In a 1975 article on Albert Camus's *The Outsider*, Vargas Llosa affirms:

> the novel can thus be read above all as denunciation of the tyranny of conventions and of the lies on which social life is based. A martyr to the truth, Meursault goes to prison, is sentenced and presumably guillotined for his ontological inability to hide his feelings and do what other men do: play a part.[10]

Later, referring to the same Meursault and his encounter with the magistrate and the priest in his cell, Mario affirms that:

> the catechistical, sectarian, domineering attitude exasperates him. Why? Because everything he loves and understands is exclusively of this earth: the sea, the sun, the sunsets, María's young flesh. With the same animal indifference with which he cultivates the senses, Meursault embodies the truth: therefore he appears monstrous to those around him. Because the truth – that natural truth that pours out of his mouth like sweat off the skin – is incompatible with the rational forms on which social life is based; that community of men and women throughout history.[11]

Like Meursault, although situated in an elaborately realist context, Alberto from *The Time of the Hero* and Zavalita from *Conversation in The Cathedral* have what Vargas Llosa in his article on Camus calls 'the vice of truth'. Alberto denounces Jaguar for having killed the Slave. Zavalita asks Ambrosio if he killed Queca on his father's orders. Their search for the truth and for justice has an existential, as well as a moral edge. Like Flora Tristan in *The Way to Paradise* (*El paraíso en la otra esquina*[12]) and like the protagonist of *Captain Pantoja and the Special Service* (*Pantaleón y las visitadoras*[13]), Alberto and Zavalita do not accept the lies of the institutions of collective history. The cult of truth is a trait of the rebel, the transgressor – that is, of the individual privileged in Vargas Llosa's novels. Power represented by the collective system always hides the truth. The affirmation of the individual and the refutation of surrounding reality – transgression – is an incandescent form of life. From the perspective of the rebel, power can be defined as an abuse of reality. Rebellion forms the threshold to the reign of fantasy.

Vargas Llosa feels a natural complicity with the transgressors: Alberto, Fonchito (who appears in both *In Praise of the Stepmother* (*Elogio a la madrastra*[14]) and *The Notebooks of Don Rigoberto* (*Los cuadernos de Don Rigoberto*[15]), Antonio Imbert (from *The Feast of the Goat*), Flora Tristan. Some of his favourite writers, like Sade and Bataille, are transgressors. Characters from his preferred novels, such as Madame Bovary and Jean Valjean, also belong to the breed of transgressors. Transgressors negate reality as they challenge it. For Vargas Llosa, they have the instincts of a deicide.

The paradoxes of power

Mario Vargas Llosa is the explorer of power's enchantment, the poet of its evil. To search for, to transgress, to retain power are the monomaniacal obsessions that guide the life of his protagonists. In vast social canvases like

The War of the End of the World, and in private portraits like *In Praise of the Stepmother*, the search, the transgression, the usurpation or the destruction of power is the basic instinct of the individual, the essential gesture of affirmation in the struggle to survive.

The way in which Vargas Llosa's characters relate to power is inseparable from their search for freedom. If power establishes an oppressive time and place, the individual strives to create their own. When the protagonist of *The Bad Girl* (*Travesuras de la niña mala*[16]) creates new identities and nationalities for herself (she presents herself as Chilean, French, English, and so on), she is recreating new personas for herself. Her negations are acts of affirmation. The Counsellor's rebellion, or that of Flora Tristan, or that of Fonchito, are no different. Militating against power, rebellion and the rebel's reinvention of identity go hand in hand.

The paradox of this kind of rebellion is how often it supposes the creation of a new structure of power. In *The War of the End of the World*, the Counsellor rebels against the Brazilian Republic in order to assert his own power and creates a religious community around his own persona. Deified by those who follow him, the Counsellor affirms his community of followers by demonising the outside world: the army and the Brazilian Republic. The Counsellor's operation in *The War of the End of the World* is similar to that of Jaguar's in *The Time of the Hero*. Jaguar and the Counsellor are social leaders who break with threatening external power in order to establish their own domain of power.

If Jaguar is a transgressor against the school's authorities, authority remains within the group of transgressors who follow him and who call themselves 'the Circle'; he is challenged by another transgressor, by Alberto Fernández, also known as 'the Poet'. Jaguar is a double figure: a rebel and, at the same time, a leader; a transgressing son in the eyes of the authorities and a violent father figure in relation to the members of the Circle. Betraying the code of ethics he himself has established, in order to cover up their transgressions from the school authorities, becomes the greatest crime. When Jaguar is hounded by some of his fellow students, who wrongly believe he has become a snitch, he treats them with contempt and disgust. Gamboa, the lieutenant who would like to investigate the most serious transgressions the students may have committed, is disciplined by the corrupt authorities of the military academy because they fear that the results of his investigation might tarnish the reputation of the school. He is therefore exiled from Lima to a miserable posting in one of the most remote regions of Peru.

The powerful can question power, and rebels can flaunt it, but in Vargas Llosa's literary world, neither can imagine their existence beyond it.

The utopia of the rebel

The culture of rebellion creates its own utopias. The members of the Circle ruled by Jaguar and the followers of the Counsellor make up mini-societies that have abolished external reality and affirmed their own. The crusaders who accompany Brunelli in 'The madman of the balconies' (*El loco de los balcones*[17]) form their own community. When the rebel leader recreates the world, he transforms the identities of those who surround him. A new name is the symbol of a new identity. Jaguar, the Counsellor and the bad girl have all lost their original proper names. They have assumed new names that identify them as transgressors.

But power has both a social and a domestic dimension. It is not based solely on force, but also in the perverse arts of the ruse. When Fonchito of *In Praise of the Stepmother* sees his father's affection usurped by his stepmother, the boy aspires to familial power. Fonchito is a master of seduction who seeks to occupy the centre of the family. In disposing of his stepmother through his deception, he has established his domain; he has restored, and, at the same time, destroyed and humiliated his father, Rigoberto. He establishes an order in which he is the new dominator.

The power of the father

The principal holder of power, the one against whom the individual rebels, is the father. The theme of the father is central to the universe of Mario Vargas Llosa. The father represents the centre of a twisted reality, the origin of an ontological evil that has perverted the universe, as is the case with the dictators, Odría and Trujillo, whose presence looms over *Conversation in The Cathedral* and *The Feast of the Goat* respectively. Facing the evidence of this original evil, the individual contemplates an essentially corrupt reality. The youth who thinks about himself and his nation at the opening of *Conversation in The Cathedral* affirms the corruption of the world with a double question ('At what precise moment had Peru screwed itself up?' 'he'd screwed himself up somewhere along the line when?').[18] It is not about questions, but about confirmation. In this case, the interrogative form of the question only serves to emphasise the affirmation. The vices that stem from the centre of a corrupt reality unfold around the protagonists. Vargas Llosa's vision takes moral instinct as its point of departure; it is the vision of a corrupt reality felt as an affront from the outset.

The idea of the father as the purveyor of reality's original sin is applicable to Vargas Llosa's entire body of work. Trujillo, Odría and Jaguar are representatives of the father. But the figure of the father is inseparable from the perception of the son: Antonio Imbert, Santiago Zavala, the Poet Alberto. The son is precisely the fighter who seeks to reform reality, to release it from its original sin in order to find a place within it. Any reformulation, however, is also an evasion. The reconstruction of one's own, utopic, reality is the direct consequence of negating it. For the sons, rebellion is a redemption of sorts, a catharsis even if they are not successful. Reality, vicious in its origin because of original sin, is also redeemed in writing and in fiction: Alberto writes little poems; Zavala is a frustrated writer and journalist; the Myopic Journalist in *The War of the End of the World* wants to write an account of the Canudos war.

The struggle of the rebel is the motor of Vargas Llosa's narrative universe. Their collective stories amount to an epic of the defeated: Zavalita against his father and against the government; Alberto against Jaguar and the school's authorities; the conspirators against Trujillo; Gauguin and Flora Tristan against the conventions of their time; the bad girl against the conventions of her society.

Rebellion has an aura of sacredness. The rebel is a hero; his essential tragedy is that his fight will not lead to a resolution in the here and now. His triumph, if it happens, will always occurs within the realm of fiction. History and its institutions (the school, the army, social rules) are too powerful and immutable. Rebels like Alberto, Mayta or Flora Tristan are never able to realise the aims of their rebellion.

But rebellion informs a way of life. If the destiny of the son is to rebel against the father, he organises his life around this rebellion. Encroached upon by the reality of the father, no son can ignore it, or indeed be free of its challenge. Rebellion generates an identity for the rebel predicated on his struggle. Once the reason for the rebellion disappears, so does the rebel's raison d'être. In the death of the father, Vargas Llosa's rebels tend to lose their sense of identity and purpose. In *The Feast of the Goat*, most of the conspirators who participated in the assassination of the dictator lose their sense of determination after the deed is done. Jaguar of *The Time of the Hero* becomes a small-time bureaucrat when the authority figures are indifferent to his transgressions; Zavalita from *Conversation in The Cathedral* ends up working for a third-rate newspaper after his father's death; and Mayta, the revolutionary from *The Real Life of Alejandro Mayta* (*Historia de Mayta*[19]), becomes an ice-cream vendor. The paradoxical drama of the rebel is that he has no identity beyond his struggle with the figure of power. He depends on and therefore affirms it, even as he attempts to negate it.

Rebellion, in Vargas Llosa's literary world, tends to be a risky interlude. In the opening of *The Time of the Hero*, Jaguar does not know that he is setting off a series of events that will lead to his decline. The novel begins with a game of chance. A roll of the dice designates Cava as the member of the Circle who will steal the chemistry exam. Jaguar orders Cava to get going: '"Hurry," Jaguar told him again, "You know, the second on the left"'.[20] From then on, the novel is a sequence of cause and effects. The theft of the exam results in the breaking of a window in the classroom, which leads to the punishment of the cadets, which leads to the Slave accusing Cava. In turn, this is followed by the death of the Slave, bringing about Alberto's accusation of Jaguar as the culprit, and Gamboa's inconclusive investigation. This process ends when society restores its codes and restricts the individuals to their original places: the institution is not interested in the investigation, and all the heroes and anti-heroes of the novel (Gamboa, Alberto and even Jaguar) end up as colourless human beings, reabsorbed into a colourless but corrupt reality. The novel registers, among other processes, the fall from power of Jaguar, who, at the end of the story, is just another ordinary person. By the last pages of *The Time of the Hero*, we know that Jaguar has married Teresa, the daughter of a seamstress who had been involved with the Slave, who loved her, and with Alberto, who has a brief romance with her before finding a girl who belongs to his higher social class. The triumphant power is not that of the individual, but rather that of institutions – that is, the school and the military institution. Only rebellion and transgression are the domain of the individual, the individual who is condemned to continue rebelling.

Jaguar loses his power, but the institution remains unaltered. Trujillo is assassinated, but the conspirators fail to eradicate a legacy of corruption. Zavalita does not accept participating in a corrupt order that will go on without him. The destiny of the rebellious son is not to replace the father; it is to go under with him, as the sources of his rebellion go on their merry way.

The possessed body

In Vargas Llosa's novels, society, politics, love and sexual relations, as well as the family, are expressed as zones in which power struggles take place. 'Power', 'the father' and 'possession' are expressions that are synonyms for each other in his literary world, in which sexual possession and torture are often brutal affirmations of power. The reality is one in which characters either dominate or are dominated. What's more, as Zavalita explains in *Conversation in The Cathedral*, 'in this country a person who doesn't screw himself up, screws up other people'.[21] This dilemma defines his protagonists. For Vargas Llosa, social life is a forest made of zoological types. The names of the cadets in *The Time of the Hero* (Jaguar, Boa), the surname of the head of *La Crónica* newspaper in *Conversation in The Cathedral* (Becerrita, or Heifer) and the titles of his books (*The Cubs, The Feast of the Goat*) are references to a reality of hunters and prey: an animalised world.

Poised against the alternate oralities – jargon, the cult of force, the clandestine eroticism of the rebel – is the written language of power: the regulations of the Leoncio Prado military academy, the declaration of the Republican government of Brazil. The slogans repeated by the members of the street gang of Piura, 'The Unconquerables', are their response to the written rules of power. The rules of subjection that govern the Circle, the religious dogmas of the Counsellor in *The War of the End of the World*, sustain alternate pacts of power to that of official institutions. The language of rebellion is based on the force of orality, an up-to-date and flexible presence opposed to the written word.

For Vargas Llosa, the body can be a site where power relations are played out. The body as an allegory of a violated nation is enacted in the torture and rape sequences that appear in *The Feast of the Goat*. The same could be said of the sexualised hazing rituals to which the military school's third year students submit their younger cohorts in *The Time of the Hero*. The cadets of the Leoncio Prado military academy line up on the parade ground by day and hold masturbation competitions by night. They search out their preferred prostitute, Golden Feet, as an expression of their rebellion and their alternative power, without thinking of the consequences of their actions on the lives of the women who service them. Rigoberto is meticulously obsessed with maintaining his body youthful before the mirror. Palomino Molero's skewered body at the beginning of *Who Killed Palomino Molero?* (*¿Quién mató a Palomino Molero?*[22]) is the expression of the brutal power of the unknown killers that generates a criminal investigation which will not bring anyone to justice. Pichula Cuéllar, losing his penis in *The Cubs* (*Los cachorros*[23]), loses a symbol of power according to the juvenile mythology of the group, and with that loss he also loses his entry into the reproduction of a social order.

But in Vargas Llosa's literary world the body can also be the manifestation of an individual utopia. Vargas Llosa's Gauguin in *The Way to Paradise* is related to Rigoberto in his bathroom. Both are searching for the purification of the body in light of the insufficiencies or degradation of the world as they have found it. The recognition of the body as an expression of identity in Vargas Llosa is also developed in *The Bad Girl*, when the protagonist repeatedly changes her look, and with it, her identity. The attention to detail with which Vargas Llosa portrays the body of his characters is further expressed in the scenes of violence (which are meticulously written in *The Feast of the Goat*) and of eroticism (which form a large part of *In Praise of the Stepmother* and *The Notebooks of Don Rigoberto*). The violation of Jurema in *The War of the End of the World* is written in extreme and painful detail; the same goes for the physical description of Henry Chirinos in *The Feast of the Goat*. The experiences of the body are the setting for its spiritual and moral identity. Vargas Llosa's work proceeds from a minute delectation of the body's pleasures and extreme miseries.

Pacts in Paradise

In some sense, Captain Pantoja's project to establish a clandestine prostitution service secretly sanctioned by the Peruvian military in the heart of the Amazon region is an allegory for Vargas Llosa's literary approach. From this perspective, Captain Pantoja is an ascetic of the brothel's disciplines; a mystic of pleasure. He renounces his environment (his superiors, his family) in order to establish a utopic community in its stead. In this community, he realises his ideal. Given that the military is inefficient and lax, he represents its ideal virtues (order, discipline) in a system that he himself has created. His objective is to sacralise a new reality that will redefine and reformulate the earlier reality. His intention to create a new world is no different from that of the novelist in the sense that Vargas Llosa gives to it. In order to complete the appearance of this new society, Pantoja attempts to substitute the referents of reality. Like Flora Tristan, like the Counsellor, like Jaguar, Pantoja is a social utopian. His drama, like that of his fellows, is that of seeing his utopia destroyed.

Pantoja's utopia is born from his personal impulses. In the organisation of the perfect service of the visitors, where everyone is both comrade and friend at the same time, Pantoja is the central character, the holder of power. The army was never able to give him what he has now: to be emperor of a floating kingdom of women with whom he navigates the Amazon, bringing happiness to the soldiers.

But his power is temporary and ambiguous. The army – that is, the reality that surrounds him – will destroy this utopia in due course. In this sense, *Captain Pantoja and the Special Service* rewrites, in a humorous key, the themes of *The Time of the Hero*. The army (power) is an agent that represents reality in its most radical version. By its very nature, it is designed to suppress imagination, freedom and everything to do with human beings exercising their individualism. Pantoja, Jaguar, the Poet Alberto and the Counsellor rise up before power. Marginalised so they become powerful in their exclusion, they gather marginalised others to them. But this is the power of an ephemeral god.

Ephemeral power creates its own illusions. There is a gallery of secondary characters, upstarts and followers in Vargas Llosa's work. They are the unconditional secondary figures who depend on other more powerful ones.

Power is lived vicariously by Balaguer, Cerebrito Cabral and Henry Chirinos in *The Feast of the Goat*; by Lituma in *Who Killed Palomino Molero?*; by Boa, Cava and Rulos in *The Time of the Hero*. All of them court, support and seek to cling to the powerful. They are a derivative species of the leader. They only feel confident within his shadow. In Vargas Llosa's work, the exercise of power is inseparable from that of violence. Power is the natural expression of a corrupt reality, a moral stain. There is no possibility of exercising it with innocence.

In the end the ambiguous, paradoxical nature of power is the framework in which Vargas Llosa explores the behaviour of his characters. In his work, the exploration of behaviour in relation to power is an inroad into the obscure regions of the human being. Interpreting the individual impulses that drive human beings to search for power – to prolong it – the work of Vargas Llosa is an homage to those who challenge it. Mobilised by their rebellion, Vargas Llosa's heroes occupy the place of the dreamers and the defeated. Their fire is indomitable. Their epic is that of an eternal transgression.

NOTES

1. Mario Vargas Llosa. *La casa verde*. Barcelona: Seix Barral, 1966.
2. Mario Vargas Llosa. *La ciudad y los perros*. Barcelona: Seix Barral, 1963.
3. Mario Vargas Llosa. *Conversación en La Catedral*. Barcelona: Seix Barral, 1969.
4. Mario Vargas Llosa. *La guerra del fin del mundo*. Barcelona: Seix Barral, 1981.
5. Mario Vargas Llosa. *La fiesta del Chivo*. Madrid: Alfaguara, 2000.
6. Mario Vargas Llosa. *The Time of the Hero*. Trans. Lysander Kemp. New York: Grove Press, 1966, p. 7.
7. Mario Vargas Llosa. *El pez en el agua. Memorias*. Barcelona: Seix Barral, 1993.
8. Mario Vargas Llosa. *La tía Julia y el escribidor*. Barcelona, Seix Barral, 1977.
9. Albert Camus. *The Rebel*. New York: Vintage, 1956.
10. A revised version of this article appears as '*L'Etranger*: The Outsider Must Die'. In Mario Vargas Llosa. *Touchstones: Essays on Literature, Art and Politics*. London: Faber and Faber, 2007, pp. 90–7.
11. Ibid.
12. Mario Vargas Llosa. *El paraíso en la otra esquina*. Madrid: Alfaguara, 2003.
13. Mario Vargas Llosa. *Pantaleón y las visitadoras*. Barcelona: Seix Barral, 1973.
14. Mario Vargas Llosa. *Elogio de la madrastra*. Barcelona: Tusquets, 1988.
15. Mario Vargas Llosa. *Los cuadernos de Don Rigoberto*. Madrid: Alfaguara, 1997.
16. Mario Vargas Llosa. *Travesuras de la niña mala*. Madrid: Alfaguara, 2006.
17. Mario Vargas Llosa. *El loco de los balcones*. Barcelona: Seix Barral, 1993.
18. Mario Vargas Llosa. *Conversation in The Cathedral*. Trans. Gregory Rabassa. New York: Harper & Row, 1975, p. 3. Translation slightly modified.
19. Mario Vargas Llosa. *Historia de Mayta*. Barcelona: Seix Barral, 1984.

20. *Time of the Hero*, p. 7.
21. *Conversation*, p. 144. Translation slightly modified.
22. Mario Vargas Llosa. *¿Quién mató a Palomino Molero?* Barcelona: Seix Barral, 1986.
23. Mario Vargas Llosa. *Los cachorros. Pichula Cuéllar*. Barcelona: Ediciones Lumen, 1967.

2

GERALD MARTIN

The early novels
The Time of the Hero and *The Green House*

Many critics would argue that Mario Vargas Llosa deserved the Nobel Prize in Literature in 1981, when, at the age of forty-five, he published his 'Tolstoyan' epic, *The War of the End of the World* (*La guerra del fin del mundo*[1]). So precocious was Vargas Llosa's talent that the 1966 publication of *The Green House* (*La casa verde*[2]), his second novel – and a fully-fledged classic – had already persuaded many readers that this thirty-year-old Peruvian was one of the twentieth century's great novelists.[3] This essay looks back at *The Green House*, the first winner of the epoch-making Rómulo Gallegos Prize in Caracas in 1967, and its predecessor, *The Time of the Hero* (*La ciudad y los perros*, 1963[4]), winner of the 1962 Biblioteca Breve and Formentor Prizes in Spain. His first book, the short story collection *Los jefes*[5] ('The Leaders'), had also won a prize in Spain in 1958 – and Vargas Llosa's first two visits to Europe, Paris in 1958 and Spain in 1959, were also thanks to European prizes. Half a century later, he finally has the full collection.

In the end the great surprise was not that his two remarkable early novels could hardly be improved on – was *Sentimental Education* an improvement on *Madame Bovary*, or *Anna Karenina* on *War and Peace*? – but rather, in the first place, that the Nobel committee waited so long to honour him, and in the second place, that after waiting so long they unexpectedly changed their collective mind, belatedly giving him, at the age of seventy-four, the ultimate recognition he so obviously deserved. The explanation for this distorted trajectory was almost certainly, again, a dual one: Vargas Llosa's political opinions and actions moved to the right after the 1960s, which is always a problem if you want to win a Nobel Prize; and another remarkable Latin American novelist, Gabriel García Márquez, distorted Vargas Llosa's destiny just a year after *The Green House* was published, with a much more accessible and transparent masterpiece that shortly thereafter acquired mythological status of its own: *One Hundred Years of Solitude* (*Cien años de soledad*, 1967[6]).

The intervention of *One Hundred Years of Solitude* and its legendary author has allowed literary historians to forget what a phenomenon Vargas Llosa was during that period in the 1960s when the so-called 'Boom' of the Latin American novel was born, baptised and confirmed. In 1962, when he completed *The Time of the Hero*, which was destined to be a sensation in Spain when it was published the following year, Vargas Llosa was only twenty-six years of age, nine years younger than Gabriel García Márquez (b. 1927), who was almost completely unheard of at the time, almost a decade younger than the instigator of the Boom, the Mexican Carlos Fuentes (b. 1928), and more than two decades younger than the Argentinian Julio Cortázar (b. 1914), author of the astonishing *Hopscotch* (*Rayuela*, 1963). By 1969, when the Boom was beginning to fragment, Vargas Llosa had written three major novels in seven years. None of them showed even the slightest sign of having been written in haste.

Because he was so young, and in some ways unformed, Vargas Llosa's route to literary stardom was different from that of his older peers. In particular, whereas the other three Boom novelists gained their recognition through Latin American publishers, Vargas Llosa became the precursor of what was to happen increasingly over the next fifty years by achieving his success through publication in Spain – a country at that time fastidiously avoided by most other writers for fear of being compromised by General Franco's dictatorship. (Before long, however, all the leading Latin American writers would be published in Franco's Spain, and several of them, including both Vargas Llosa and García Márquez, would live there.)

Vargas Llosa began a doctorate on the poet Rubén Darío at the Complutense University in Madrid in 1959, but moved on to Paris when his one-year grant expired, and turned to teaching and broadcasting. But both his first books were in line with Spanish expectations, which is possibly why they both won Spanish prizes. The Spanish novel was dominated at the time by books about adolescents trying to grow up in a grey and morally corrupt society, where freedom was strictly limited and change a distant hope. Vargas Llosa's first collection of stories, *Los jefes*, was very much in this mode. The title story reveals a problematic that Vargas Llosa has pursued from that time to the present day: the matter of motivation, of sincerity, the way in which those who claim to represent moral or political ideas inevitably find themselves involved in a struggle for power with their co-religionaries or, indeed – worse – find themselves acknowledging that power was what they were always concerned with and ideals were merely a front for personal ambition. The narrator of 'The leaders' is one of the organisers of a strike by high-school students over the matter of an examination schedule; but as the conflict unfolds he confesses: 'I felt anxious and doubtful, because deep down I knew that what was at stake was not the exam schedule, not even a question of honour, but a personal vendetta.'[7]

The second book, *The Time of the Hero*, explored the same theme, but it was a revelation: although once again a work about adolescence, this first novel was light years ahead of Vargas Llosa's Spanish contemporaries. Its technical prowess, inspired in part, perhaps, by his living and working for two years in a Parisian milieu, dominated by the technically obsessive *nouveau roman*, put all of them instantly in the shade, at the very moment when Latin America was experiencing the first years of the 1959 Cuban Revolution: suddenly everything seemed possible, both to writers of Latin American novels and to their readers. Vargas Llosa's first novel reflected all of this. Although his worldview has never been less than sceptical, it is arguable that his early works were moderated by a spirit of openness and political rebelliousness that would be much less evident in the disillusioned 1970s and 1980s. Thus *The Time of the Hero* and *The Green House* are probably the most optimistic novels that he ever wrote: the world they portray is grim, but some social progress is shown to be possible and the author criticises society because he sincerely wants change and is prepared to work for it.

Forty years ago, in 1971, I wrote a brief article on the already great Peruvian novelist entitled 'Mario Vargas Llosa: New Novel and Realism'.[8] My contention was that this young writer was different in literary orientation from all the other major Latin American writers of his generation, and from the new movement, to the extent that there was one, as a whole. The best-known currents within the new novel were a sort of labyrinthine metaphysics largely emanating from the River Plate cities, whose best-known exponents were Jorge Luis Borges and Julio Cortázar, and an essentially tropical magical realism centred on the Caribbean zone, which was inspired by the antecedents of Miguel Angel Asturias and Alejo Carpentier, and exemplified in the work of writers as different as Gabriel García Márquez and Guillermo Cabrera Infante.

In essence, I argued that Vargas Llosa's orientation was that of the great bourgeois realists of the nineteenth century (Balzac, Flaubert, Tolstoy) and their twentieth-century successors (most notably Dos Passos and Faulkner): psychological, sociological, historical or, in a word, critical. Needless to say, there was no assumption of any simplificatory intention in this assertion; on the contrary, all Vargas Llosa's works, like those of his great mentors Flaubert and Faulkner, show an obsessive concern with form and structure. At the same time, I noted that Vargas Llosa himself might have been thought to be unhappy with his own writing, since whenever he talked about those stark, sober and deadly serious works of his, he spoke in terms that made it sound as if he really wanted to be playful, whimsical and lightly fantastic, like his fellow participants in the Boom; as if the author of *The Time of the Hero*, *The Green House* and *Conversation in The Cathedral* (*Conversación en La Catedral*[9]), all among the greatest of Latin American novels, and arguably the very greatest of all Latin American 'realist' novels, would rather have authored such frothy concoctions as Cabrera Infante's *Three Trapped Tigers* (*Tres tristes tigres*, 1965),

Cortázar's *Hopscotch* or Fuentes's *Change of Skin* (*Cambio de piel*, 1967). My point seemed, for a time, a prophetic one. From that precise moment, which happened to coincide with Vargas Llosa's separation from the Cuban Revolution and the Latin American left, the influence of French fiction on him diminished; works like *The Green House* and *Conversation in The Cathedral* ceased to appear, and the new Vargas Llosa, playful, parodic and satirical (neither so angry nor so young), emerged. The author of *Captain Pantoja and the Special Service* (*Pantaleón y las visitadoras*, 1973[10]) and *Aunt Julia and the Scriptwriter* (*La tía Julia y el escribidor*, 1977[11]) really did belong, heart and soul, to the new Latin American novel, and his over-determining literary influences, indeed, were now his own fellow Latin American writers (of course, Vargas Llosa, being who and what he is, usually managed to improve on the models), rather than his former, deadly serious, highly committed French idols, from Flaubert to Sartre. It is still worth noting, however, that both Vargas Llosa and Sartre distanced themselves from the Cuban Revolution at the same time and, indeed, in the same letter, and that a few years later Vargas Llosa would return to politics, idealism and disillusionment with *The War of the End of the World*, in which his disillusionment was now not only more acute, but also permanent.

Yet there is always more to Mario Vargas Llosa than meets the eye. For one so calm, urbane, well-mannered – indeed, so cool and apparently rational – the Peruvian author has held some disconcerting views about the demonic function of writing: that writers, whether they know it or not, seek to avenge themselves on their families, society, life and God himself; that they feed on carrion, like vultures, engaging in every form of perversion, from voyeurism downwards; and feel compelled to expose, exhibit, humiliate and prostitute themselves like striptease artistes, for the sake of their critical mission. Thus, he has converted many of the most important experiences of his life unashamedly (though, doubtless, misleadingly) into the subject matter of his fiction, most notoriously in the case of *The Time of the Hero*, in which the military academy in which he studied as a secondary school student is mercilessly depicted under its own name and with all its most minutely secret details exposed and revealed (copies of the novel were ceremonially burned on the academy parade ground soon after its publication); and of course in *Aunt Julia and the Scriptwriter*, which will be studied in a later chapter of this book.

The Time of the Hero

The Time of the Hero, as mentioned, appeared in 1963, when its author was a mere twenty-seven, at the very beginning of the Boom of the Latin American 'new novel'.[12] It was remarkable for its narrative efficiency, technical expertise, controlled passion and bleakness of vision. It was based on cinematic montage out of Flaubert, in the sense that it achieved density by carefully cutting and cross-stitching a very long novel into the dimensions of an average-sized text. It gave a highly critical but convincing portrayal of the Peruvian military, and a prescient one too, since it was written at a moment when the new wave of neofascist military regimes would shortly be striking their first blow with the 1964 coup in Brazil. It is also one of the most forensic depictions of Latin American machismo, giving a brutal but effective insight into the effects of the ideological state apparatuses and the mass media on the consciousness of susceptible adolescents in 1950s Peru, well before the New Left came to theorise such phenomena.

As in the short story 'Los jefes' ('The leaders'), the plot of *The Time of the Hero* revolves around an act of rebellion against a school examination. At first, however, no matter of principle is at stake: a group of cadets in the Leoncio Prado military academy, who have formed a self-defence group known as the Circle, conspire to steal the questions for an upcoming chemistry examination. Their crime is discovered and the entire year loses its weekend privileges. A cadet known as the Slave finds this unbearable, because he wants to see his new – and first ever – girlfriend; in order to resolve the problem, he squeals on Cava, the cadet who was designated to break into the office where the questions were kept. Cava is expelled from the academy, and at the end of the first of the novel's two halves the Slave dies of a gunshot wound. The second half sees a division among the cadets as a result of this death; one of the middle-class students, Alberto, known as the Poet, accuses Jaguar, one of the working-class cadets and the leader of the Circle, of murder. The director of the academy decides that the matter must be hushed up for the sake of the institution's good name and refuses an investigation (the kind of decision that governments take all the time).

What sounds commonplace in summary is utterly transformed in the telling. No author had previously applied such critical realism so efficiently to Latin American society through the medium of the novel; but there was much, much more to this book. Formally, the text was invisibly structured through a ghostly architecture built on essentially Faulknerian techniques – *Los jefes* ('The Leaders'), spare and austere, had owed its largest debt to Hemingway – that Vargas Llosa would only theorise years later, when he wrote his famous critical appreciation of García Márquez's narrative fiction, *García Márquez. Historia de un deicidio*[13] ('García Márquez: history of a deicide'). The four main concepts are: 'communicating vessels', a technique through which realities from different times and places are first juxtaposed and then merged (Faulkner used this most notably in *Light in August* and *The Wild Palms*); 'Chinese boxes', the technique of narrating one story within another, or within a frame; the 'hidden datum', the technique of withholding information and releasing it at the most dramatically appropriate moment, a modernist technique that demands assiduous reader participation and turns all novels into detective stories; and, finally, the 'qualitative leap', out of Hegel, Marx and other philosophers, through which the narrative achieves a level of intensity that seems suddenly to burst it through to another dimension of reality. The last two methods are used throughout Vargas Llosa's fiction; the first two determine, respectively, the entire conception and structure of *The Green House* (based on two giant communicating vessels, the Amazon jungle and the city of Piura) and *Conversation in The Cathedral* (a novel constructed like a Chinese box in which almost all the action either takes place inside or becomes the subject of a long conversation between two of the characters in a down-at-heel bar called The Cathedral).

It is this ghostly architectural design – organising the novel's social space and historical time, and precisely focusing the novel's events and the reader's responses – which explains the impact of these early novels. Their remarkable fusion of moral and aesthetic emotion is rarely matched in twentieth-century fiction, and unparalleled in the history of the Latin American novel, which has excelled in many things, but not in the supreme virtues of the realist text, which Flaubert brought to such a fine art with *Madame Bovary*[14] and Faulkner with, for example, *Absalom, Absalom!* It could not be claimed that Vargas Llosa reaches Faulkner's level of poetic eloquence – few writers do – but he takes Faulkner's technical expertise to levels that Faulkner never dreamed about.

In fact, *The Time of the Hero* exhibited two features generally overlooked by its readers and critics. First, it explored the nature of fiction and the status of the novel as a historical genre. As much as anything, based on its use of hidden data and qualitative leaps, it is a murder mystery and also a detective story: who killed the character known as the Slave? However, as in all Vargas Llosa's works, which are always about something altogether different, there is no solution to the mystery and no satisfactory answers to any of the questions. Second, in addition to the self-consciousness that characterises the work of this deceptively straightforward novelist (who uses the least 'literary' language in contemporary Latin American fiction and only rarely allows the discussion of educated 'ideas' in his texts), the work is also self-referential. This is not simply because all the characters are 'storytellers', in both senses of the word (narrators, liars), or because one of the two central characters, the middle-class Alberto, is called the Poet (he writes love letters for his classmates, as well as highly profitable pornographic stories); but rather because the very last scene of the novel, a tour de force, is simultaneously a parody of the soap-opera approach to human reality (one of Vargas Llosa's vices); a satirical spoof of the mixed motives that have led his readers through a long, sordid and frequently violent narrative, which is just about to fizzle out on them like a damp squib; and yet – despite all the foregoing – an existential triumph for one of the characters and a happy ending to a love story.[15]

Vargas Llosa, through a highly imaginative merging of strands of first- and third-person narration, applies his virtuosity to Faulknerian techniques in order to skew the reader's experience of the novel in the direction of one of its least appealing characters: a thug, a petty tyrant and possibly a murderer. Infinitely complicated and only explainable in outline terms in this brief essay, it is organised in two chronological halves, as mentioned above, and has five narrative strands. (It is also organised, less obviously, into two geographical segments: the Academy and the City, the inside and the outside.[16]) The cover-up of the Slave's death completes the education of adolescent boys, who, while they learn about maths and chemistry in school, are also learning, both inside and outside it, that society is corrupt, and that in future, after they graduate, it will be every man for himself.

Three of the five strands are narrated in the third person and two in the first person. There is what might be called a core narrative (third-person narration), which is the effective 'mainstream' of the book, while the other four connect to four central characters: Alberto, the Poet, who seems to be the central character (third-person narration); that involving Ricardo, the Slave, a weak but decent, lower-middle-class cadet, incapable of surviving in the piranha pool that is the military academy (third-person narration);[17] Boa, a crude, masturbatory adolescent from the lower – even 'lumpen' – classes (first-person narration as undifferentiated stream of consciousness); and Jaguar, a once innocent, working-class cadet, involved in a life of crime even before he arrives at the academy, but also fearless and a natural leader. (We never learn the real names of the two working-class characters, as if reflecting society's prejudice that the lower classes are 'all the same' and need not be individualised.)

All four strands relating to these individual cadets end at the moment they enter the academy – in other words, they are all flashbacks making up a very large collective prologue – and each of them comes to an abrupt conclusion as their protagonist's life joins the institutional world and their narrative thereby merges with the core narrative. Given that the two working-class characters enjoy the privilege of first-person narratives, their consciousness is brought much closer to that of the reader. Moreover, the strand relating to Jaguar continues the longest and is the novel's paramount example of a hidden datum, as most readers are unable to reconcile its sensitive first-person narrator – whose identity is not revealed until the very end – with the brutal Jaguar observed in the core narrative and through the eyes of the other cadets. In other words, the reader's presumed social prejudices, which are fully validated by the conventional perceptions of Jaguar's fellow cadets, are prevented from affecting his or her estimation of both the inner life and the extra-academic life of the character who takes over as principal protagonist at the very last moment. By this means, Jaguar is able to attain some kind of 'heroic' status at the end: he gets the good-hearted girl he has always sincerely loved, takes a respectable job in order to give her a decent family life, and yet remains loyal to those who helped him in earlier times, whereas his adversary Alberto, a character who shows some good instincts and with whom the reader is encouraged to identify, reneges on his brief moment of social conscience and decides to revert to his middle-class social type by marrying for status and money, while fully intending to cheat on his wife and live a life of luxury and dishonesty. Neither outcome is satisfactory – Jaguar is undoubtedly 'recuperated' by conventional society, as the Marxists used to say – but there is little doubt as to which is considered more admirable.

Critical orthodoxy has been to declare a plague on all the characters, assuming that this is what Vargas Llosa himself has done. Not only is this not the case, but he goes on to use similar techniques in his next two novels, with similar objectives and similar results. We will only be concerning ourselves here with the first of them, *The Green House*.

The Green House

One of the three or four greatest novels ever written in Latin America, *The Green House* is a compelling representation of the lives, dreams and illusions of ordinary Latin Americans. The fact that its author wrote it at the age of twenty-nine, under the pressure of immense audience expectation after the success of *The Time of the Hero*, makes the achievement all the more remarkable. Nevertheless, despite the acclaim with which it was greeted – it was very much a necessary work if the Boom was to be sustained – it has not been as popular with readers and critics as other novels by Vargas Llosa. One suspects that it is a question of the breadth of ambition going unnoticed, and in that sense it is akin to the Guatemalan novelist Miguel Angel Asturias's *Men of Maize* (*Hombres de maíz*, 1949), written in another version for another generation. Neither novel can be fully appreciated unless the reader is prepared to work very hard, because messages as complex as theirs cannot be communicated without highly complex literary structures.

The novel does not seem to 'say' anything at all; its characters are at once irredeemably unreflexive and determinedly self-absorbed. Yet it is an account of the transition from a traditional to a modern society (from the development of Latin America from the nineteenth-century world it still remained in the 1920s and 1930s, to the world of the 1960s when the book was written), and about the relation between the city and the country, condensed in the juxtaposition of a series of events that take place in the Peruvian Amazon and others that occur in the coastal city of Piura. Undoubtedly, this juxtaposition implies others, between Europe and native America, male and female, culture and nature, calculation and spontaneity, domination and liberation, but these are for readers to trace amidst the interwoven forest of details and labyrinth of signs.

It is depressing that so many critics who have been able to respond to works typical of the new novel of the 1960s and 1970s, conceptually pretentious or metaphorically impenetrable and opaque, have so largely failed to perceive the extraordinary richness in a realist novel as vast and ambitious as this. Again, the text is intricately structured: indeed, it is clearly Vargas Llosa's outstanding architectural achievement, one in which each formal device is perfectly conceived for the purpose to which it is put and in which the overall design is almost breathtaking in its simultaneous complexity and coherence. Again, too, it is self-referential: the Amazon's shifting geography, branching its way seasonally through the forest, like Piura's susceptibility to envelopment in sand, reflects the novel's striking combination of openness and closedness. It is a text in which history has meaning for the author but none for the characters, for whom it is merely life, as open and mysterious as the Amazon or any other unconquered territory, or as closed as the oppressive and unequal societies that have existed in Latin America since the conquest in the sixteenth century.

The Green House, written when the impact of the Cuban Revolution was at its strongest and while Vargas Llosa himself was exploring his own full potential as a novelist, represents the high point of his political radicalism, an unmistakable if not radical critique of patriarchy, capitalism and imperialism characteristic of the era. (The story of Jum, the indigenous leader who rebels against the encroaching capitalists and is brutally tortured to secure his silence, is just one of several examples.) It is the only work by Vargas Llosa in which women can be interpreted as triumphing. (*The Feast of the Goat*, *The Way to Paradise* and *The Bad Girl* (*La fiesta del Chivo*, *El paraíso en la otra esquina* and *Travesuras de la niña mala*[18]) all have redoubtable female protagonists, but none of them triumphs over their masculine partners and antagonists in the way that Chunga, Lalita and Bonifacia do in *The Green House*.) Equally, it is the only one in which the call of the wild and the primacy of nature herself survive the process of exploitation and disenchantment. Simply in terms of an achievement of the imagination, though, one must underline the fact that here, for the first time in his career, Vargas Llosa took the risk of writing both about a world he only knew indirectly and about characters whom he knew hardly at all, with almost no trace whatever of an authorial alter ego. Vargas Llosa did base his novel on personal experience of a brief visit into the jungle, however, a scenario that would recur in several works. Typically, for a writer often branded a naturalist, and a devotee of the perfectionist Flaubert, he made a second journey into the Peruvian Amazon to check details and to add to the authenticity. (The jungle is a scenario that recurs in several later books and becomes an important part of the writer's imaginative storehouse.) The result is a memorable picture of a cruelly divided Peru, riven by every internal tension imaginable in a contemporary nation, and the novel reflects this in its structure, in both obvious and more subtle ways.

This work is especially important, because although Vargas Llosa has a penchant for big books, this is his only truly panoramic, or what I elsewhere call 'Ulyssean' novel, which mythologises, simultaneously, the nation, the continent and, more secretly, the author's own autobiographical experience.[19] It is not only a symbolic encapsulation of the history and geography of Peru, but also, implicitly, of Latin America as a whole. The story begins in the Peruvian Amazon jungle, with a group of soldiers and nuns (the military and the Church) kidnapping the children of indigenous tribes in order to save them from barbarism and educate them in Christianity and other Western values (the justification for the sixteenth-century conquest, though Vargas Llosa never talks in such abstract terms). Behind this action we soon see that the soldiers are also being used to support determined capitalist entrepreneurs invading tribal territories for their own enrichment, especially through the exploitation of rubber. Eventually, somewhat surprisingly, one of the soldiers marries one of the Indian girls, Bonifacia (who may be the rebel Jum's daughter) and takes her back to his home town of Piura, a northern city situated near the Pacific coast, in one of the driest regions of the country. Unfortunately, things do not turn out as the newlyweds hope: Lituma's return to his home town restores him to a world of lower-class machismo, and he ends up in prison after being provoked into a calamitous duel in the bar known as The Green House (hence the title of the novel, though it also suggests the Amazon jungle itself), whereupon his wife is seduced by one of his best friends and becomes a prostitute.

The Green House was founded early in the twentieth century by the mysterious Don Anselmo, who becomes a legend in the city. His strand is the central one in a plot that, again, could have been taken straight out of a Latin American soap opera. It narrates the founding of the brothel, Anselmo's scandalous relationship with a blind and mute adolescent, her death in a fire and his decline to the point where he ends up, also blind, as a harp player in a revived Green House run by his daughter.

The book is effectively in two segments, like *The Time of the Hero*. One corresponds to events that take place in the jungle around the mission and garrison of Santa María de Nieva, and the other to the city of Piura. On the edge of the northern desert, near the coast, Piura happens to be the first city founded by the Spaniards on their arrival in what is now Peru. This counterpointed story – that of the jungle and the city – is told in four narrative sequences plus an epilogue, with each of these sequences broken up laterally, so to speak, by five strands that run through the entire novel (though two fuse in the second half of the book, leaving four strands there instead of five) and adopt different narrative modes to reflect the different kinds of reality they convey, or the different kind of narrative effect that Vargas Llosa seeks to produce.[20] In other words, the narration of these two worlds is divided into dozens of episodes, which are shuffled like cards by a writer who is probably a virtuoso player of patience. Like the pre-cinematographic Flaubert, and all subsequent cine-montage specialists, Vargas Llosa is an expert – *the* great expert in Latin American fiction – in the knowing production of specific effects, undoubtedly one of the great tests of narrative art in the twentieth century.

The Green House had to resist the inevitable criticism that the structures and techniques integrated into its texture are too abstract and that its art is too automatic. Vargas Llosa was more than equal to the charge: the apparently mechanistic strategies become ever more complex, until an astonishing and quite unpredictable monumentality emerges, without the author himself changing pace, launching climaxes or in any other way modifying his imperturbable posture. Part of the explanation lies in the lucidity with which he sets his objectives. His two basic devices – communicating vessels and Chinese boxes – operate here at both macro and micro levels, creating a remarkable alternation of mirror and mirage.

There is almost no interiority in *The Green House*: virtually everything is visual, as in a film, or auditory, as in a radio drama. The only moment at which there is any sustained interiorisation is during what turns out to be the dying soliloquy of one of the major characters – in an important sense, *the* major character, Anselmo – and of course, precisely because the device has not been used before, its effect is immeasurably heightened. The emphasis on the external, the visible and the audible, a common enough device since Flaubert, and more so since the French *nouveau roman*, creates a striking effect of mysteriousness when applied first to the Amazon forest and then juxtaposed with contemporary urban consciousness: 'people who make maps don't realise that the Amazon is like a hot woman, she don't stay still a moment. Here everything moves, the rivers, the animals, the trees. What a crazy place we ended up in, Fushía.'[21]

> As it crosses the desert, the wind from the Cordillera heats up and hardens: armed with sand, it follows the river, and when it reaches the city it hangs between earth and sky like some dazzling breastplate. There it empties itself: every day of the year, at twilight, a dry fine rain like sawdust, which only stops at dawn, falls on squares, roofs, spires, belfries, balconies and trees, and paves Piura's streets white.[22]

By the time we are through with *The Green House* we can see the novel's inner logic – a path through the jungle; we can see the effectiveness of its techniques and where they have been leading. Thus we come to realise, after hundreds of pages, that *The Green House* is counterpointed between Santa María and Piura for a reason that goes beyond – though it also reflects – the jungle/city thematic of the novel, namely because two characters, Lituma (the Sergeant) and Bonifacia (the Jungle Girl), meet and get married, linking through their relationship the two hopelessly incompatible realities of urban and rural Peru – and Vargas Llosa somehow, through this relationship, shows us in a new way how every marriage brings together not only two different people, not only a man and a woman, but two different families, two different histories, two different traditions and often two different 'worlds'.

Later we also perceive that the moment of their marriage is not only the spatial – and cultural – but also the temporal dividing line of the novel (like the temporal dividing lines in *The Time of the Hero*: first the book's two halves, before and after the death of the Slave; second, the narration of the cadets' lives before and after entering the military academy), and that, both structurally and symbolically, everything that takes place in the jungle is chronologically prior to everything that happens in Piura (other than Anselmo's early experiences there) – at which point we also understand why each of the two is known by their own name in their birthplace but by a stereotyped nickname in other regions (compare the use of nicknames in *The Time of the Hero*). We therefore come to see that the novel is also very much about that 1920s theme, Latin American regionalism, and about innumerable attempts by the characters, usually vainly, to achieve some kind of unity and reconciliation across Peru's regional, racial and even sexual divide. Then we see further that this point of departure based on a man and a woman, Lituma and Bonifacia, allows the careful and precise integration of diverse strands threading through the entire novel, some of which last only thirty days and others sixty years of historical time, while occupying the same number of pages of narrative time. (Even trying to describe these patterns produces a sense of dizziness!) Vargas Llosa understands so completely the relation between structure and process that he is acutely aware at all times of the reader's plot-constructed consciousness. Even so, how he found the sheer narratorial imagination to know how this would all fit together in the mind of his reader, both in terms of individual effects and the overall design, remains a mystery, but the technical mastery behind this mystery creates literary effects – a magical aesthetic – which few other modern novelists have ever achieved.

The vertebral sixty-year-long story, that of Anselmo the harpist, founder of the brothel called The Green House, and fountain of myth and local legend in the novel – though it turns out that he is not from Piura, still less its popular quarter the Mangachería, but from the jungle – is also used, in another tour de force, to replicate (and even parody: 'In the first month after his arrival in Piura, nothing happened') the narrative techniques of the nineteenth-century realists and, no doubt, the 'pre-literature' of the 1920s 'novelists of the land in Latin America', whom Vargas Llosa used to scorn in his early years as a novelist. Then, gradually, this mode is dissolved and fuses into the stream-of-consciousness techniques used in those same 1920s works by Joyce and, later, Faulkner and Vargas Llosa himself (in other words, this strand alone summarises the evolution of the twentieth-century novel), ending with Anselmo's dying meditation, as the absent novelist suddenly addresses his central character at the end of his journey through life and this novel:

> And one more time ask yourself if it was better or worse, if life has to be like that, and what would have happened if [Toñita] hadn't, if you and she, if it was all a dream or if things are always different from dreams, and then one last effort and ask yourself if you ever really resigned yourself and if it's because she died or because you are old that you are so accepting of the idea of dying yourself.[23]

Questions like these could be addressed to any character in a novel at the end of their fictional life, but Vargas Llosa elicits a much greater impact because of the way in which he has prepared this moment and the way he has it framed. Anselmo in his tower – explorer, conqueror, exploiter, creator of fantasies and fountainhead of myth (from epic hero to popular street singer) – is one of the most complete and radical visions of the patriarchal complex, presented by Vargas Llosa with an almost perfect blend of ambiguities, which at once holds, recreates, exposes and subverts. It is an unusual achievement in Latin America, where, on the whole, the partisan character of narrative psychology – based on a largely unmediated and none too subtle real history of violence and repression – has led most novelists into presenting villains as villains even unto themselves. Like the Mexican Juan Rulfo in *Pedro Páramo* (1955), Vargas Llosa shows us a far more human and thus tenacious social and psychological reality, without in any way diminishing its lamentable and despicable aspects. The novel appears to end, like *The Time of the Hero*, on a note of reconciliation. A work predicated on the impossibility of crossing the social dividing lines that Peru's geography itself embodies, seems to close in a mood of compromise, which can either be viewed as a triumph of the underdogs in making some kind of space for themselves, or as an acknowledgement of their defeat and another triumph of the status quo.

After *The Green House*, and with an exasperated pessimism and loathing, Vargas Llosa would bring us, in *Conversation in The Cathedral*, Latin America's most complete and desolate picture of one of its great cities – Lima – dominated by the political corruption necessary to maintain an unjust and immoral society.

By now, however, for all its mesmeric brilliance, it was becoming clear that Vargas Llosa was lamenting the human and social condition much more than critiquing specific societies, and that, like Borges and so many others before them, he was saying that society was everywhere corrupt, but even worse – hopeless – in the place where he was born.

Vargas Llosa's subsequent trajectory has been marked by several magnificent novels over the course of forty years, but in *The Green House*, with its seamlessly interwoven substructure of myth, fantasy and ideology, he came as near to the perfectly integrated novel as he ever would again. Nevertheless, he evidently recognised that what he had achieved was a book for connoisseurs, and he no doubt reflected that although he was now in the same league as the great modernist writers who had inspired him – Faulkner, and his peers Proust, Joyce and Woolf – those writers had never reached an audience as wide as he himself was seeking. (None of them, moreover, was as political as he was determined to be.) He had mastered his craft and demonstrated this to the literary establishment; now he would use his literary expertise and experience more tactfully and economically to put across his wider message in an ever more complex and challenging world.

NOTES

1. Mario Vargas Llosa. *La guerra del fin del mundo*. Barcelona: Seix Barral, 1981.
2. Mario Vargas Llosa. *La casa verde*. Barcelona: Seix Barral, 1966.
3. It is worth noting that when Vargas Llosa taught a course on the Latin American novel at Columbia University in the autumn of 1975, he included *The Green House* in his list of required reading, to highlight his own contribution to Latin American literary history. A reproduction of the required reading for his course is on the sixth page of the set of images reproduced after John King's chapter (pp. 168–73).
4. Mario Vargas Llosa. *La ciudad y los perros*. Barcelona: Seix Barral, 1963.
5. Mario Vargas Llosa. *Los jefes*. Barcelona: Editorial Rocas, 1959. All the stories in *Los jefes* have been included in *The Cubs and Other Stories*. In this chapter the translation of the short story collection is given as 'The Leaders' and the translation of the individual story is given as 'The leaders'.
6. Gabriel García Márquez. *Cien años de soledad*. Buenos Aires: Sudamericana, 1967.
7. Mario Vargas Llosa. *The Cubs and Other Stories*. London: Faber and Faber, 1991, p. 49.
8. Gerald Martin. 'Vargas Llosa. Nueva novela y realismo', *Norte* 12(5–6), 1971, pp. 112–21.
9. Mario Vargas Llosa. *Conversación en La Catedral*. Barcelona: Seix Barral, 1969.
10. Mario Vargas Llosa. *Pantaleón y las visitadoras*. Barcelona: Seix Barral, 1973.
11. Mario Vargas Llosa. *La tía Julia y el escribidor*. Barcelona: Seix Barral, 1977.
12. Before publication the novel was at different times entitled 'The impostors', 'The time of the hero' and, eventually, 'The city and the dogs' (*La ciudad y los perros*).

It is always troubling when translators and/or publishers ignore an author's wishes, and in this case Vargas Llosa was unfortunately overruled.

13. Mario Vargas Llosa. *García Márquez. Historia de un deicidio*. Barcelona: Seix Barral, 1971.

14. Vargas Llosa himself points this out in his second major critical work, *La orgía perpetua. Flaubert y* Madame Bovary. Barcelona: Seix Barral, 1975.

15. This conclusion is a tour de force in many ways, not least in its simultaneous use of communicating vessels and Chinese boxes to relay not only the moment when Jaguar found the courage to persuade Teresa of his love, but also the conversation in which Jaguar narrates this story – matter-of-factly, without any of the drama with which the novelist invests it – to his friend Flaco Higueras, who is captivated at first, but soon tires of what is, after all, another man's story.

16. The novel is called 'The city and the dogs', and not 'The academy and the city' (because the first-year students are nicknamed 'dogs' by the older cadets), but of course the underlying juxtaposition is the same.

17. Both the Slave and the Poet, as characters, have personality traits and biographical experiences that correspond to partial self-portrayals by Vargas Llosa.

18. Mario Vargas Llosa. *La fiesta del Chivo*. Madrid: Alfaguara, 2000; *El paraíso en la otra esquina*. Madrid: Alfaguara, 2003; *Travesuras de la niña mala*. Madrid: Alfaguara, 2006.

19. See Gerald Martin. *Journeys through the Labyrinth: Latin American Fiction in the Twentieth Century*. London: Verso, 1989.

20. The five strands are: the story of the jungle mission of Santa María, ending with the marriage of the Indian girl Bonifacia and the soldier known only as the Sergeant (in reality, Lituma); a thirty-day journey down the Amazon as the old boatman Aquilino takes the jungle brigand Fushía to end his days in a leper colony; the story of Don Anselmo in Piura, the history of his brothel, The Green House, and his scandalous affair with Toñita; the story of the Machiavellian governor of the region, Julio Reátegui, and his devious relationship to the military and to commercial traders (in only the first two parts of the novel); the story of Lituma and his friends in the Mangachería quarter of Piura, his time in prison and his relationship with Bonifacia, now a prostitute, after his release. There are also prologues to each of the four parts and epilogues to each of them at the end.

21. Mario Vargas Llosa. *La casa verde*. 12th edn. Barcelona: Seix Barral, 1972, p. 51. (Translation Gerald Martin.)

22. Ibid., p. 31.

23. Ibid., p. 370.

3

EFRAÍN KRISTAL

The total novel and the novella

Conversation in The Cathedral and The Cubs

Conversation in The Cathedral (*Conversación en La Catedral*, 1969[1]) is arguably the greatest novel about Peru, and a compelling literary statement about corruption in Latin America. It is also unsurpassed as a work of narrative fiction in its ability to explore how individuals, communities and even an entire social world can be undermined by the corrosive effects of corruption. As David Gallagher pointed out in a seminal essay published in 1973, *Conversation* is the culmination of Vargas Llosa's literary explorations of Peru of the 1960s, in as much as 'it finds its way to the proper formal structure and the proper language' to offer a damning picture of a nation in which every individual is compromised or corrupted in one way or another. Gallagher calls it a literary investigation of a nation's 'original sin', summed up in a question, in its opening paragraph, the most quoted line from any Peruvian novel: '¿En qué momento se había jodido el Perú?' (politely: At what point was Peru ruined?)[2]

The question is asked, in an interior monologue, by Santiago Zavala, the novel's protagonist, and Vargas Llosa's most complex and best-developed character. Santiago wonders when his own life was ruined as he ponders on the misery and degradation of Peru. In this novel, the ruin of a nation and the ruin of myriad individual destinies are one and the same. *Conversation in The Cathedral* is a series of concentric stories that encompass the experience of a nation whose epicentre is the story of Santiago. As a young man he abandons a life of privilege to reject the social milieu of his father, Don Fermín, whose wealth and social position depend on shady business dealings with powerful men from whom he gains political influence. Many critics of the novel have made the mistake of associating Don Fermín with the traditional Peruvian oligarchy. He is actually a self-made man from the lower middle classes who gained a measure of power through his willingness to participate in unlawful activities. Paralleling Fermín's trajectory is Cayo Bermúdez, the sleazy and brutal head of a secret police, who climbed up the social ladder through the use of ruthless force. When the reader first encounters either Don Fermín or

Cayo, Vargas Llosa has not yet revealed that the former stems from the lower middle classes and continues to have dealings with the criminal world, or that Cayo Bermúdez came from the same pauperised social world as Don Fermín's chauffeur, Ambrosio. For Ambrosio, Cayo Bermúdez is a thug worthy of contempt, and Don Fermín is a gentleman worthy of respect. Indeed, his employment with Santiago's father amounts to as much respectability as he could ever have fathomed, given the violence and cruelty of Ambrosio's original social milieu. In *Conversation*, Vargas Llosa offers a detailed and nuanced picture of the disproportion between the public respectability of his protagonists and either the sordid realities they endure, or the brutality and abuse to which they subject their victims. It is also clear that in this social world, no individual is immune to humiliation. When the novel closes, Santiago Zavala, as well as the reader, has become fully aware that true decency is incompatible with social success in this society, and that the corrupt social system can trump the hopes or the desires of any individual, even the most powerful or treacherous.

Even before coming to terms with the full dimensions of corruption in Peru, Santiago chooses social failure over success as a way to repudiate his bourgeois family. Santiago's father is a respected member of Peruvian society, a power broker in the business and political arena, and as his eldest and favourite son, Santiago is expected to follow suit. Instead, the young man becomes involved with radical groups whose aim is to promote a socialist revolution. Santiago's family tolerates the young man's decisions to suspend his university studies and work for a low-brow newspaper as the passing fancies of a young man who needs to be indulged and protected until he grows out of his protracted adolescence. His father uses his political influence to release Santiago from jail when he is arrested for his association with communists. When he marries a young woman who could have been hired as a household servant, his rupture with his family is definitive: he will not be able participate in the reproduction of a social order with a wife from an inferior social rank. In this social world, women solidify the bonds between powerful families through family ties. Marriage is also a way, as is the case with Santiago's father, to incorporate new players into the coteries of the ruling sector.

Santiago's marriage to an unacceptable woman in *Conversation* is equivalent to the castration of Pichula Cuéllar, the protagonist of *The Cubs* (*Los cachorros*, 1967[3]), where Vargas Llosa had already explored an upper-class individual's fall from grace, as he is gradually excluded and eventually forgotten by the members of his own social milieu. In fact, as Guadalupe Fernández Ariza has pointed out, *The Cubs* is closely associated with *Conversation*, with the two works sharing some of the same characters.

For example, in *The Cubs*, the ambitious Chispas is destined to become a member of the Peruvian upper classes when his cousin Cuéllar is long forgotten. In *Conversation*, Chispas is Santiago's brother (thus the protagonists of the two works are first cousins), and gladly embraces the social role Santiago rejects: a life of privilege thanks to their father's wealth and political connections.[4] *The Cubs* is a study in the self-punishment and exclusion of an individual who is not fit for social reproduction. As a youth, Cuéllar was emasculated by a dog in a freak accident, and his physical handicap makes him useless to a society whose main function is to reproduce itself. He belongs to a social milieu in which inheritance and power fill the void made by the absence of other values and by an indifference to human misery. The indifference of his peers, the 'cubs' of the Peruvian upper classes, to his plight only increases as Pichula compensates for his frustrations. Unable to participate in sexual rites of passage, his sometimes aggressive, and mostly unsettled and self-destructive behaviour leads him to suicide.

The Cubs was originally published in 1967 as a collaborative effort between Vargas Llosa and the photographer Xavier Miserachs, for a project called 'The Image and the Word' sponsored by the editor Carlos Barral, who was keen to produce collaborative projects between writers and visual artists.[5] The images disappeared from future editions of the book, never appearing in the English translation, but they complement the book effectively: images of boys in the schoolyard that correspond to Pichula's innocence are followed by images of an angry dog and the empty shower room where the emasculation could have taken place. Only after this do the photographs begin to show female characters: first, schoolgirls in tidy uniforms; then young women as they are coming of age. The tensions of adolescent courtship in the narrative are accompanied by images of dancing and outings by girls and boys; they are followed by images corresponding to Cuéllar's risk-taking, including a striking photograph of a hand protruding from a dangerous wave, and the empty wreck of a fatal automobile crash. The last image forefronts a young couple with a baby in a stroller, enjoying a social event in the garden of a well-appointed home, and this image is intended to complement the closing of the narrative.

With a mastery of both point of view and narrative time, Vargas Llosa concludes the novella, alternating between two grammatical voices: a second-person collective masculine voice that expresses the cold reaction of the protagonist's peers to his suicide, and a neutral third-person voice that accelerates the narrative time to show how the classmates, now adults, have reproduced the world of their parents. The effect suggests that the memory of Pichula Cuéllar, indelibly set in the mind of the reader, has been thoroughly erased from the minds of his former friends:

Sad case, we said at the funeral, how he suffered, what a life, but he got his just deserts. They had grown up and we all had wives, cars, children who studied in the best private schools, they were building themselves little summer houses by the beach, and we began to gain weight, our hair was turning grey and our bodies were softening, and we began to feel stomach-aches after eating or drinking, and little age spots and wrinkles were showing up in their skin.[6]

The destiny of Pichula Cuéllar, like that of all the characters in Vargas Llosa's narrative fiction of the 1960s – of the early short stories, *The Time of the Hero* (*La ciudad y los perros*[7]) and *The Green House* (*La casa verde*[8]) – depends on his inclusion or exclusion from the groups and social hierarchies that either defend the existing social order or rebel against it in vain. Vargas Llosa's most ambitious and successful attempt to explore this theme is *Conversation in The Cathedral*, a rich, textured and absorbing portrait of the consequences of the demographic transformations taking place in Peru during the twentieth century. The novel is set against the emigration of millions of indigenous peoples from the Andes to Peru's urban centres. This population shift generated a complex human universe, bolstering the social rise of individuals such as Don Fermín, and of the upper-middle classes, the new ruling sector that displaced the traditional landed oligarchy from its former grip on economic and political power.

If the central events of *The Cubs* correspond roughly to Vargas Llosa's high school experiences in Lima in 1947 before his father made him enrol in the military academy he made famous in *The Time of the Hero*, *Conversation* corresponds roughly to the period that follows, giving pride of place to the years when Vargas Llosa was a university student and a journalist for the newspaper *La Crónica*.[9] The narrative core of the novel is set in a historical period that covers the political transition from the presidency of Manuel Odría (1948–56) to the first presidential election of Fernando Belaúnde Terry (1963). Odría came to power in a coup d'état, but was elected president after a caretaker government by another general. That being said, many in the Peruvian left considered the entirety of his government to be a dictatorship, a point of view shared by Santiago, as well as the novel's implied author. Indeed, Don Fermín is actively involved in proposing deceptive and illegal strategies to legitimise the dictatorship, including the repression of Odría's political opposition in a compromised electoral process. Santiago abhors the dictatorship, but has no illusions that a true re-establishment of democracy through free and fair elections will better the situation of his country.

This was also the view held by the young Vargas Llosa – many years before he repudiated the Cuban Revolution – and of his friend and mentor, the poet and essayist Sebastián Salazar Bondy, best known outside Peru for his essay

Lima la horrible ('Lima the horrible', 1964), a devastating attack on the image of the city as emblematic of the hypocrisy of the Peruvian ruling classes. Bondy criticises their patriotism and fondness for the purported glories of Peru's colonial period, as they mask the misery inflicted on the Peruvian lower classes made up primarily of indigenous peoples. It is no coincidence that Salazar Bondy's essay resonates with the atmosphere of corruption and hypocrisy beneath the surface of Lima's respectable society that informs *Conversation in The Cathedral*. The effect of a novel that unmasks any pretence about the ostensive decency of Peruvian society is already encapsulated in its title. As the title intimates, the centrepiece of the novel is a conversation, but it does not take place in a cathedral, as the reader might assume before reading the novel. Rather, it takes place in a seedy bar called The Cathedral, not too far from the actual Cathedral of Lima. Appearing intermittently in the novel, the edifice serves both as a symbol of the very myth of Peru's glory, which Salazar Bondy decried, and as a sad witness to the degradation of a nation. Vargas Llosa was closely associated with Salazar Bondy, who nurtured and promoted his early literary career. When Salazar Bondy read Vargas Llosa's first novel, *The Time of the Hero*, in manuscript form, he exhorted his younger friend to publish it immediately because of its revolutionary significance:

> Your novel captures the contradictions of the underdeveloped, deformed and unbearable society we live in, but things will explode, in fact, they are already exploding. This is why you should not wait much longer to publish your novel.[10]

And on the eve of Belaúnde's electoral triumph, Salazar Bondy offered an analysis of Peru's political situation, which can also be read as a fair gloss of the political message of *Conversation in The Cathedral*:

> We are on the eve of Peru's presidential elections after years of dictatorship, and yet I know that elections do not bring about the radical solutions required to address Peru's most pressing problems. Whatever the outcome of the elections – even if they are not foiled by a military intervention – the crisis of our nation will go on unabated. A small and powerful export and financial oligarchy owns the means of production, and will continue to run the affairs of this nation, as it has for over one hundred and fifty years. I can only take hope in the genuine resistance that is beginning to emerge from the grass roots, even though it is sometimes repressed by brute force, or neutralized by other means. The revolutionary potential of the popular sectors is often diffused from within by sympathisers on account of vagueness or unproductive action. Take for example the student movement: university students express their contempt for the bogus values of the bourgeoisie by protest alone, and this is hardly enough to make a

difference. More disappointing is the fact that some students become conformists and fall prey to the pursuit of personal success, to a thirst for money, and to corruption.[11]

Salazar Bondy's statement in 1963, when he was actively guiding the early literary career of Vargas Llosa, also prefigures some of *Conversation*'s characters. In the novel, Santiago Zavala is an example of one of those university students unable to translate his contempt for the capitalist system into anything other than a sense of personal frustration, while his brothers, Chispas and Popeye (akin to Cuéllar's peers in *The Cubs*), are examples of young men who support the candidacy of Fernando Belaúnde Terry as they pursue lucrative business careers.[12] Salazar Bondy died in 1965, when he was in his early forties; Vargas Llosa dedicated *The Cubs* to his memory, and other traces of his influence are evident in *Conversation*.

Conversation is a novel about a dictatorship that does not give pride of place to the dictator. In the novel, Odría appears once, and only fleetingly. From a Marxist perspective akin to Vargas Llosa's youthful convictions, it is not the individual in power, but the capitalist system that accounts for the corruption of a social world. One could add that this explains why the shifts from democratically elected presidents to military dictatorships taking place in Peru from the fall of Odría until the election of Belaúnde Terry are not central to the novel, though it is set precisely in this historical period.[13] The ideological underpinnings of *Conversation* are far from those that inform *The Feast of the Goat* (*La fiesta del Chivo*, 2000[14]), Vargas Llosa's other novel about a dictator. In *The Feast of the Goat* the dictator plays a prominent role, demonstrating how the agency of powerful men, or of adept politicians who can manipulate political moments of transition, can make a decisive difference in the unfolding of historical situations. When he wrote *Conversation in The Cathedral*, Vargas Llosa did not think that individual agency was meaningful within the confines of a capitalist system, and this assumption is at play in the novel. According to Jean Franco, *Conversation* offers the portrait

> of a society that neutralizes rebellion and turns young people into either failures or conformists. The novel lacks a dialectical process, which would offer a way out. The regime and the powerful are constantly threatened by treachery and blackmail, but the revolution never breaks out. The stability of the dominant class is invariably guaranteed, and the self-realisation of individuals loses all meaning in such a thoroughly corrupt environment.[15]

Its first Peruvian readers saw in *Conversation* a powerful indictment of the miserable social reality of their nation, but the novel gained a much larger audience because it is a remarkable literary work that appeared to capture the discomfort of a degraded world on the eve of transformative changes, a sentiment that resonated with readers around the world who were concerned with the predicaments of Latin America after the Cuban Revolution.

With this novel, Vargas Llosa reconciled the most daring literary techniques of Joyce and Faulkner (the crossing of temporal and spatial planes, the use of interior monologue, a free use of indirect speech) with expressions of popular culture (film, music, sensationalist journalism) to explore an indecent social world. Each of its chapters contains mysteries and allusions that can only be deciphered on a second reading, but even on first reading the force of the action and the gripping dilemmas of the characters are compelling. Santiago Zavala thought of his father as a member of the Peruvian upper-middle classes, whose comfortable lives depend on the exploitation of the lower classes, but he discovers that Don Fermín had been a closeted gay man, well known in criminal milieus. His father's double life is revealed to him when he discovers that Ambrosio, Don Fermín's chauffeur and lover, had assassinated Hortensia, a drug-addicted prostitute who threatened to reveal his boss's sexual orientation.

The narrative axis of the novel is a four-hour conversation between Santiago and Ambrosio in The Cathedral, around which many other conversations, stories and situations are grafted. The encounter is accidental – Ambrosio has returned to Lima after many years spent hiding from the law in the Peruvian provinces – but the conversation is pressing for both of them. Santiago wants to understand why Ambrosio loved his father, and Ambrosio wants to understand why Santiago rejected him. The conversation does not lead to an understanding between the two men, but when it concludes, the reader comes to terms with a world that shattered the aspirations of both men. The complex narrative structure is particularly striking when Vargas Llosa intertwines conversations and events on the same page that may be taking place simultaneously in different places, or that took place at different points in time. And he often associates the mood of one narrative situation with another; this technique is particularly effective when the association foregrounds the emotional impact of a revelation that will take place at a later moment in the novel. For example, in a section of the novel in which Santiago's politically committed girlfriend is breaking off their relationship because she feels it is in the way of political objectives they ought to share, Vargas Llosa intertwines two poignant snippets of a conversation in which Don Fermín breaks off his relationship with Ambrosio. On first reading, it is impossible to understand the context of these snippets because it has not yet been revealed that the two men have been sexually involved, or that Ambrosio murdered a woman to protect Don Fermín's reputation. It is moving enough, however, for the reader to hear Ambrosio's anguish when he says 'me está botando' ('you are getting rid of me', p. 127), when Don

Fermín has said half a page earlier, 'No estoy pensando en mí, infeliz, sino en ti' ('I'm not thinking about me, you wretch, but about you', p. 127). In a similar vein, in the initial chapters Don Fermín's intermittent voice asks a series of questions with the same idea: '¿Lo hiciste por mí?' ('Did you do it for me?', p. 52).[16] These subliminal touches reveal the depth of affection between the two men, against which the break-up of Santiago's relationship with his socialist girlfriend feels like an adolescent phase.

There is an element of sentimental pathos in the development of the homosexual relationship between Ambrosio and Don Fermín (and *Conversation* is not immune from melodrama),[17] but given the centrality of their mutual affection to the work, the novel's early critics were mistaken in making the value judgement that Don Fermín's homosexuality is condemned by the narrative voice. The main antecedent for this relationship in Vargas Llosa's oeuvre is in *The Green House*, in the story of Don Anselmo, the adult man who falls in love with Toñita, the young deaf and mute girl who survived a violent attack by highway robbers who murdered her family. Anselmo's relationship with an underage and physically impaired girl will spell the downfall of the house of prostitution he established. The eponymous Green House is condemned by the local priest, and burned to the ground by others who consider that Anselmo violated common decency beyond repair in his relationship with Toñita.

Thirty years after its publication, when the novel's political themes have lost their topicality, it is easier to appreciate that the literary world of *Conversation in The Cathedral* is a work of fiction in which Vargas Llosa transmogrified personal experiences and historical events with his powerful literary imagination: one does not need to know anything about the details of Peruvian history to appreciate the genius of its literary construction or its moral dimension. *Conversation* is a close cousin to André Malraux's *The Human Condition*, because they are both moral novels set within a political context. Santiago Zavala's torment, like that of Malraux's protagonists, is of a conflicted individual who does not know what to do about the human misery that surrounds him. Santiago has no doubts about the problems that plague his corrupt country, but he agonises about the solutions:

> The worst thing was to have doubts. Clenching your fists, grinding your teeth, Ambrosio, APRA is the solution, religion is the solution, Communism is the solution, and believing it. Then life would become organized all by itself and you wouldn't feel empty anymore, Ambrosio.[18]

And Santiago also laments his own doubts: 'if everybody set himself to being intelligent and having his doubts, Peru would go on being screwed up forever'.[19]

If Malraux's novel, as a moral novel in a political context, is a significant literary antecedent to *Conversation*, an even more important antecedent is William Faulkner's *Absalom, Absalom!* Mary E. Davis has shown that the multiple conversations and multiple narrators of *Conversation* are an homage to *Absalom*.[20] One could add that the influence is also thematic. Faulkner's novel evokes the biblical story of Absalom, King David's son, who rebelled against his father. The conflict between son and father is central to Faulkner's novel. Henry Sutpen is the son of Thomas Sutpen, who has amassed a great fortune, and the young man decides to repudiate both his father and his inheritance. In a dormitory at Harvard University, Quentin Compson – a young man from Mississippi with a fraught relationship with his own father – discusses Henry's rejection of his father in response to the interrogation of his roommate, Shreve McCannon. McCannon, a Canadian, asks: 'Tell me about the South. What's it like there? Why do they live there? Why do they live at all?'[21] The answer to these questions initiates a long conversation, but also a process of introspection about the predicaments of the post-bellum South. In *Conversation* and *Absalom*, the rejection of a father who has succeeded through corruption becomes the focus of an exploration that reveals the corruption of an entire social world. In both novels, a dialogue that takes place years after the events is the narrative core that incorporates other voices, intermingled with one another and adding complexity and social pathos. In both novels, the story of a young man who has repudiated his father sheds light on the failure of an entire society, and in both novels the theme is presented through a complex literary structure.

José Miguel Oviedo's critical work, *Mario Vargas Llosa. Invención de una realidad*, is still the best place to go to begin to unravel the complexities of Vargas Llosa's mastery of narrative form in this novel.[22] Oviedo offers a painstaking account of Vargas Llosa's techniques: he offers diagrams in which he indicates how the various conversations taking place in different times and places are put together in a technique he calls 'the telescopic dialogues'. Oviedo also shows that the meticulous shifting of spatial and temporal planes in the novel allows for a powerful sense of development: the first part of the novel focuses on Santiago Zavala's life as a university student; the second on a prostitute whose clients are among the most powerful men in Peru; the third on the journalistic milieu that reveals the double life of Don Fermín; and the fourth and final section offers a window onto the private lives of several key characters that shed retrospective light on all the rest. Oviedo also shows how to identify the voices of many characters by certain linguistic leitmotifs, which appear and reappear throughout the novel. For example, when the word 'son' appears at the end of a spoken clause, the careful reader will know that it is Ambrosio speaking to Santiago.

The experiences of Santiago Zavala and his family form part of a web of human relations that include numerous characters from a wide range of social settings and situations: house servants, journalists, union labourers, small- and big-time criminals, including the henchmen of President Odría; members of the bourgeoisie and petit bourgeoisie; people who live in or frequent shanty towns, expensive homes, brothels, universities, bars and elegant clubs. The story of a frustrated young rebel is the vehicle for an unprecedented and unsurpassed literary exploration of Peruvian urban life. The reader becomes Santiago's travelling companion on his journey of self-awareness, while over-hearing the monologue in which Santiago reflects on his own and his country's predicaments. By the second reading of the novel, the reader is able to appreciate Santiago's situation as clearly as the character himself when he begins his conversation with Ambrosio, who has returned to Lima years after committing murder in order to save Don Fermín's reputation. The conversation, an attempt to reach an understanding between the two men, fails. For Ambrosio, the political abstractions with which Santiago rationalised his rejection of Don Fermín are nothing but an insolent rant: 'I want you to know that you do not deserve the father you had, I want you to know that. You can go straight to shit hell, boy.'[23] And while Santiago is able to reconcile himself to the memory of his father, whom he comes to see as another victim of the social and political system he despises, he is unable to understand why Ambrosio, a heterosexual man who belongs to the classes most exploited in Peru by men like his father, was willing to become his father's lover. Santiago Zavala's muted tragedy – a rejection of family and nation that justifies his decision to lead a mediocre life – is symptomatic of a corrupt social order; his conclusion about his own situation is poignant: 'He was like Peru, he'd screwed up somewhere along the line. He thinks: when? He thinks: there is no solution.'[24] The same futility is even more affecting when Ambrosio – alone and on the verge of destitute poverty – tells Santiago about his future plans: 'He would work here and there and after that here and there, and then, well after that he would have died, wasn't that so, son?'[25]

In the compassion that Santiago Zavala is able to feel for his late father, and in his earnest, but failed attempt to arrive at some understanding with Ambrosio, the greatest theme of Vargas Llosa's maturity as a writer has already emerged: the search for reconciliation between human beings after illusions have been lost. More than a milestone in Vargas Llosa's career, *Conversation* is one of the great literary creations in the Spanish language. It is also the conclusion to the first phase of Vargas Llosa's career as a writer of narrative fiction. His next novels would revisit some of his earlier themes with a measure of humour and irony, and he would transition from a literary worldview in which social orders can overwhelm the agency of any individual, to an exploration of literary worlds in which individual agency makes a difference.

NOTES

1. Mario Vargas Llosa. *Conversación en La Catedral*. Barcelona: Seix Barral, 1969. *Conversation in The Cathedral*. Trans. Gregory Rabassa. New York: Harper & Row, 1974.
2. David Gallagher, 'Mario Vargas Llosa'. In *Modern Latin American Literature*. Oxford University Press, 1973, pp. 122–43.
3. Mario Vargas Llosa. *Los cachorros. Pichula Cuéllar*. Barcelona: Editorial Lumen, 1967. Translated as *The Cubs*, in *The Cubs and Other Stories*. Trans. Gregory Kolovakas and Ronald Christ. New York: Harper and Row, 1979. In addition to the English translation of *Los cachorros*, *The Cubs and Other Stories* includes all the short stories from *Los jefes* ('The Leaders').
4. The connections between the novella and *Conversation in The Cathedral* are traced by Guadalupe Fernández Ariza in her critical edition of *Los cachorros*. Madrid: Cátedra, 1987.
5. Years later, Vargas Llosa would collaborate in similar projects with his own daughter, an accomplished photographer who illustrated his books on Tahiti, Iraq and Palestine (Morgana Vargas Llosa. *Las fotos del paraíso*. Madrid: Alfaguara, 2003; Mario Vargas Llosa. *Diario de Irak*. Madrid: Aguilar, 2003; Mario Vargas Llosa. *Israel/Palestina. Paz o guerra santa*. Madrid: Aguilar, 2006).
6. Vargas Llosa, *Los cachorros*, pp. 102–3. (Translation Efraín Kristal.)
7. Mario Vargas Llosa. *La ciudad y los perros*. Barcelona: Seix Barral, 1963.
8. Mario Vargas Llosa. *La casa verde*. Barcelona: Seix Barral, 1966.
9. For the impact of Vargas Llosa's experiences as a journalist on his creative process, see Marie-Madeleine Gladieu. *Mario Vargas Llosa*. Paris: L'Harmattan, 1989, pp. 29–41. Gladieu demonstrates that several anecdotes in Vargas Llosa's novels – particularly from the period of *Conversation*, *The Cubs*, and *Aunt Julia and the Scriptwriter* (*La tía Julia y el escribidor*. Barcelona: Seix Barral, 1977), were inspired by journalistic articles from the newspaper *La Crónica*. It is of special interest to note that the central anecdote that inspired *The Cubs* was also a journalistic article.
10. Sebastián Salazar Bondy. Unpublished letter to Vargas Llosa. 6 July 1962. Mario Vargas Llosa Papers CO 641, Correspondence, Box 1, Manuscripts Division, Department of Rare Books and Special Collections, Princeton University Library. (Translation Efraín Kristal.)
11. Sebastián Salazar Bondy. Prologue. *La encrucijada del Perú*. Montevideo: Araca, 1963, pp. 7–8. (Translation Efraín Kristal.)
12. Chispas is also a character of *The Cubs*, in which he is a happy, successful businessman, and he reappears in *Al pie del Támesis* ('On the banks of the Thames') (Lima: Alfaguara, 2008), as a man who sacrificed his innermost desires to pursue a life of financial gain.

13. After his coup d'état in 1948, Odría himself had been democratically elected, and the election of Manuel Prado y Ugarteche was followed by two military coups d'état before Fernando Belaúnde Terry's election in 1963.

14. Mario Vargas Llosa. *La fiesta del Chivo*. Madrid: Alfaguara, 2000.

15. Jean Franco. 'Lectura de *Conversación en La Catedral*'. *Revista Iberoamericana* 37(76, 77), July–December 1971, pp. 766–7. (Translation Efraín Kristal.)

16. All translations Efraín Kristal.

17. The story of Hortensia, the woman Ambrosio murders, is also the stuff of melodrama: she was used, deceived and abandoned by an airplane pilot, her only true love, and becomes a drug addict and a prostitute whose clients include politicians. Desperate for money to feed her expensive lifestyle and drug habit, she blackmails Don Fermín. For the significance of the inflections of Mexican cinema in Vargas Llosa's recourse to melodrama, see the chapter by Carolina Sitnisky in this volume.

18. Vargas Llosa, *Conversation*, pp. 99–100.

19. Ibid., p. 139. (Translation slightly modified.)

20. Mary E. Davis. 'La elección del fracaso. Vargas Llosa y William Faulkner'. In José Miguel Oviedo (ed.). *Mario Vargas Llosa*. Madrid: Taurus, 1981, p. 42.

21. William Faulkner. *Absalom, Absalom!* New York: Vintage, 1987, p. 424.

22. José Miguel Oviedo. *Mario Vargas Llosa. La invención de una realidad*. Barcelona: Seix Barral, 1977, pp. 204–64.

23. Vargas Llosa, *Conversation*, p. 598.

24. Ibid., p. 3. (Translation slightly modified.)

25. Ibid., p. 601.

4

MICHAEL WOOD

Humour and irony

Captain Pantoja and the Special Service and *Aunt Julia and the Scriptwriter*

As critics have noted, in the early 1970s Mario Vargas Llosa was a man in transition from one set of political beliefs to another,[1] but he was also a novelist in search of a new complexity, and he found it for a while in a genre that was not his first choice: comedy. His achievements in *Captain Pantoja and the Special Service* (*Pantaleón y las visitadoras*, 1973[2]) and *Aunt Julia and the Scriptwriter* (*La tía Julia y el escribidor*, 1977[3]) are all the more remarkable because the writer was, in several respects, turning away from what he knew. At the same time he was anxious not to be disloyal to his past, and in comedy he discovered a means of expressing certain truths that continued to lurk in realms of encroaching falsehood. *Captain Pantoja* reminds us of the closeness of mania to certain kinds of virtue; and *Aunt Julia and the Scriptwriter* ironically celebrates an art that escapes madness, but only just.

In a 1999 prologue to *Captain Pantoja and the Special Service*, Vargas Llosa tells us that the novel is based 'on a fact', 'a real event   that I got to know well during two trips to the Amazon', and that his early drafts were very different in tone from the final, and quite wonderful result. 'As incredible as it seems   in the beginning I tried to tell this story seriously. I discovered that was impossible, that the story demanded farce and laughter'.[4]

The author goes on to speak of his pleasure in writing the book, and of the ease of the writing. The relative ease, I think he must mean. This is an extraordinarily accomplished and skilful novel, full of technical invention and variation, and we should not underestimate the hard work, the serious work that must have gone into it.

Even in its final version the novel does not entirely abandon its old seriousness, which lingers among the joking and the guffaws. Of course, good comedy is always serious in its way – as serious as anything gets – because comedy as a genre is about our chances of happiness. Tragedy, by contrast, is about our inevitable misery, and melodrama is about misery that could have been averted but was not. Most drama, and indeed most novels, hover somewhere between tragedy and melodrama, and happiness, in such works, either fails to appear even as a possibility or mysteriously gets lost. It gets lost in comedy sometimes too, but comedy is not about plausible success, or literal happy endings. It is about the *chances* of happiness, about our willingness to imagine what things are like when they go right, when our lives are lucky. If we think this is not serious, we are saying that only darkness matters or deserves our concentrated attention.

But although this argument will serve as a general framework for what follows, my chief focus is more local and more specific, more closely related to the style and content of two particular novels. *Captain Pantoja and the Special Service* does not entirely abandon the seriousness of its early drafts because seriousness is its subject and its comic mode. Seriousness is what the book is being funny about. And in *Aunt Julia and the Scriptwriter* the earnestness of the narrator, the youthful would-be writer, serves as a foil to the solemnity of Pedro Camacho, the pompous and prolific author of radio serials, both of them embroiled in increasing disorder and both of them objects of intimate and affectionate mockery.

The seriousness of farce

Here is Captain Pantoja, in his first report to his superiors in Lima, writing about what he fears may be the difficulties of working with the disreputable demi-monde of Iquitos, and particularly with the pimps of the women he plans to employ in his officially sanctioned, albeit publicly denied, military brothel (p. 33):

> since these individuals unquestionably could become a source of problems. But from his unforgettable days as a cadet, the undersigned knows well that there is no mission without its difficulties and that there are no difficulties that cannot be conquered by energy, will power and work.

There is a splendid mix of idioms here: the pimps as 'these individuals' and also 'a source of problems'; the language of mission, energy, will and work; the syntax of the self-persuading slogan ('there are no difficulties that cannot be conquered'); the touch of sentiment in the captain's memory of his good old unforgettable times as a cadet. The word 'difficulties' is itself marvellously evasive. These are not the usual difficulties of the military academy, or indeed of the army on most days or in most places. And Vargas Llosa is already laying the ground for an elegant double joke, an irony worthy of Flaubert. First step: we are laughing because the language here is comically, solemnly inappropriate to its subject. Second step, not yet taken: platitudes do work; Pantoja overcomes all his difficulties, at least all his difficulties of this type.

Indeed his success becomes his problem, and the comedy, without ceasing to be comedy, consequently acquires a new dimension.

An officer reports on a try-out of the visitors' service. What has happened at this moment is that the pilot of the plane has been scaring the Madame of the group, Leonora Curinchila, alias Chuchupe, by his elaborate aerial acrobatics, and she has passed out. Here is how this sounds in the language of the military document (p. 73):

> The reason for her light-headedness was that she had been greatly frightened during the flight from the Itaya River to the Napo River due to the plane's shaking in the wind and to the pilot, who, according to the assertion of the aforementioned, had performed continual risky and pointless acrobatics, intending to amuse himself by increasing her terror, which her nerves could not withstand. Once the said woman had recovered, she attempted to assault the pilot with words and crude gestures, and it was necessary for Capt. Pantoja to intervene in order to put an end to the incident.

There is the same gap as in the previous example: between a solemn, would-be stabilising and respectable lexicon and a disreputable or trivial event. Except that now the comedy arises not so much from the unsuitable subject as from the unruly antics, and from the colourful dialogue we can readily imagine behind the deadened language. The remark about Chuchupe's nerves seems to be free indirect speech, almost a quotation, but we have to supply her abusive words and rude gestures ourselves. And we do, of course, laughing in large part at their absence from the visible field of the language.

Here is Captain Alberto Mendoza reporting on an early mission, the real thing, no longer just a try-out. Six women service eighty-three men, described as 'users', 'within the time limit prescribed by regulations and to their total satisfaction' (pp. 115–16):

> In view of the fact that the woman least requested by the troops was Dulce María, she was assigned the group of only thirteen men. Attached is the list of the 83 users with given name, surname, number of service file and ticket of deduction from payroll. Deportment of convoy while quartered in Lagunas was proper. Only one incident occurred: upon the arrival of the transport, Reinaldino Chumbe Quisque recognised his maternal half-sister (the so-called Lunita) among the Special Service and proceeded to insult her and to administer corporal punishment to her, fortunately of mild consequences, before being restrained by the military police. Chumbe Quisque was denied servicing, and locked in the guardhouse with six days of hard labor for bad character and conduct, but was later granted amnesty from the second part of his punishment on appeal by his half-sister, Lunita, and the other specialists.

The captain goes on to recommend the extension of the visitors' service both to officers and to non-commissioned officers. Again, we imagine the missing insults, and picture the arguments leading to the amnesty behind the language that belongs to other fields of activity entirely. Think of all the ways we might describe a man hitting a woman without doing too much harm – as distinct from 'corporal punishment, fortunately of mild consequence'.

And here is Pantoja reporting on the spontaneous creation of the school song, so to speak, of the visitors' service, what he describes as the Hymn of the Special Service, sung to the tune of 'The Mexican Hat Dance' (p. 118):

> That as a friendly gesture after the final toast   the specialists sang for the undersigned a little musical work they had secretly composed for the occasion and which they proposed be adopted as the Hymn of the Service. (b) That after the hymn had been performed several times with real enthusiasm by all the specialists, the undersigned acceded to said request, a measure he hopes will be ratified by headquarters, keeping in mind the advantage of stimulating enterprises that, like this one, denote interest and love of the personnel for the organisation of which they form part, foment the fraternal spirit indispensable for the realisation of group labour and reveal high morale, youthful spirit and even an element of ingenuity and mischievousness, which, in small doses, of course, never go too far in adding a little spice to the completed mission.

The combination of solemnity, cliché, mildly out-of-control enthusiasm, and self-conscious caution is extraordinary, and you would think this particular joke could not go further. It can, though. The hymn mentions patriotism and the nation and the army, but fails to mention the navy, provider of the riverboat the service uses. An admiral protests, in the severest terms, and Pantoja is forced to apologise for his 'unpardonable carelessness', explaining that the hymn was adopted 'in an unpremeditated and somewhat hasty manner, without submitting it to previous critical evaluation of its form and content' (p. 130). We can almost see the evaluation that Pantoja did not undertake – see its language anyway – and we recognise exactly where we are in all these examples, and throughout much of the novel. A language of discipline and control, above all, a language of paperwork, a language designed to leave an administrative trace while evacuating all personality, has been invaded, in spite of itself, by the sheer daily disorder of the world, by the unpredictable doings of persons. You will remember that Pantoja received his initial instructions about the service because the soldiers posted to Iquitos and environs were raping women left and right. 'The entire Amazon District is up in arms', a general says (p. 4). Forty-three pregnancies in six months. The chaplains have married twenty or so couples, but the general says, 'this depravity requires more radical measures than forced marriages' (p. 6).

Captain Pantoja and the Special Service is a satire of Church and army, as many critics have said, and a comment on the stubborn, mechanical-mindedness of Pantoja, a man who needs to take orders, loves to take orders. He is a charming fellow, Donald Shaw says, if a little naive, but he is like a robot.[5] But in the context I am trying to develop, the novel is, above all, an undoing of Sartrean seriousness, as Vargas Llosa suggests in his prologue, a portrait of existential seriousness as farce. It is the seriousness itself that is the farce; a failure to allow for everything seriousness denies, a wish that it would all go away, or at least keep quiet. This, we realise, is what the army wanted all along, since by the end of the book even the officers most indignantly opposed to the visitors' service are seen happily enjoying the services of prostitutes. It is going to be the return of the good old times, one of them says. 'This will be the peaceful country of the good old days once again' (p. 240). The good old times: when the soldiers were not causing havoc and when the solution to the havoc was not itself a form of institutionalised disgrace. When Pantoja is reproached for breaking out of clandestinity and putting on his uniform for the funeral of a prostitute, he says he did it because there was no longer any point in trying to keep the secret – everyone already knew about the service. 'Was that a reason', one Colonel Lopez asks, 'for him to convert rumours into apocalyptic truth?' (p. 241).

The language of the novel, then, or much of it, is a comic expression of helplessness, a language full of what it cannot contain – in either of the senses of that word. But there is more. If the language of the army keeps failing, the army's organised practices, as Pantoja understands them, achieve extraordinary success. The visitors' service works; everyone likes it. Well, everyone except the officers who pretend to be shocked and the civilians who are not getting a look-in, and for a while the radio commentator who is not getting his bribe. And Pantoja's wife and mother, of course. So not quite everyone. But the prostitutes and their handlers like working for the army – regular, clean conditions, decent pay – and the soldiers like the service, if anything too much. This is what I have described as the second step of Vargas Llosa's elegant joke. A local bishop threatens to excommunicate everyone associated with the visitors' service. A general apologises, says the whole thing should never have got off the ground, and blames Pantoja for its success. 'At least he could have organised the thing in a mediocre, defective way. But that idiot has converted the Special Service into the most efficient unit of the armed forces' (p. 174). When the high command discusses the affair, another general says, 'I'm not concerned with the negative things about the Special Service, but the positive ones   What's serious are its fantastic successes' (pp. 86–7).

Seriousness is a farce for two reasons, then: because it fails hopelessly, and because it improbably succeeds. But we are talking about different forms of seriousness, even if they are both comic. The first, as we have seen, is chiefly, but not always linguistic: a matter of evasion, of hiding things in language and through language; of leaving life's hypocrisies alone, leaving them in the shade, or in the hammock. The second is represented entirely by Pantoja himself, and could not come into being without him. He is not a humourless, rigid figure; he plainly enjoys his work, and he is human enough to fall for one of the prostitutes; and he is not quite robot-like in the way Shaw suggests. But he is a comic character in a strictly Bergsonian sense, because he does everything, appropriate or inappropriate, with model efficiency, and does not know how to do it otherwise. He is not adaptable, or is adaptable only within a framework of maniacal efficiency. This is his gift, and the grounds of his unlikely success. He treats a brothel service as if it were an essential army manoeuvre, and he succeeds because he is blind to all sense of the ridiculous, to say nothing of the immoral, and because he takes care of all the details.

There is an important point about comedy here. We laugh at failures of adaptation, at the person falling into the manhole, even when this turns out to be a lucky break, when the manhole leads to heaven, for example. Here it seems as if the laugh might be on us, since the person is in heaven and we are not; but of course we also laugh when the manhole leads to disaster, which is why laughter is often thought of as cruel. This is not so. Laughter of this kind is strictly neutral. It sees a human being failing to swerve where a swerve would be appropriate – failing to fail, in Pantoja's case – and it marks the failure, the missed swerve. It is not the fall that is funny; it is the inability to notice or step around the manhole. In this respect, the comedy of Pantoja's efficiency rejoins the comedy of the failed language: a key aspect of the real, human world is betrayed or ignored, and the comedy insists on the betrayal.

But then another element enters the comedy at this point, because Pantoja is not only a Bergsonian puppet. He is a man who loses his wife and child – even if they are restored to him at the end. He loses the prostitute he loves; and his very success is taken away from him. His mother says he seems to be sorry not to be doing his disreputable work, and back at his job as 'a real soldier again' (p. 235). He says he is not sorry, but they were three years of his life. Three years of success. 'They gave me a very difficult assignment and I executed it. Despite the difficulties, the lack of understanding, I did good work. I built something that had life, that was growing, that was useful'(p. 235). Mission, difficulty, work. All the key words return, and are just as ridiculous now as they were before. Useful is a word in the same vein. But life and growth are something different, and we know why the usually stolid captain is weeping when he is told that his mobile brothel is going to be closed and that he should resign from the army. 'Hell', his general says, 'no one is going to believe that I've seen an Army captain cry because they shut down a whorehouse'(p. 228).

He is not crying because the brothel is being closed. He is crying because the brothel was not a brothel to him; it was the army, it was what the army wanted of him, and what he provided. It is true that there is a scary edge to the comedy here; and we could imagine another novel about a man who just obeyed orders, who would do anything the army asked of him. But Pantoja is a loyalist and an enthusiast, not a monster of obedience, and this is not that other novel.

Pantoja, we might say, is a man who does not understand the novel's epigraph, from Flaubert's *Education sentimentale*: 'There are some men whose only mission in life is to serve as go-betweens; intermediaries; one crosses them like bridges and passes beyond them.' He does not know that that is who he is, who most people are. And he is not going to know; he is not going to wake up, in spite of the repeated calls for him to do so. But he is also a man who, in spite of himself, and in spite of his unawareness, undoes that epigraph. He is not just a bridge, he is a person. And the whole thrust of the novel's comedy, its brilliant assault on seriousness of all kinds, is to defend the stubborn particularity of the person against all ideas of service, usefulness, getting somewhere, tidying things up, refusing the raw, unwashed data of the world. You may remember that the general who hopes the old times have returned also says that two nightmares are over: 'At last, at last, the two nightmares of the Amazon ended once and for all' (p. 240). What are the two nightmares? The visitors' service, of course, and the insane religious sect led by Brother Francisco, a group centred on the theory and practice of crucifixion, which started by nailing small animals to crosses, and then moved on to a child and an old lady, finally arriving at the founder himself, who welcomed and stage-managed his own martyrdom. What could be the connection?

For the general, the two nightmares are simply two nuisances. The only connection is that there are two of them. But the novel invites us to think otherwise – we heard about Brother Francisco almost as soon as we heard about Pantoja, and before we heard about Pantoja's mission. The two nightmares are sexual desire and religious need – or perhaps they are those two things in their extreme, unmanageable, asocial form. I do not think the novel offers us any prescription for dealing with them, and I do not think it should. But it does tell us, its comedy of seriousness tells us on every page, the one thing institutions like to forget: that the unmanageable is unmanageable, not simply something for which we have not yet found the right management techniques.

There is a wonderful passage where all this comes together, and where we see the disorderly humanity of Pantoja in conflict with his idea of service, and where he almost understands what is happening to him. He blames his work for inflaming his own desire. 'It's something very mysterious, something that's never happened to anyone. A sense of the unhealthy obligation, same as a sickness'(p. 168). One of the last things we hear about him is that he is going to check up on the breakfasts of his men, off there in the cold zones of Lake Titicaca. 'I don't know why you have to go yourself to see the soldiers' breakfast, you maniac'(p. 244). This is his wife's phrase, and 'maniac' is precisely the word. But it is not just his sense of duty or adaptation to the context that makes Pantoja who he is. As we have seen, he is the reverse of adaptable, except in one special sense. His friend among the prostitutes is wrong to suggest that he would become crazy if he ran a madhouse. He would run the madhouse like a barracks, because he would believe this was the only way to do it. The inmates might even have a better time under his directorship. But he is right about himself. His sense of obligation is unhealthy, a form of disease. Not because obligations are unhealthy, or because Pantoja will walk conscientiously into any manhole the army opens up for him, but because he loses himself in his duty, and sees himself getting lost. Because he cannot acknowledge his desire except through a sort of erotics of obligation. Because his seriousness is a mania, and he will never get a chance to laugh at himself as we laugh at him.

Serious literature or trashy fiction?

If the chief technical device of *Captain Pantoja and the Special Service* is the alienating language of the official document, a formal record, so to speak, of the gap between unruly life and ordered writing, the chief formal arrangement of *Aunt Julia and the Scriptwriter* is a series of parallel events, ostensibly opposed in tone and content and implication, that finally collapse into each other, fully revealing the weakness of a distinction that was always on the verge of breaking down. The supposed distinction is between serious literature and trashy fiction; and if the comedy of *Captain Pantoja* arises from an effect of distance, from the lack of resemblance between life and what a text can make of it, the comedy of *Aunt Julia and the Scriptwriter* arises from a failure of distance, the sheer slump, it seems, of life into a bad novel. But is it a bad novel? What is a bad novel?

In his 1997 prologue to a new edition of the book, Vargas Llosa says he based it on a writer of radio serials whom he knew, 'whose melodramatic stories devoured his brain for a while', adding to this material 'an auto-biographical collage', a fictionalised version of his own first marriage.[6] Eleven of the work's twenty chapters relate, in the first person, the tale of one Mario Vargas, called Varguitas by almost everyone, the nickname a marker of the youthfulness he is very anxious to deny. He is 18, therefore, in the Peru of the mid-1950s, not old enough to have a passport or to get married without his parents' permission. He marries his Aunt Julia – more precisely his uncle's sister-in-law – because he genuinely loves her, but also because he is told he cannot, and because he is still in the grip of her first words to him: 'You've just gotten out of high school, haven't you?' 'I hated her instantly', he says (p. 8).

> My slight run-ins with the family in those days were all due to the fact that everybody insisted on treating me as though I were still a child rather than a full-grown man of eighteen. Nothing irritated me as much as being called 'Marito'; I had the impression that this diminutive automatically put me back in short pants.

It would be unkind and unjust to say the fictional Mario is 'a child of eighteen' rather than the 'full-grown man' he says he is, because he shows himself capable of great resolve and courage as the plot thickens and the marriage approaches, meeting massive family resistance. But we need to note the irony in the phrase about the complete man – the older Mario's sceptical take on his former self's pretensions – and a great deal of the fun and the subtlety of this novel lies in the uncertain status of its narrator: old enough to fall seriously in love, young enough not to be able entirely to distinguish his love from rebellion. He never stops calling Julia, *Aunt* Julia.

The Mario chapters (I, III, V, VII, IX, XI, XIII, XV, XVII, XIX, XX) alternate with nine chapters presenting versions of the radio serials of the man whose brains were devoured for a time by them. It is important to notice that these sequences are simulations, prose narratives recounting episodes that in their broadcast versions are dramatised, spoken by actors, directed by the author himself, and accompanied by lurid and ingenious sound effects. This is what Vargas Llosa means by saying that 'episodes   without being scripts, seem like scripts by Pedro Camacho' (p. 9). We read the plot, we have to imagine the show; so here, something resembling the gap between what we read and what we think, so characteristic of *Captain Pantoja*, appears in an interesting new form (p. 18):

> On one of those sunny mornings in Lima when the geraniums are an even brighter red, the roses more fragrant, and the bougainvilleas curlier as they awaken, a famous physician of the city, Dr. Alberto de Quinteros   opened his eyes in his vast mansion in San Isidro and stretched his limbs.

For Pedro Camacho, this is high sentimental art, everything in its right place, and just a little better than life: the weather, the flowers, the famous doctor, the spacious residence. For us, it is a pile-up of clichés, starting with the co-opting phrase 'one of those', and passing through the predictable plants, and the mannered placing of the first and last adjectives. Because we are reading what the fictional audiences are hearing, Vargas Llosa has taken pains to give us verbal equivalents of Camacho's favourite stylistic touches. In an actual radio show written by a vain and solemn fifty-year-old man, it would be enough to insert a male character who is fifty years old and make sure he has the right sort of adventures – the author would have done what he could to present an idealised version of himself. In the prose account we are given, figures are described again and again as having reached 'the prime of life' (pp. 60, 102, 137, 214, 255, 291, 331), with the appropriate facial and moral characteristics in attendance: 'broad forehead, aquiline nose, penetrating gaze, the very soul of rectitude and goodness' (pp. 19, 60, 102, 137, 178, 210, 255, 291, 331). These phrases occur, in this order, in every episode, with only the tiniest of variants. In the Spanish original, one of the fifty-year-old men, a professional rat-killer, lacks kindness, has only the very soul of rectitude. And one of these admirable mature citizens is a woman. Camacho's style generally is full of pompousness and platitudes – an intriguing counter-point to the violence of the actions he relates – but these repetitions are especially telling, and allow us to see how Vargas Llosa has set about achiev-ing an irony that comments on these serials, 'but without turning them into mere caricatures'.[7] The plots of the serials are extravagant to start with – dealing with incest in high society, the execution of an illegal immigrant, the self-mutilation of a rapist, various murders – and become catastrophic. By the end of the novel – which adds an epilogue to Pedro Camacho's rise and fall as a writer – all the episodes have turned to disaster, with every character in the show dying in an earthquake or a combination of shooting and panic at a soccer match. These stories mirror Camacho's own crack-up. He has done himself in by working too hard, and cannot remember the plots of his own stories, or which names go with which characters, so people keep changing their jobs and biographies, and he has even resurrected a few corpses by mistake, giving a role in one episode to a character he had killed off in previous one. For a while, his more sympathetic and cultured listeners think he may be employing the technique of having his characters recur in different contexts, like Balzac, or, for that matter, Faulkner or García Márquez. But the sequences are too disorderly for that, and alas, Camacho is just having a breakdown, the effect of exhaustion, and identified by a kindly doctor as 'deliquescence' (p. 343).

Meanwhile, Mario tells us about his job at the local radio station, where he meets and befriends Camacho and avoids his supposed studies at the uni-versity. It is a very nice touch that he says in his second sentence that he thinks he was studying law – 'I was studying at the University of San Marcos, law, as I remember' (p. 3). It is not just that he is not doing it; he is not even sure what it is. What he really wants is to be a writer, and the text is littered with his descriptions of stories he has written or is writing, all failures for one reason or another. His romance with Aunt Julia seems to be most of all a threat to this fantasy vocation, and neither Mario nor we can know at this stage that this story will be one of his great successes as a writer, indeed indistinguishable from the novel we are reading.

After many difficulties, to use one of Pantoja's words, Mario manages to marry Aunt Julia, and if the climax of the late radio serials is total extinction, the highpoint of his story is the comic quest, in village after village, for a mayor who will marry a man who is only eighteen years old and does not have his parents' permission. The trials of Mario and Julia, accompanied by two loyal friends, assume the proportions and the pace of a picaresque novel, every misadventure more unlikely and more entertaining than the last. Even at the last moment, when they have found a compliant mayor, there is a snag – two snags. They need another witness, and having conscripted their taxi-driver for the job, meet yet another hindrance. 'What a misfortune', the taxi-driver says (p. 315). What does he mean? He means they cannot have a wedding without a toast, and takes off to buy a couple of bottles of wine. Luckily he does come back, and the ceremony concludes. In his dreams, Mario begins to suspect he is in one of Camacho's radio serials (p. 313), and later uses the medium as a metaphor to criticise his mother's sentimentality: 'Mama dearest, don't begin another of your radio serials' (p. 353).

Of course, the differences are considerable. The picaresque novel and the catastrophe drama are not at all the same genre, and melodrama as the image of easy emotion is a long way from melodrama as the expression of a psychotic crisis. But this is where it is worth pausing to look closely at what Vargas Llosa is doing, since here, as in *Captain Pantoja*, he is experimenting with extreme forms of disarray and disjunction, only to show that at some point we may have difficulty keeping the extremes apart. It is true that Pantoja does not know his diligence is a mania, even a disease, and we find it funny for that reason. But then we make the equation that he cannot make; similarly, in *Aunt Julia and the Scriptwriter*, Camacho does not understand the degree to which his hectic programmes are a mirror of his breaking mind – he thinks he merely has a few memory lapses. However, where the reader makes the connection in *Captain Pantoja*, the book makes the connection in *Aunt Julia and the Scriptwriter* – or, more precisely, the book lays the clues all along the parallel paths of its two sets of stories. *Aunt Julia and the Scriptwriter* is slower and less perfectly pitched than *Captain Pantoja*, but it is also more complex. The story of Camacho's mania is matched by the story of a young man's madness. Taken together, the two stories confirm each other's most interesting implications, and also invite us to think further and think otherwise – to suspect, for example, that the mania is not only mania, and the madness is not madness at all.

The two stories do not simply alternate; they are twinned. Mario meets Aunt Julia on the same day he first hears of Camacho (p. 20). Aunt Julia herself thinks that their romance, even before it really resembles a romance, is 'A perfect subject for one of Pedro Camacho's serials', because it involves 'The love affair of a baby and an old lady who's also more or less your aunt' (p. 90). Mario does not respond to the challenge in the word 'baby', but he does take care to record it for us. And because Aunt Julia recounts the plots of some of the radio serials to Mario, Camacho gradually becomes part of their affair: 'little by little, Pedro Camacho became a constituent element in our romance' (p. 91). Sometime later, Aunt Julia actually meets Camacho. She and Mario visit the writer in his miserable abode, and become privy to his great secret: when he can, he likes to dress up as the characters he is writing about: a judge, a doctor, an old lady, a sailor, a cardinal. At one point, Mario is outraged to discover that Aunt Julia has a suitor 'in his fifties', one of those all too presentable fifty-year-olds Camacho constantly writes about (p. 155).

There are more subtle, and more troubling crossovers. Mario's colleague at the radio station finds and enjoys in real news items all the violence Camacho discovers in his imagination, in his 'systematic genocide of his characters' (p. 274). Mario as narrator appears to borrow phrases from the third-person narratives of the serials – 'meagre salary', for example (p. 102). And when Mario, needing to support a wife, finds himself working like a maniac, he thinks he is following in Camacho's footsteps (p. 439).

The implication, finally, is not only that life itself is a poor scriptwriter, and not at all that there is no difference between the scribblings of the apprentice writer and the prolific fantasies of the experienced hack. The implication is that writing, any kind of writing, as long as it registers the difference between an *escribidor* and an *escritor*, is a vocation or it is nothing at all. 'For him, to live was to write', Mario says of Camacho (p. 130). It is not what he writes that matters; it is that he writes, even with his extravagant plots, strings of clichés, bundles of social prejudices and terrible solemnity about his own work ('We artists don't create out of a desire for fame and glory, but rather out of love of humanity', p. 50). He is nevertheless the model of the writer, a man who sacrifices everything to his art. The fact that his art is largely ridiculous actually enhances the pathos rather than reduces it. The madness of art, in Henry James's phrase, is bad enough when great art results. But the madness remains whatever the outcome. Mario's friend Javier is being funny and sarcastic when he says, 'A guy who's capable of killing off every last one of his characters in a story by having them die in an earthquake is worthy of respect' (p. 264). But his comment is only slightly displaced. The person worthy of respect, and pity, is the one who is capable of going mad for the sake of his own fictional characters.

Of course, this proposition is itself ironic, as Vargas Llosa says, or can only be made from a certain ironic distance. But it offers a not easily answerable challenge to literature and culture, and Mario puts the matter perfectly when he gives himself a little time to reflect on 'the life of Pedro Camacho' (p. 195):

> What social milieu, what concatenation of circumstances, persons, relations, problems, events, happenstances had produced this literary vocation   that had somehow come to fruition, found expression in an *oeuvre*, and secured an audience? How could he be, at one and the same time, a parody of the writer and the only person in Peru who, by virtue of the time he devoted to his craft and the works he produced, was worthy of that name?

Mario's ambition is to be a real writer, not a half-writer, and Camacho is the only real writer he knows: 'The person I'd met who came closest to being this full-time writer, obsessed and impassioned by his vocation, was the Bolivian author of radio serials'(p. 195). Of course, Mario does not end up in anything like Camacho's madness and distress, and he does not write sentimental melodramas. He writes, among other things, a comedy about sentimental melodramas. But this fact only displaces, but does not remove, his question. Perhaps every real writer has a parody of a writer as his or her shadow, and the writer's relation to the shadow may resemble Pantoja's relation to his mania. Comedy, for a while, was Vargas Llosa's way of negotiating the curious double truths of laughter and insanity.

NOTES

1. See especially Efraín Kristal. *Temptation of the Word: The Novels of Mario Vargas Llosa*. Nashville, Tenn.: Vanderbilt University Press, 1998, pp. xiii–xiv.
2. Mario Vargas Llosa. *Pantaleón y las visitadoras*. Madrid: Santillana, 2000. Further in-line citations refer to *Captain Pantoja and the Special Service*. Trans. Gregory Rabassa. London: Faber and Faber, 1987.
3. Mario Vargas Llosa. *La tía Julia y el escribidor*. Madrid: Alfaguara, 1997. Further in-line citations refer to *Aunt Julia and the Scriptwriter*. Trans. Helen R. Lane. London: Picador, 2007.
4. Mario Vargas Llosa, 'Prólogo', *Pantaleón y las visitadoras*, p. 9. (Translation Michael Wood.)
5. Donald L. Shaw. 'Humor e ironía en *Pantaleón y las visitadoras*'. *Antípodas* 1, December 1988, p. 63.
6. Mario Vargas Llosa, 'Prólogo', *La tía Julia y el escribidor*, p. 9.
7. Ibid., p. 9.

5

JUAN E. DE CASTRO AND NICHOLAS BIRNS

The historical novel

The War of the End of the World

A total novel

The novels published by Mario Vargas Llosa in the 1970s marked a significant turn in his writing. Unlike those of the 1960s, arguably the most complex examples of high modernist literature in the Latin American canon, the novels of the 1970s – *Captain Pantoja and the Special Service* (*Pantaleón y las visitadoras*, 1973[1]) and *Aunt Julia and the Scriptwriter* (*La tía Julia y el escribidor*, 1977[2]) – are characterised by their deft use of humour, their storylines filled with narrative incident and pastiche, and their overall accessibility to general readers. These novels, despite their commercial success, had raised questions among a significant minority of critics, including some of the most influential, about a possible decadence of the Peruvian novelist or a commercialisation of his literature.

The publication of *The War of the End of the World* (*La guerra del fin del mundo*[3]) in 1981 signalled for many a return to the ambitious novelising of Vargas Llosa's first period. For instance, Peruvian critic Antonio Cornejo Polar found that 'with *The War of the End of the World*, Vargas Llosa again shows his ability to propose extremely vast and complex narrative projects and to develop them with unusual efficacy and ingenuity'.[4] The Uruguayan Angel Rama, another great Latin American literary critic of the period, was even more enthusiastic, proclaiming the novel 'a masterpiece', and predicting that in 'one hundred years   it will be mentioned as one of the key novels of this second half of the twentieth century. Rama even declared Vargas Llosa to be 'our greatest living classic [writer]'.[5] The doubts that, at least for some, had been generated by the turn in Vargas Llosa's writing had been answered by the publication of a work that equalled the highest achievements of his earlier period.

Vargas Llosa's return to writing a grand-scale novel did not imply an unmodified regression to his earlier high modernist techniques. Writing about *One*

Hundred Years of Solitude, but implicitly describing his own early novels, Vargas Llosa had declared García Márquez's masterwork a 'total novel', 'one of those demential creations that compete with reality on an equal plane, countering it with an image qualitatively equal in vitality, vastness, and complexity'.[6] However, *The War*'s 'totality' is achieved in a manner which diverges significantly from Vargas Llosa's 1960s novels, or, for that matter, from García Márquez's magical realism. For instance, instead of the complex juxtaposition of dialogues that characterised his earlier novels, there is now a mastery of the classic narrative realist style, though punctuated by periodic switching between past and present tense and the presence of various focalisers and narrative voices through which the novel is told. Not in vain does Rama argue, in an evaluation that has now become commonplace, that with *The War* Vargas Llosa wrote Latin America's '*War and Peace*, even if one hundred years later'.[7]

Besides its return to traditional narrative techniques, *The War* represented other significant departures from Vargas Llosa's earlier masterpieces. Instead of a searing examination of Peruvian reality, as was the case in his novels of the 1960s, *The War* is set in Brazil. It tells a story of the 1896–7 military repression of the 30,000-strong millenarian community of Canudos formed under the charismatic leadership of Antônio Conselheiro, the prophet-like ascetic who rejected the newly founded secular republic (1889) as aligned with the Antichrist. The Canudos rebellion took place in the north-eastern state of Bahia, an impoverished, semi-arid region containing largely mixed-race inhabitants. After a stand-off of over a year, and a series of futile attempts by the Brazilian army to defeat the rebels, Conselheiro and his followers were apprehended and killed by Brazilian army forces in October 1897. The Canudos episode is a significant one in Brazilian history, well-known to many Brazilians both for its intrinsic importance and, as we shall see shortly, the literary residue that it left. Thus this was also Vargas Llosa's first historical novel, retelling a story that had previously been told in a classic of Brazilian literature and culture: Euclides da Cunha's non-fiction account *Rebellion in the Backlands* (*Os Sertões*, 1902). Using filmic terminology, Rama even describes the novel as a 'remake' of da Cunha's earlier semi-sociological account of the event.[8]

Despite the fact that, as is so often the case, serendipity played a role in the development of Vargas Llosa's interest in Canudos – he had been commissioned to write a screenplay for a film on the rebellion that was never made – it is possible to see in this specific historical event a perfect embodiment of what by the late 1970s had become central concerns for the Peruvian author.[9] The opposition between rationality and irrationality, the links between religion and politics, the limits of violence as a political tool, the tensions between tradition and modernisation, and the tragic cultural divisions that characterise Latin America, among other topics, are incarnated with unusual clarity in the Canudos rebellion as Vargas Llosa depicts it in the novel. The settlement of Canudos by Antônio Conselheiro is an explicit rejection of modernity; he rejects maps, censuses and the metric system. In the novel, Canudos exemplifies a conflict between European ideas of progress, fanatically embraced by the Brazilian army, and backwardness, exemplified in the monarchic millenarianism of Conselheiro. In this, Vargas Llosa is underscoring his own vision regarding the contradictions of Brazilian and Latin American modernisation.

One can also see in these topics a reflection of the ideological changes Vargas Llosa had experienced by the late 1970s, the period when he began to write *The War*. Vargas Llosa, who had gone through 'a socialist period', and had even 'claimed that his conception of literature was socialist', publicly distanced himself from the Latin American left.[10] Even if it is difficult to characterise Vargas Llosa's earlier novels as overtly 'socialist', given their refusal to identify any possible social actor as capable of effectuating meaningful social change, the fact is that *The War* can be seen as reflecting his new-found preoccupation with the destructive potentiality of the radical and revolutionary movements that at the time were still spreading throughout Latin America.

The limits of utopia

Though no longer a supporter of socialist movements, the Vargas Llosa of 1981 is not yet the influential advocate of free market doctrines he is today. In fact, in a book of essays published the same year, *Entre Sartre y Camus* ('Between Sartre and Camus'), he identified publicly with the liberal anti-communism of Albert Camus. Vargas Llosa argued that his reading of this French author had led him to conclude that:

> Modern experience shows us that to disassociate the struggle against hunger, exploitation, colonialism, from the struggle for the freedom and the dignity of the individual is as suicidal and absurd as disassociating the idea of freedom from true justice, which is incompatible with the unjust distribution of wealth and culture.[11]

As Efraín Kristal notes, *The War* is the first of his novels in which Vargas Llosa 'explored a new theme in line with the concerns of anti-authoritarian liberalism: the fragility of a civilised coexistence assailed by fanatics, political opportunists, and well-intentioned but misguided idealists'.[12] Vargas Llosa's non-socialist liberalism had roots in many different strands of thought: from Albert Camus's scepticism towards absolutes to Karl Popper's idea of an open society.

Indeed, the novel provides a description of Canudos in terms that remind one of the values celebrated by the post-socialist Vargas Llosa in his writings on Camus. Thus the near-sighted journalist, the only one of the characters in the novel with personal experience of both modern Brazil and Canudos, states about the latter: 'It was the realm of obscurantism, and at the same time a world of brotherhood of a very special kind of freedom' (*The War*, p. 460). In Vargas Llosa's Canudos, obscurantism and fanaticism are presented as necessary conditions for the establishment of a community grounded on religious solidarity and eager to defend its sovereignty. Canudos is founded on Antônio Conselheiro's overwhelming charisma. To be sure, he gives a sense of meaningful purpose to his followers' lives, but this new-found meaning is predicated on a sense of devotion to their leader and their adherence to his teachings. The Little Blessed One, a young boy who models his sense of piety on his leader and grows old before his time, becomes the Conselheiro's deputy and administrator. The Lion of Natuba makes up for his deformed body, by his inner strength and zeal, spurred on by gratitude to Conselheiro. The half-caste Big João gains a sense of self-worth when he offers his considerable physical strength in service of the messianic cause. The bandit João is sanctified by Conselheiro and becomes 'Abbot João'. Father Joaquim, an inconspicuous parish priest, gains courage and self-confidence in the reflected glare of his leader. The storekeeper Antônio Vilanova (whose entrepreneurial energies provide sustenance to the community, and who, in a different context, might well have been the sort of grass-roots businessman Vargas Llosa later celebrated) is pugnacious and aggressive in ordinary life, yet his reverence for Conselheiro moves him to diffidence and self-effacement. Women such as Catarina and Maria Quadrado also become integral parts of Conselheiro's retinue. The empathetic presence of Maria Quadrado, a compassionate element of Mariological Christianity, tempers Conselheiro's harsh distinction between those he considers to be worthy of salvation ('the Elect') and those who are not ('the dogs').

Conselheiro's capacity to effect dramatic personal change in his followers – bandits become responsible members of the community, murderers become saints – leads the near-sighted journalist to wonder temporarily 'if God sent him' (p. 419). Yet ultimately the utopian community is rooted in the denial of rationality, and therefore in the impossibility of falsification of Conselheiro's beliefs, and in the negation of true freedom based on the possibility of making conscious and rational choices.

The fatal limitations of Canudos become evident in two passages near the end of the novel. The first one takes place when the settlement is on the verge of being destroyed by the overwhelmingly superior Republican army, after a period of heroic resistance during which Conselheiro's followers defeated two military expeditions that had come to Canudos to repress their rebellion. For unexplained reasons, Antônio Conselheiro has fallen ill – the ability of Canudos to withstand the Republican armies is presented as directly linked to his health – and has developed 'a little watery trickle'. Arguing that Conselheiro's diarrhoea is 'his essence part of his soul', the Little Blessed One decides to take communion with the excrement. The novel laconically notes that 'All the women of the Sacred Choir also took communion, in the same way' (p. 510). (The Sacred Choir, which looks after Conselheiro's personal needs, is comprised of some of the more devout women in Canudos. It is also the only visible opportunity for women to participate publicly in the patriarchal society of Canudos.) In this episode, the obscurantism and fanaticism of the community have reached a sort of grotesque apex.

Another link between Canudos and death follows the passing of Conselheiro, when the destruction of the settlement is imminent. The Little Blessed One, who believes to be channelling his dead leader, negotiates with the army that the wounded and sick children, women and aged be permitted to surrender. However, Abbot João orders their execution (pp. 553–4). In this case, as in the refusal of the population of Canudos to abandon the settlement, fanaticism leads to destruction.

Conselheiro's main concern is not the creation of a sustainable social order that will bring the inhabitants of Canudos out of poverty and misery and into prosperity. He is a pastor concerned with the salvation of his flock as he anticipates the imminent coming of the apocalypse and the final judgement, the 'end of the world' that gives the novel one of its meanings (another is the suggestion that the events of Canudos are taking place in the periphery of modern civilisation). Conselheiro is opposed to the centralised, bureaucratic administration in both the provincial capital, Bahia, and the national capital of Rio de Janeiro, which he considers to be sacrilegious. Indeed, he interprets the displacement of the Brazilian monarchy and the separation of Church and state by a secular political order to be both an outrage to piety and a portent that the apocalypse is in the offing. His political aim, therefore, is to resist any influence coming from the newly founded Brazilian Republic, which is why the first public act of his community is the public burning of edicts sent from the capital city of Rio to Canudos. Conselheiro's vision is not geared to the political empowerment of individuals who feel disenfranchised from a national order to which they aspire to belong. Rather, he is intent on resisting the arrival of modernising forces that he considers an affront to the religious worldview with which he inspires his followers. In the novel, the lives of the inhabitants of Canudos appear to be as barren as the lands in which they live until they embrace a spiritual leader who gives them a sense of meaning, purpose and fulfilment, even as they await the imminence of their deaths.

Conselheiro, however, does not just have followers, but sympathisers. Chief among these is Galileo Gall, a Scottish anarchist who comes to Canudos to report for the leftist French journal *L'Etincelle de la Révolte*. Gall was trained as a phrenologist, and his investment in a pseudoscience predisposes readers of the novel to scepticism regarding his convictions, including his belief that 'the revolution will free society of all its afflictions'. In the novel, Vargas Llosa underscores Gall's fundamental lack of understanding of the historical events unfolding before his very eyes, and the reader is intended to mock his political projections tinged with a residue of Eurocentrism. Even though he sympathises with the rebels, the rebellion matters to him to the extent that it might also matter to the like-minded Parisian audience for whom he writes, and who might be persuaded that the model for a world revolution akin to his anarchist hopes is taking place in South America.

In Vargas Llosa's novel, Gall is clearly a foil who embodies anachronistic and misguided European scientific, philosophical trends (phrenology, anarchism, utopian socialism, and the like). Vargas Llosa is far more understanding of the Canudos rebels than he is of Gall's misguided projections onto a world he does not understand. Vargas Llosa's authorial voice does not share the assumptions of those Brazilians in the novel who judge their fellow countrymen and women from Canudos with racist prejudice or with a patronising attitude. Rather, he depicts the rebel population as victims of religious fanaticism, and of a tragically misguided and unnecessary military repression by the Brazilian republic. From this point of view, Gall's assumptions about Canudos as the starting point for a world revolution that should inspire his Parisian audience is nothing short of laughable. The reader is meant to mock Gall when he likens the peasants of Canudos to the followers of the legendary Rob Roy. Given his personal contempt for Britain, informed by his Scottish background, it is ironic that the authorities of the Brazilian Republic, who become aware of him, are persuaded that he is a British spy, in cahoots with seditious forces in Brazil that would like to re-establish the monarchy.

The baggage Gall brings to bear in Canudos is not just ideological, it is also sexual. Gall is a sexually frustrated man. Knowing sexuality only as lust in his youth, he had vowed to renounce sexual activity ten years before his arrival into Canudos. Before reaching Brazil, Gall was persuaded that chastity would fortify his revolutionary zeal. In Canudos, however, he feels sexually tempted and begins to wonder if his decision was necessary. In his most damning act in the novel, he forces himself on Jurema, the wife of a local tracker whom Gall had hired to guide him through the backlands. Jurema had steadfastly resisted Gall's advances, and his despicable conduct belies his lofty ideals for a just society for all men and women. It is clear, in the novel, that Gall's political fanaticism is linked to his repressed sexuality, and that his libidinal energy is sublimated into his enthusiasm for revolutionary causes.

One could add that just as Gall displaces his unhealthy sexuality onto political sublimations, Conselheiro's religious fanaticism displaces the spiritual consolation of traditional Christianity for violence and self-destruction.[13] The questionable nature of the seditious zeal that animates both Conselheiro and Gall is akin to Vargas Llosa's scepticism with respect to revolutionary movements. Although the novel makes it plain that Conselheiro has capitalised on the disenfranchisement of a people neglected and abused by their own government, Vargas Llosa's novel is informed by an underlying distrust of any revolutionary action intended to remedy the plight and misery of the abused. Indeed, he depicts it as unhealthy and even pathological. The novel gives pride of place to two cases in which revolutionary movements arise from an unsound displacement of spirituality as well as an unsound sublimation of sexuality.

Why Brazil?

Vargas Llosa goes to explicit length – indeed, perhaps intruding his own authorial voice – to say that the Canudos rebels are not like the deeply conservative peasants who rebelled against the French revolutionary regime in the Vendée rebellion of 1793. The Canudos rebels fight against those who have overthrown the monarchy. They are anti-antimonarchists. But they are not fighting to restore the monarchy as such. Why is this so? In one sense, Conselheiro is just exploiting uncertainties felt by the peasants when the Brazilian monarchy was replaced by a secular Republican order.

When Vargas Llosa published the novel in 1981, most people who called themselves socialist or revolutionary would have felt little in common with religious messianics at ease with a monarchy and defiant of a secular state. In works such as Eric Hobsbawm's *Primitive Rebels*, radical historians had traced continuities between millenarian optimism and modern movements for social change, but had also characterised them as 'pre-political', a statement, coming from a Marxist, of at best limited praise.[14] Most contemporary radicals, though, felt their beliefs were reactions to present social conditions and did not rely on a historical genealogy of predecessor movements. But Vargas Llosa must have felt that the forward-looking, progressive rhetoric of the left of the 1970s masked a deep adherence to retrogressive, traditionalist scenarios that stood in the way of actual progress. In this, he had considerable intellectual backing. Influential works published after the Second World War by Karl Löwith and Norman Cohn traced many modern ideologies to Christian roots, and suggested that modernity had adapted Christianity, rather than, as its advocates often contended, categorically advancing beyond it.[15] Cohn, in particular, focused on, and popularised, the idea of 'millenarianism'. Millenarians were Christian splinter groups in the Middle Ages who believed that the year 1000 (the first millennium) would bring the apocalypse. After the millennium, some Christian communities continued to expect that the day of reckoning would soon redeem the world from sin. Outside an explicitly Christian context, our contemporary use of words like millenarian, apocalyptic, chiliastic and eschatological come from this mid-twentieth-century intellectual milieu. Indeed, the reading of Conselheiro's movement as a radical rather than Christian restoration movement would not be possible without the earlier reading of medieval Christian heretics as proto-revolutionaries. Löwith and Cohn linked modern revolutionary movements to these earlier splinter groups, implying that they had in common a wish to provide immediately gratifying solutions for worldly problems that, in reality, were far less easily soluble. This was complementary to the anti-communism of sceptical centre-leftists (like Karl Popper and Isaiah Berlin, both figures greatly admired by Vargas Llosa). These liberal thinkers, wary of communist absolutism, looked, as Vargas Llosa does, to liberalism to present a modernity uninhibited by the ghosts of the past.

And those ghosts were not so visible in a Hispanophone Latin America that had almost immediately adopted the republican models pioneered in the hemisphere by the United States. Brazil was different. When the Portuguese government was in exile in Brazil during the Napoleonic Wars, Brazil became the seat of the Portuguese monarchy, in 1808; and in a bloodless secession within the Portuguese royal family, Brazil became an independent monarchy in 1821. The Brazilian Republic is not established until 1889, which corresponds to the period when the novel is set. The context of the historical rebellion in the Brazilian backlands, on which Vargas Llosa draws for his novel, is not a conflict between a progressive revolutionary force against a reactionary order (as Galileo Gall would like to believe), but a disenfranchised population that is resisting the forces of secular modernity as they look to a religious leader for guidance. The novel's supreme irony is predicated on the fact that the Republican government commits an act of genocide against its own people because it had misunderstood the intentions of the rebels, who are not participating in an international conspiracy to restore the Brazilian monarchy (as the press in Rio de Janeiro has reported), and who, in turn, have interpreted the advent of a secular government as a portent of the end of the world.

The total novel: against ideology

The first modern novel, Miguel de Cervantes's *Don Quixote*, is a humane but ruthless undermining of the chivalric novels read by its great protagonist. When Abbot João, under Conselheiro's benevolent matchmaking eye, is about to declare his sexual interest in Catarina, he tells her 'chivalric tales'. Echoing Cervantes's sense of the chivalric as delusive, Vargas Llosa can be seen as mounting a Cervantine critique of ideology when he targets a Christianity made into fanaticism by outsize distortions, perhaps even a direct attack on Christian absolutism. Vargas Llosa would perhaps see elements of irrationalism in the established religion.[16] Indeed, he might well not disagree so much with Galileo Gall's characterisation of religion as 'a dream of sick men' – exacerbated in its novel reincarnation as leftist ideology (p. 264). Vargas Llosa's exposure of the buffoonery of both Gall and Conselheiro stands directly in the Cervantine tradition of using novelistic realism to tear down the walls of ideological fakery and self-deception.

Vargas Llosa is also inspired by Gustave Flaubert, the first novelist to see narrative fiction as a fully-fledged art form. Vargas Llosa's admiration for Flaubert is well known, and he wrote a famous monography on *Madame Bovary*. In *The War*, the most important Flaubertian antecedent is arguably *Bouvard and Pécuchet*. In Flaubert's posthumous novel, two doltish copy clerks compile a Dictionary of Received Ideas, ludicrously taking pride in the unoriginality of the thoughts they record. For much of its length, *The War* can also be read as a giant compendium of received ideas, and this gives a new dimension to Vargas Llosa's interest in the notion of the 'total novel'. From the perspective of *The War*, the 'total novel' is not only a work of narrative fiction that gives the illusion that the reader has entered into a self-contained universe, it is also a work that offers a sweeping range of ideological positions, presented with some measure of distance and even scepticism. In *Bouvard and Pécuchet*, Flaubert makes it a point to explore standpoints and beliefs that are farcical, and many positions held by characters in *The War* can also be characterised as such. And yet, what gives *The War* its particular poignancy is the fact that positions that might be considered farcical are held by individuals who will participate in a horrible human tragedy.

Another major inspiration for Vargas Llosa's *The War* is clearly Tolstoy's *War and Peace*. As previously mentioned, some of the initial reviewers of the novel saw it as a Latin American *War and Peace*. What was meant here was not just the large scope of the novel, but the way that Vargas Llosa, like Tolstoy, forestalls any attempts to make definitive sense of history. *The War* comes close to Mikhail Bakhtin's idea of the novel as most complete when it is 'contested, contestable, and contesting'.[17] Though far different in emphasis, intention and effect to Bakhtin's idea of the novel as a vehicle for 'heteroglossia', or multiple speech, Vargas Llosa's idea of the 'total novel' posits the novel as an open, liberal form that critiques chivalric nostalgia, self-important bluster or world-historical illusions. What makes the novel total is neither the subject nor the scale, but the fact that Vargas Llosa does not endorse a particular protagonist or point of view. Millenarians and revolutionaries may be travestied, but bourgeois liberals are not protagonists. Epaminondas Gonçalves, a leader of the Progressive Republican party, is self-important, ineffective and deluded.

The general Moreira César is incompetent. Likewise, the near-sighted journalist is a far lesser character than either the da Cunha he is intended to half-represent or the Vargas Llosa who engenders them. Some critics in search of a character the novelist endorses have fastened on the Baron de Canabrava, the wealthy local magnate, at first suspected of backing the rebels, but who turns out to be one of their strongest opponents. Critics as different as Rama and Gene Bell-Villada have not only claimed that Vargas Llosa sympathises with the Baron, but have also seen that sympathy as an index of Vargas Llosa's willingness to endorse even the landed aristocracy, given his discomfiture with the left.

An unsettling incident near the end of the novel provides both argument and counter-argument for this thesis. In the second most violent scene of forced sex in the novel after Gall's rape of Jurema, the Baron assaults his wife's maid, Sebastiana, a woman of African descent and a former slave. He does so in front of Estela, his wife, who is paralysed and catatonic in bed, unable to speak due to an illness. This shocking scene, towards the end of the novel, is an episode of sexual perversity. Some have argued that, from Vargas Llosa's authorial perspective, the Baron's conduct is superior to that of Gall and Conselheiro because his depravity, unconscionable though it may be, is private. However one judges the episode, one cannot believe that Vargas Llosa, who has spoken again and again against misogyny, homophobia and other aspects of traditional Latin American patriarchy, which he sees as illiberal and just the sort of pathologies a modern, open society would countermand, is in any way endorsing Sebastiana's victimisation. The Baron's behaviour is a private, not a public, evil, but still an evil; furthermore, the very name Sebastiana links the episode to the Sebastianism of which Conselheiro's rebellion is an instance. This coincidence of names suggests the Baron's behaviour is a privatised version of the same irrational impulse, less catastrophic when manifested in private life, but no more commendable. Yet it is not just this specific incident, but the very idea of the total novel as conceived by Vargas Llosa that renders the Baron unadmirable. A total novel that solicits the possibility of a liberal society is, by definition, one that allows for pluralism.

Thus the Baron is not exemplary. The novel does not endorse him. His sexual transgression does not enable him to be complacent about his world. Looking out of his window, he senses 'puzzlement and uneasiness' (p. 541). After this, the final mopping-up of the Canudos rebels by the army is anti-climactic. Likewise, the old woman's belief that Abbot João was taken up to heaven has a small degree of pathos, to the extent that the reader even feels sorry for those whose delusions had been an object of such savage derision for most of the novel.

The War is consistent with Mario Vargas Llosa's break with the consensus of the Latin American left. Nearly thirty years later, the original context has faded and a very different world has replaced it, one in which liberalism has new enemies, and in which even those who proclaim liberal slogans may indeed be among the worst of those enemies. But in its evisceration of the hopes of revolution, Vargas Llosa provided his readers with arguably his most daring and capacious work, a 'total novel' that captured the follies of a past age and warned against their re-enactment in the present and future.

NOTES

1. Mario Vargas Llosa. *Pantaleón y las visitadoras*. Barcelona: Seix Barral, 1973.
2. Mario Vargas Llosa. *La tía Julia y el escribidor*. Barcelona: Seix Barral, 1977.
3. Mario Vargas Llosa. *La guerra del fin del mundo*. Barcelona: Seix Barral, 1981. Further in-line citations refer to *The War of the End of the World*. Trans. Helen R. Lane. New York: Penguin, 1997.
4. Antonio Cornejo Polar. 'Mario Vargas Llosa. *La guerra del fin del mundo*' (book review). *Revista de Crítica Literaria Latinoamericana*, 8–15, 1982, p. 219.
5. Angel Rama. '*La guerra del fin del mundo*. Una obra maestra del fanatismo artístico'. In Rama. *Crítica literaria y utopía en América Latina*. Antioquía, Colombia: Universidad de Antioquía, 2006, p. 296. (Translation Juan E. de Castro and Nicholas Birns.)
6. Mario Vargas Llosa. '*Cien años de soledad*. Realidad total, novela total'. In Gabriel García Márquez. *Cien años de soledad. Edición conmemorativa*. Madrid: Santillana, 2007, p. xxv.
7. Rama, '*La guerra del fin del mundo*', p. 296.
8. Ibid., p. 297.
9. Efraín Kristal has described the process by which the screenplay became the novel in *Temptation of the Word: The Novels of Mario Vargas Llosa*. Nashville, Tenn.: Vanderbilt University Press, 1998, pp. 124–6.
10. Ibid., p. 7.
11. Mario Vargas Llosa. *Entre Sartre y Camus*. Río Piedras, Puerto Rico: Huracán, 1981, p. 460.
12. Kristal, *Temptation*, p. xiv.
13. Vargas Llosa has spoken of, and condemned, a 'dogmatic lay religion' in his acceptance speech for the Irving Kristol Award given to him by the American Enterprise Institute: 'Confessions of a Liberal' (www.aei.org/speech/22053), accessed 28 June 2011. For a fuller version of Vargas Llosa's intellectual anti-dogmatism, see Mario Vargas Llosa. 'Updating Karl Popper'. *PMLA*, 105(5), 1990, pp. 1018–25.
14. Eric Hobsbawm. *Primitive Rebels: Studies in Archaic Forms of Social Movement in the Nineteenth and Twentieth Centuries*. Manchester University Press, 1959.
15. Norman Cohn. *The Pursuit of the Millennium: Revolutionary Millenarians and Mystical Anarchists of the Middle Ages*. London: Pimlico, 1993. Karl Löwith. *Meaning in History*. University of Chicago Press, 1964.

16. Vargas Llosa has been open about his agnosticism, an admission which undermined his 1990 presidential race in Peru. See Braulio Muñoz. *The Storyteller: Vargas Llosa between Barbarism and Civilization*. Lanham, Md.: Rowman and Littlefield, 1992, p. 38.
17. Mikhail Bakhtin. *The Dialogic Imagination*. Trans. Caryl Emerson and Michael Holquist. Austin: University of Texas Press, 1981, p. 332.

6

FIONA J. MACKINTOSH

Innocence and corruption

Who Killed Palomino Molero? and *The Storyteller*

Published within one year of each other, *Who Killed Palomino Molero?* (*¿Quién mató a Palomino Molero?*, 1986[1]) and *The Storyteller* (*El hablador*, 1987[2]) are superficially very different, the former focusing on a melodramatic small town murder mystery, and the latter delving into the myths and cosmology of a Peruvian Amazonian tribe, the Machiguenga. The town of Talara in northern Peru links the two stories, in that it is the scene of the murder of Palomino Molero and is the home town of Saúl Zuratas's mother in *The Storyteller*.[3] Both novels have an identifiable biographical point of origin; *Palomino* stems from Vargas Llosa's involvement in the 1983 Uchuraccay Investigatory Commission, set up after the murder of eight journalists,[4] and *The Storyteller* harks back to Vargas Llosa's visit in the mid-1950s to the Alto Marañón region of the Peruvian Amazon, which sparked his long-lasting engagement with the debate about the place of indigenous cultures in a modern, Westernised society. They have in common a concern with the problematic nature of concepts such as 'truth' and 'authenticity' within the context of specific racial and social tensions.

Who Killed Palomino Molero?

Who Killed Palomino Molero? is, as its title proclaims, a self-conscious detective-style narrative; for the setting Vargas Llosa returns to Talara in the 1950s, and to his 'two most recurrent characters',[5] Lituma and Silva. The two policemen are seeking to solve the mystery of the horrific mutilation and hanging of a young bolero singer from Piura, Peru, recently enlisted in the air force. In this novel, Vargas Llosa utilises his familiar counterpoint narrative technique to interweave the murder mystery with an amorous subplot that adds comic relief.[6] Often perceived as being among Vargas Llosa's lesser works, *Palomino* nevertheless treats its detective model with the wit and sophistication associated with 'geographically and politically aware detective fiction',[7] and indeed sets up a parallel literary investigation that sends the reader hunting for 'intertextual clues' to Vargas Llosa's other works, making it more of a 'post-modernist fiction loosely based on the epistemological format of the detective story'.[8]

Though the novel appears to be a standard third-person narrative, the reader's suspense and curiosity is focused through the thoughts and reactions of Lituma, who acts as the classic foil to Teniente Silva. While Silva (whose methods are traceable to Vargas Llosa's readings of Karl Popper[9]) reasons his way through situations, Lituma gets emotionally involved, and, in doing so, draws the reader into his perspective on the unfolding events. For instance, his impatience towards his chief's digressive interrogation tactics mirrors the reader's, whose hermeneutic strategies in trying to piece together the mystery are frustrated at every turn: 'When would Lieutenant Silva start asking her questions?' (*Palomino*, p. 65). 'How would he do it?' (p. 67). Subverting the generic detective model, this novel frustrates closure, since the apparent – but unsatisfactory – solution of Palomino's mysterious death brings no catharsis to the two investigators; initially alienated from the event by horror and incomprehension, at the end they remain alienated and isolated since none of the local people will accept their version of events, preferring to see a larger plot involving corruption, contraband and Ecuadorian military intelligence. This frustrating circularity, returning to the point of departure without any sense of relief or 'epistemological closure'[10] is underlined in a bathetically comic way; the novel opens and closes with an identical oath from Lituma, 'Sons of bitches' (pp. 3, 151). At the opening it expresses horror at the sight of Palomino's corpse; at the close of the narrative it expresses disgusted resignation to the fate he will now suffer of being posted to the sierra, far from home, in 'recognition' of his having (apparently) solved the crime.

Gringos *and* cholos: *class, race and corruption*

The social context to this novel – which implicitly draws on or exorcises Vargas Llosa's own involvement in the Uchuraccay Investigatory Commission – is the typical racialised hierarchy found in many of Vargas Llosa's novels.[11] At the top are the *gringos* of the International Petroleum Company (IPC), and just below them the aviation officials represented by Colonel Mindreau. Below Mindreau are the ordinary air force men, who within their rank are hierarchised by race; into this category fall Teniente Dufó ('suitably' white) and Palomino Molero (*cholo*, or mixed-race). Lituma, who describes himself as 'a purebred *cholo*' (p. 101), is annoyed by the behaviour of the 'whites' (p. 100) and the 'big guys', who usually manage to avoid justice (pp. 118, 124). Lituma and Silva are positioned between the air force and the ordinary people, represented by Doña Adriana – proprietress of the local *fonda* or snack bar – and her fisherman husband, Don Matías, alongside a cast of minor characters, such as the taxi-driver Don Jerónimo, the barman Liau the Chinese, and Lituma's group of Piuran friends, 'the Unconquerables', who meet at La Chunga's bar (another intertextual reference to other Vargas Llosa works). The principal site of intersection of conflicting elements in this racial and social hierarchy is the emblematic figure of Palomino Molero, the 'kid' whose pathetic and grotesque corpse, described as being more like 'a scarecrow or a broken marionette' (p. 3) than a corpse, is found hanging crazily in a tree at the start of the novel. While the Colonel blames man's baser nature in general for what happens to Palomino, he nevertheless introduces clear racial and social prejudice to his comment: 'There is an element of bestiality in all of us. Educated or ignorant, all of us. I suppose there's more among the lower classes, the *cholos*. Resentment, complexes' (p. 128). In addition to feeling indignation at the Colonel's gross generalisation, the reader is encouraged to position him or herself with the *cholos*, since our perspective on the events narrated is largely that of Lituma. The whole novel implicitly comments on these distinctions and confrontations of race and class, since this racialised hierarchy is the necessary backdrop to the 'impossible love' (p. 18) between Palomino and Alicia Mindreau, daughter of the Colonel at the airbase.

Cinematic elements

Although detective fiction provides the most obvious generic model for *Palomino*, the novel is also heavily dependent on cinema and cinematic techniques. The cinema features as a kind of window onto the life of the upper classes as imagined by those lower down the social scale ('Like the gringos at the IPC [the airmen] … live like movie stars', p. 27). It also materially reinforces the power structures inherent in the society, since the priest has the right to censor films by virtue of the outdoor cinema being projected onto his church wall.

There is a continuous symbolic play of light and darkness which highlights moments of dramatic suspense, sometimes ironically. For example, towards the end of the novel when Silva and Lituma are on the beach, there is an interpolated description of the moonlight that shows up the outline of the houses belonging to the *gringos* and to the high-ranking workers of the IPC. This obvious use of light seems clearly to be symbolising in cinematic vernacular the fact that the shadows of larger interests will always loom over individual destinies; this apparent symbolism turns out to be a false lead for the reader-detective, since rather than representing the truth of the case, it reflects the misplaced beliefs and hasty conclusions of the locals in Adriana's *fonda.* The bright moon is linked in Lituma's mind to the romantic *boleros* he imagines Palomino singing to the guitar; in stark contrast to this untroubled picture is the figure of Colonel Mindreau, whose sudden apparition is described as a shadow: '"Good evening," said the shadow' (p. 120). The lighthouse that dominates the shoreline adds to this literary chiaroscuro, playing first across the backdrop of the sea, then silhouetting the Colonel: 'The beacon from the lighthouse momentarily revealed the short, imperious figure dressed in khaki' (p. 133). This figure is seen gradually to blur into the more general shadows, as Lituma and Silva – in a kind of tracking shot – turn to watch him recede from view as they head back to town. 'The colonel's figure, a shadow lighter than the shadows around it, stood in the same spot' (p. 133). Being among the shadows is symbolic of his joining the dead, as he will shortly when he commits suicide.

When Silva subsequently reads the Colonel's suicide note, and finds out that the Colonel has killed not only himself but also his daughter, this dreadful discovery is linked in Lituma's description with the effect of a blinding light: 'Lituma saw [Silva] blink and squint, as if the glare were blinding him' (p. 136). But the traditional association of light with revelation and truth is continually undermined. First, since the motives for the crime remain murky, did the Colonel subject his daughter to incestuous abuse, and did he personally kill Palomino and Alicia for their transgressive love across racial and social hierarchies? Second, if the community refuses to acknowledge what has been discovered, preferring theories of contraband and corruption, then the 'facts' are condemned to remain in the world of fiction. This ironic paralysis, brought about by the blinding light of 'truth', recalls the moment early on in the novel when Silva became aware of the pressure on him to solve the crime, before accusations of a cover-up could begin to take hold: 'In the blinding light, it seemed as if things and people might simply dissolve at any moment' (p. 25). In both cases, light leads to a sense of dissolution, rather than to clarity and order.

In addition to the emphasis on light and shadow, there is a strongly cinematic emphasis on imagining and replaying particular scenes. This is used both for heightening dramatic tension and suspense in the case of the main 'detective' plot, where many possible scenarios for the murder of Palomino are imagined and then discarded by Lituma, and also for comic effect in the case of the amorous subplot between Silva and Doña Adriana. For instance, when we finally reach the moment of the much anticipated seduction scene, what we are presented with is not the actual scene as it happens, but Doña Adriana's verbal replaying of it for her own amusement and to satisfy the voyeuristic curiosity of Lituma (and, through his eyes, the reader). In the retelling, her scornful goading and challenging of Silva (not the expected reaction of an upright married woman) elicits both the embarrassed incomprehension of Silva within the narrative, and its echo in Lituma's embarrassed disbelief at the narrative he is being told. The juxtaposition of the two perspectives – that of Lituma reacting in real time to the replay, and within it that of a 'humiliated, emasculated, failed' Silva[12] reacting to Doña Adriana's sudden adoption of the role of provocative taunter – makes for a great comic moment, shown in italic in the English translation (p. 147).

> *But, but* ... stammered the lieutenant ...
> 'But, but ... ' stuttered Lituma ...
> *You have no right to make fun of me like that*, stuttered the lieutenant.
> 'He was totally destroyed. You should have seen him.'
> 'I'm not surprised, *Doña* Adriana ... I'm destroyed just listening.'

In Lituma's mind, imagined scenes frequently almost overpower his senses, to the extent that he becomes emotionally carried away by them. The whole murder investigation threatens to dissolve into a sentimental song lyric (reminiscent of Pedro Camacho's melodramatic radio serials in *Aunt Julia and the Scriptwriter*[13]), as he imagines the passion of Palomino, who was prepared to defy society and risk his life for love: 'It was a kind of waking dream, again and again he saw the happy couple ... he a half-breed *cholo* from Castilla; she a white girl of good family. There are no barriers to love, as the old waltz said. In this case the song was correct' (p. 82).

Yet the precise nature of the relationship between Palomino and Alicia remains one of the unsolved mysteries of the book. Earlier, during the course of their investigations, Lituma's sentimental imaginings had intruded on the questioning of Alicia Mindreau, since the flat, unemotional tone of Alicia's narration made him instinctively reject her version of events. However, he is still 'seeing' Alicia with Palomino in his mind's eye (p. 101). We are reminded that everything we see is reconstructed through Lituma's partiality; indeed at one point he even doubts whether he is really seeing and hearing her: 'it was as if the girl were not there and had said nothing, as if it was all a figment of his imagination' (p. 104). His instinctive revulsion at her apparent coldness becomes racially charged – 'Damn, but these whites are complicated people' (p. 103) – reminding us of the racial tensions at all levels. Lituma's imagined vision of the two improbable lovers becomes recurrent and abhorrent; he describes Alicia and Palomino as 'two extra images' (p. 124) (in the Spanish, '*intrusas*' is more clearly negative), since they give him no peace and Alicia's manner offends his romanticised reading of their story.

The fitting climax to this novel, which is based around repeated scenes, real or imagined, is the Colonel's claim (made immediately prior to his suicide) that his daughter is suffering from delusions. In his own definition, '"delusions" [he uses the English word] means illusions, fantasies, deception, and fraud' (pp. 125–6). Yet ironically, his attitude towards Palomino Molero seems equally to have been characterised by a delusion born of the rigid racial and social hierarchy in which he desperately believes: 'The daughter of a base commander does not fall in love with a recruit ... Colonel Mindreau's daughter does not fall in love with a guitar player from Castilla' (p. 129). That he has to state this in the present tense makes it more of a timeless statement of fact around which his worldview is based than a denial of any real event in the past. It is as though by repeating this 'truth', he can delude himself into thinking that the past never happened, a state of mind only encouraged by the conflicting versions of the past that are variously presented.

The truth about love and truth

Like the ending of Isabel Allende's *Eva Luna* (1985) (published a year before *Palomino*), which also draws on forms of popular culture to comment on the relationship between fiction and reality, the inconclusive ending of *Palomino* leaves it open as to which version of the truth we accept, and, as a secondary issue, which version of love. Can the love portrayed in Palomino Molero's stereotyped and clichéd songs really exist? Lituma raises the question of what is and is not believable when he counters Doña Adriana's scepticism about the Colonel's suicide with reference to her telling of the failed seduction scene, thus playing off one strand of the narrative against the other, one 'incredible' truth against another: 'But I believe the story you told me. And it's much more fantastic than the suicide of Colonel Mindreau' (p. 149). This link to fantasy is brought out by Booker, who reads the text as indebted to the fantastic, since we are 'in the complex situation of not knowing whether the mystery has been solved or not'.[14] Through the parody of the Holmes–Watson, teacher–disciple model that Silva and Lituma reproduce, we see a process of learning about truth as the novel advances. Lituma is cautioned by Silva that 'The truths that seem most truthful, if you look at them from all sides, if you look at them close up, turn out either to be half truths or lies' (p. 86). Most ironically, the ultimate truth that both are forced to accept is that the reward for seeking truth is banishment and alienation. As Booker notes, 'the final hints ... that Peruvian society itself is the real culprit in Molero's death ... transform *Palomino Molero* into a work of social criticism'.[15]

The Storyteller

The Storyteller has at its core the art, power and purpose of narrative – whether oral or written – within a culture. The novel's clearly symmetrical structure, consisting of six alternating chapters set within the narrative frame formed by the opening and closing chapters, juxtaposes and indeed brings into conflict the oral and written modes of storytelling and their corresponding worldviews. In Chapters 3, 5 and 7 we have the mythical history and cosmogony of the Machiguenga Indians of the Peruvian Amazon, apparently told in an oral style of narration by a Machiguenga *hablador* or storyteller; Chapters 2, 4 and 6, and the frame (1 and 8), consist of a conventional Western written narrative of personal recollection, reflection and (possible) enlightenment, by an unnamed narrator-novelist closely resembling Vargas Llosa himself, an autobiographical gesture that recalls *Aunt Julia and the Scriptwriter*. Through the alternating of these two very different narrative styles, Vargas Llosa provokes a consideration of whether the oral and written can be reconciled,[16] and thereby raises broader questions about the survival of indigenous cultures within modern society, questions perennially addressed by a well-established tradition of 'anthropological aspiration and practice' among prominent Latin American writers.[17]

The pivotal figure linking the two alternating narrative strands (though the link only emerges gradually and ambiguously) is that of the narrator's old university friend, Saúl Zuratas; a Peruvian born to a Jewish immigrant father and a Talaran *criolla* mother, he is known by the symbolically resonant nickname 'Mascarita' – Mask Face (*Storyteller*, p. 8) – which literally refers to the characteristic birthmark covering half of his face. The narrator, escaping Peru for an artistic and literary holiday in Florence, happens upon a photographic exhibition by 'one Gabriele Malfatti' (p. 4) about the Machiguenga, in which there is a picture of an *hablador*. This incident in the opening chapter sparks off the narrator's subsequent reminiscence about his old friend Mascarita, who, as an apathetic law student, had turned his attention increasingly to anthropology, and in particular to the study through fieldwork of the Machiguenga Indians. Mascarita's increasing identification with – and defence of – these 'primitive' people was always countered by the narrator's opinions that they should adapt to modern civilisation. However, when the narrator visits the Amazon and talks to a missionary couple named Schneil, he learns of the *habladores*, whose multiple roles in Machiguenga society seem to encompass collective memory, news-bearer, go-between and orator, as well as teller of stories. He becomes intrigued by this figure in which he sees a kind of parallel to his own vocation as a novelist in Western society. He, in turn, develops a fascination with the Machiguenga, but specifically with the idea of the *hablador*.

The narrator's efforts to find out more about these mysterious figures are continually frustrated, since references in the anthropological literature seem to disappear after the 1940s. As he pursues his research, he periodically reflects on the difficulties of writing a novel in which the voice of an *hablador* would be heard: 'the difficulty of inventing, in Spanish and within a logically consistent intellectual framework, a literary form that would suggest, with any reasonable degree of credibility, how a primitive man with a magico-religious mentality would go about telling a story' (pp. 157–8). Like the photographer Malfatti, who seeks to capture their image 'without dema-goguery or aestheticism' (p. 4), he aims to present the Machiguengas in an 'authentic' way, but complains that 'the voices of the ones that I'd contrived sounded all wrong' (p. 106). This drive for authenticity is highly significant to the central ethical problem posed by the novel about speaking for the other. Both Vargas Llosa himself (whose manuscripts for this novel reveal a far greater amount of revision and rewriting of the *hablador* chapters than of the rest) and the writer-narrator wish to write a book in which the Machiguengas would speak, but how can they do that from the position of outsider?[18] As Mark Millington puts it, the problem is 'how the other culture can be related to and its alterity preserved rather than its being assimilated and understood in alien terms', and more specifically 'how the other culture … is to be represented within a form as fundamentally Western as the novel'.[19]

The Machiguenga and the question of 'authenticity'

Within this novel, therefore, the alternate *hablador* chapters have a highly ambiguous status, and are likened by Jennifer Geddes to 'a series of unmask-ing moments';[20] initially they seem to offer a rare and exotic insight into Machiguenga mythology by a genuine Machiguenga *hablador*, but through the 'communicating vessels' of the narrator chapters, we are made increas-ingly sceptical as to their authenticity. Repeated textual clues in the oral narratives gradually point us towards Saúl being the *hablador*; for example, he has a talking parrot, in Spanish a 'lorito *hablador*' (emphasis added), which makes a linguistic connection between the possessor of the parrot and the mythical possessor of storytelling gifts. Saúl's potential conversion to the culture and values of the Machiguenga tribe he has been studying is also prefigured in his own name, through its biblical intertext – Saul's conversion on the road to Damascus (Acts 9:3–19). So, once we suspect Saúl of being the voice, the *hablador* chapters then appear to be a transcription of Saúl's oral narratives in his new-found role, a conjecture that is strengthened by the appearance and transformation of other elements of Western culture in the *hablador*'s discourse – Kafka's Gregorio Samsa from *The Metamorphosis*, Adam and Eve, or the Holy Trinity. However, once the reader becomes apprised of the narrator-novelist's own doubts as to whether Saúl really *is* the *hablador* pictured in Malfatti's photographs (much as he would like this to be the case from a literary and romanticised point of view), these chapters change status yet again: 'The change in the sign of the enunciation changes the nature of what is enunciated'.[21] The narrator declares defiantly: 'I have decided that it is he who is the storyteller in Malfatti's photograph. A personal decision, since objectively I have no way of knowing' (p. 240). We are only 'invited (not persuaded)'[22] to believe in Mascarita's eventual incorporation into their tribe as the mythical storyteller figure; as the narrator ruefully admits, 'it was too unreal and too literary to be plausible' (p. 185).

Even if we as readers can believe in Saúl's cultural 'conversion' as a successful bridging of the two cultures, his whole narrative is clearly framed by, and contained within, the Western novelistic framework, which therefore seems like a neocolonialist encroachment on the other's territory. Ideological critics such as Misha Kokotovic have viewed the novel in terms of an infiltration, contamination or colonisation of Machiguenga cultural purity by the invasive forces of Western culture,[23] whereas Elizabeth Dipple's objection is also aesthetic – she considers that 'this writer's struggle [applicable both to Vargas Llosa and to his narratorial alter-ego] with both the technical and ideological aspects of fiction is . . . that he actively suffers from a fragile sense of not being inside the mask he would don, of failing at some level to participate'.[24]

A specific polemic has grown up around these questions of representing the other, relating to Vargas Llosa's use of sources for this novel. Going more closely into the sources consulted by Vargas Llosa (which he carefully lists in a final acknowledgement), a question is raised: does/did the *hablador* really exist in ethnographical terms? Both Efraín Kristal and Lúcia Sá have explored this question, and each claims that rather than being an 'authentic' aspect of Machiguenga culture, the figure of the *hablador* is in fact Vargas Llosa's creative invention (or distortion of the sources) to serve his obsession with the primacy of storytelling within a culture.[25] The mode Sá calls 'essayistic underpinning' makes the reader assume that the description of the Machiguenga world is 'authentic', and allows Vargas Llosa's twisting of Machiguenga cosmogony[26] to go unnoticed, though as Kristal notes, the novel 'does not purport to document the complex historical, political, or anthropological reality of the Peruvian Indians'.[27] The most crucial source in terms of determining whether or not Vargas Llosa did invent the concept of the *hablador*, and, significantly, the one source not appearing in Vargas Llosa's acknowledgements, is that of the couple Wayne Snell and Betty Elkins de Snell from the Summer Institute of Linguistics. Vargas Llosa met the couple (on whom the novel's missionary linguists the Schneils are based) on his first trip to the Amazon in 1958.[28] In a 2001 interview, Vargas Llosa not only describes this meeting, but also says that he heard directly from the Schnails [*sic*] about the Machiguenga *hablador*:

> It was fascinating when they talked about the difficulties they'd had in making contact ... How they'd finally succeeded in being accepted and had lived with them. At that point something came up – one of those *magical* moments in my *life as a writer* – something which *was forcibly engraved on my memory* and from which resulted *El hablador*. Mr Schnail [*sic*] told, as a passing anecdote, that in that community of one or two families, a Machiguenga suddenly appeared who was just that, an *hablador* ... *I never forgot that episode and I began to formulate, at first without being aware of it, in an unconscious way*, the embryo of what would many years later become the story of *The Storyteller*.
>
> What was it that made such an impression on me? Maybe it was the thought that this storyteller was my fellow-being, that in a primitive way, he was a teller of stories.[29]

Since critics such as Sá and Kristal appear to have found no evidence in the published anthropological literature (either by the Snells themselves or others) for this figure, we are left with the vexed question of what they actually told Vargas Llosa about the Machiguenga. In other words, and rather fittingly in the circumstances, in trying to establish the truth about a practitioner of (unrecoverable) oral narration, we are reliant on an unrecoverable oral narrative of sorts as a source.

What seems possible is that in this 2001 interview, Vargas Llosa (as he did in *Aunt Julia*) is rewriting – whether consciously or otherwise – his own memory in terms of 'his' fictional past in *The Storyteller*; not only has he changed the original couple's surname (Snell to Schnail), in accordance with the name change they had previously undergone in his novel (Snell to Schneil), but his description in this recent interview of their original inspirational anecdote neatly echoes and effectively corroborates in retrospect the same key episode in the development of his fictional alter ego in *The Storyteller*.

We can compare the 2001 interview to the fictional version of 1987, which occurs at the moment in the novel when chance has allowed the narrator a second visit to the Amazon to make a TV documentary on the Machiguenga, and he re-encounters the Schneils. 'Making the first contacts had been very difficult for the Schneils. A full year after these first attempts had gone by before he, and only he, had succeeded in being received by a Machiguenga family' (*Storyteller*, p. 84). 'It was only at the end that, quite incidentally, there arose the subject which, seen from afar, blots out all the others of that night and is surely the reason why I am now devoting my days in Firenze to weaving together the *memories and fantasies of this story*' (pp. 89–90; emphasis added). 'One morning ... Edwin had gone off to visit another family of the community ... there were at least twenty people gathered together, a number of them from distant hamlets ... [They] were squatting in a half circle, facing a man ... declaiming. He was a storyteller' (p. 176). 'I told them that ... the existence of those storytellers ... had been, for twenty-three years, a great stimulus for my own work, a source of inspiration and an example I would have liked to emulate' (p. 174).

The narrator credits the figure of the *hablador* with having forged 'that curious emotional link between the Machiguengas and my own vocation (not to say, quite simply, my own life)' (p. 157). We can see clearly how in both this fictional text and the subsequent interview, a thrilling idea is planted in the novelist's mind which then becomes a developing obsession over several decades, because of the parallel felt between the (potential) roles of oral and written storytellers. The phrase 'memories and fantasies of this story' clearly signals the game Vargas Llosa is playing throughout. So if we accept the lack of evidence for the existence of *habladores* in the anthropological literature, it appears that in his own discourse relating to this novel, Vargas Llosa is taking on the fictive memories of the narrator of *El hablador* and using them, in circular fashion, to talk about the process of creating that narrative. In this way, the fiction is feeding itself, the product is retrospectively contaminating the process of its own creation; it justifies and authenticates the central storytelling figure, but with reference to an irrecoverable source, thereby performing the impossibility of authenticity and confirming the manipulated nature of memory. As the narrator says, 'memory is a snare, pure and simple: it alters, it subtly rearranges the past to fit the present' (p. 95).

Speaking and listening

Through this fiction, which can be either truthful or lying, depending on the level at which one is reading, Vargas Llosa provokes thought about the roles of storytellers within a culture (whether oral or written), but also, more generally, about what it is we wish for from storytelling, why we desire it and what need it satisfies for Vargas Llosa and for readers/listeners. Perhaps, like the wistful narrator who wants to believe that Saúl did indeed find 'spiritual sustenance, an incentive and a justification for his life, a commitment' (p. 241) by becoming an *hablador*, the reader should allow him or herself to be moved by this 'more or less coherent story' (p. 241), recognising that all human beings need to constitute and reconstitute themselves through fictions in order to survive in a modern world such as that presented in the final chapter, which is characterised by a 'colourful ... multitude' (p. 245) and a loss of identity and community.

In the central *hablador* chapter, we experience a revelation about story-telling, since it appears that the actual origin of this ritual is to be found in the act of listening and of learning to listen. Seripigari Tasurinchi listens to glow-worms, and gradually learns to understand them. Mascarita listens to the parrots, the guardian-companions of whose company he belatedly becomes aware, and he too begins to learn from them. And most importantly, both men learn to listen to the earth. 'I listen closely, the way he did. Go on listening, carefully, respectfully. After a while the earth feels free to speak ... I hear, I am beginning to hear. Now I can hear. One and all have something to tell. That is, perhaps, what I have learned by listening' (p. 131). The reader is drawn into the implied audience within the narrative, by the *hablador* addressing his audience directly. They become bound to one another by a linguistic contract – he is urged to speak, and they are urged to reflect on what he says to them, as are we the readers: 'They fulfilled their obligation, perhaps. Are we fulfilling ours? Are we walking? Are we living?' (p. 66).

So the birth of storytelling is not only dependent on the reciprocal act of listening, but also on an attitude of hesitation, of uncertainty and provision-ality. Kit Brown talks of a 'delicate balance between order and chaos' in relation to Machiguenga mythology.[30] Vargas Llosa appears to signal the delicate balance between storytelling and the acts of hesitation and listening; so perhaps against the more dubious political grain of containing and dis-torting Machiguenga lore within a modern Western mindset and narrative framework, we can recuperate from this text the value and importance of hesitation, uncertainty and, above all, listening as crucial components of trying to construct a narrative about or around the other.

In this respect, it is instructive to append a thought that Vargas Llosa jotted down in a notebook at the time of writing *El hablador*: 'Thought: The problem is in the chapters with the storyteller speaking: you still can't tell the difference. Western conjecture. I need to try and come up with a phrasing in Spanish that ... [unfinished]'.[31] Preserving that hesitation, that sense that there is still – and always will be – something elusive and inexpressible about the other culture, while continuing the struggle to get closer to it, is surely an appropriate gesture for Vargas Llosa, the self-appointed speaker and storyteller.

NOTES

1. Mario Vargas Llosa. ¿Quién mató a Palomino Molero? Barcelona: Seix Barral, 1986. Further in-line citations refer to Who Killed Palomino Molero? Trans. Alfred Mac Adam. London: Faber and Faber, 1988.
2. Mario Vargas Llosa. El hablador. Barcelona: Seix Barral, 1987. Further in-line citations refer to The Storyteller. Trans. Helen Lane, London: Faber and Faber, 1990.

3. Efraín Kristal. *Temptation of the Word: The Novels of Mario Vargas Llosa*. Nashville, Tenn.: Vanderbilt University Press, 1998, p. 29.
4. Ibid., p. 150.
5. Ibid., p. 151.
6. For an analysis of this counterpoint technique, see Kenneth M. Taggart. 'La técnica del contrapunto en *¿Quién mató a Palomino Molero?*' In A. M. Hernández de López (ed.). *Mario Vargas Llosa. Opera Omnia*. Madrid: Pliegos, 1994, pp. 151–8.
7. Philip Swanson. 'The Politics of Detection: Uncovering and Obscuring in the Post-Boom Fiction of Mario Vargas Llosa and Juan José Saer'. University of Manchester, Centre for Latin American Cultural Studies, Working Paper 2, May 2003, p. 2.
8. M. Keith Booker. 'Detective Fiction, the Fantastic, and the Role of the Reader: *Who Killed Palomino Molero?* in Postmodernist Context'. In Booker. *Vargas Llosa among the Postmodernists*. Gainesville: University Press of Florida, 1994, pp. 139–61, quote on p. 141.
9. Kristal, *Temptation*, pp. 152–3.
10. Booker, *Among the Postmodernists*, p. 141.
11. For a discussion of how *Palomino* relates to the Uchuraccay commission, see Roy Boland. 'Demonios y lectores. Génesis y reescritura de *¿Quién mató a Palomino Molero?*' *Antípodas*, 1, 1988, pp. 160–82.
12. Swanson, 'Politics of Detection', p. 8.
13. Mario Vargas Llosa. *La tía Julia y el escribidor*. Barcelona: Seix Barral, 1977.
14. Booker, *Among the Postmodernists*, p. 155.
15. Ibid., p. 143.
16. Julianne Newmark. 'Language, Absence and Narrative Impossibility in Mario Vargas Llosa's *El hablador*'. *Latin American Literary Review*, 31, 2003, pp. 5–22, quote on p. 5.
17. Sara Castro-Klarén. 'Myth, Ideology and Revolution: From Mayta to Tasurinchi'. In Castro-Klarén. *Understanding Mario Vargas Llosa*. Columbia: University of South Carolina, 1990, pp. 189–223, quote on p. 222.
18. I refer to Mario Vargas Llosa Papers CO 641, Manuscripts Division, Department of Rare Books and Special Collections, Princeton University Library.
19. Mark I. Millington. 'Insiders and Outsiders: Cultural Encounters in Vargas Llosa's *La casa verde* and *El hablador*'. *Forum for Modern Language Studies*, 31, 1995, pp. 165–76, quote on p. 175.
20. Jennifer L. Geddes. 'A Fascination for Stories: The Call to Community and Conversion in Mario Vargas Llosa's *The Storyteller*'. *Literature and Theology*, 10, 1996, pp. 370–7, quote on p. 376.
21. Castro-Klarén, 'Myth', p. 209.
22. Ibid., p. 208.
23. Misha Kokotovic. 'Mario Vargas Llosa Writes Of(f) the Native: Modernity and Cultural Heterogeneity in Peru'. *Revista Canadiense de Estudios Hispánicos*, 25 (3), 2001, pp. 445–67, quote on p. 458.
24. Elizabeth Dipple. 'Outside, Looking In: Aunt Julia and Vargas Llosa'. *Review of Contemporary Fiction*, 17(1), 1997, pp. 58–70, quote on p. 60.
25. Lúcia Sá. 'Perverse Tribute: Mario Vargas Llosa's *El hablador* and its Machiguenga Sources'. *Journal of Iberian and Latin American Studies*, 4(2), 1998, pp. 145–64, especially pp. 150ff.

26. Ibid., p. 156.
27. Kristal, *Temptation*, p. 158.
28. Ibid., p. 163.
29. Mario Vargas Llosa. 'El hablador y la selva'. In Raymond Williams (ed.). *Mario Vargas Llosa. Literatura y política*. Mexico City: Planeta, 2001, pp. 93–8, quote on p. 96. (Translation Fiona J. Mackintosh; emphasis added.)
30. Kit Brown. '*El hablador*. Génesis de la novela, creación artística y mito'. In Ana María Hernández de López (ed.). *Mario Vargas Llosa. Opera Omnia*. Madrid: Pliegos, 1994, pp. 73–80, quote on p. 75. (Translation Fiona J. Mackintosh.)
31. Mario Vargas Llosa Papers CO 641, Series I: Notebooks, Box 5, Folder 8, Notebook H8, Manuscripts Division, Department of Rare Books and Special Collections, Princeton University Library. (Translation Fiona J. Mackintosh.)

7

The political novels

The Real Life of Alejandro Mayta and *Death in the Andes*

Set during the years of the Sendero Luminoso (Shining Path) terrorist campaign that wrought havoc on Peru's social and political systems, *The Real Life of Alejandro Mayta* (*Historia de Mayta*, 1984[1]) and *Death in the Andes* (*Lituma en los Andes*, 1993[2]) coincide in their exploration of political violence within revolutionary contexts: both depict a nation that has become apocalyptic as a result of Sendero Luminoso's actions; both look to the past to identify the origins of the destructive forces that have taken over the nation; and both cast the Andes as the place of origin of Peru's political crises, with turbulence in *la sierra* setting the course for the nation's urban centres. Vargas Llosa also grapples with the role of Peru's indigenous populations in bringing about this social upheaval in both novels. In *The Real Life of Alejandro Mayta*, this question is subordinated to explorations of political ideology and of how history is written – vehicles for a critique of socialism's legacy in Latin America – but in *Death in the Andes*, the representation of the indigenous lies at the heart of the author's assessment of the state and fate of the nation. Hence this essay's attention to the representation of Peru's indigenous populations in both novels, and to the role that Vargas Llosa posits for them in determining Peru's political stability and future.

The Real Life of Alejandro Mayta

The Real Life of Alejandro Mayta recounts the investigation into a failed rebellion led by Alejandro Mayta and a young military officer named Vallejos in Jauja, a town in the Peruvian highlands, in 1958. In each of the novel's first nine chapters, an anonymous first-person narrator, a Vargas Llosa persona researching the uprising for a novel, interviews participants in the rebellion and individuals connected to its organisers. The narrator claims to have chosen Mayta as his subject because the latter was a former classmate. Also, like Mayta, the narrator had been caught up in the leftist fervour of the 1950s and 1960s, only to be disillusioned, and he views Mayta's actions as the road that he himself might have taken. The supposed narrative present of the novel, where the novelist interviews his informants, is 1983. He conducts his research in the context of a nation devastated by Sendero violence and on the verge of being invaded by military forces from the USA, the Soviet Union, Cuba and elsewhere. The novel's past, narrated primarily by a third-person voice, focuses on the preparation and execution of the rebellion. These sections, which are often viewed as excerpts from the narrator's novel, are interwoven with the narrator's interviews in the style of Vargas Llosa's trademark 'communicating vessels', developing leads suggested by the informants. Many details about the insurrection, in fact, emerge not from the interviews themselves, but rather from the narrator's reconstructions of the events at Jauja. The novelist-narrator's meditations on the inaccessibility of the details of the uprising, his questioning of the reliability of information from his informants, and his juxtapositions of contradictory versions of events constitute an additional narrative frame. These metafictional and metahistorical sections also trace the narrator's creation of information to substantiate an interpretation of the incidents that makes sense of the few undisputed facts in his possession.

In the final chapter of the novel, the narrator interviews Mayta himself. During the interview, the narrator reveals that his friendship with Mayta, the latter's homosexuality – which had supposedly played a key role in his relationships with several of the narrator's informants – and, lastly, the apocalyptic political situation, are the narrator's embellishments. Both the frame story of the narrator's research into the insurrection and the version of the past that is presented to us hinge on the truth of these data. Besides casting doubt on the existence of some of the interviewees, the revelation that the interviews were fabricated invalidates most of the testimony, almost all of the background on Mayta, and the narrator's ostensible motivation for writing about the rebellion: the act of creation is being used to surmount the despair of political chaos. The revelation of invented data also demonstrates that the supposedly historical present of research into the rebellion is as fictional as the novelistic reconstruction of the past, conflating what had appeared to be different levels of narration.

If the narrator seems at times like a detective confronting witnesses and trying to find out 'what really happened' at Jauja, his task is also comparable to a historical investigation: like the historian, he compiles, compares and attempts to synthesise information in order to reconstruct the past. However, his findings ultimately cast doubt on historical discourse's presumed truth-value by suggesting that either there is no single truth hidden in the past or that it is forever inaccessible. 'I wonder if we ever really know what you call History with a capital H,' an informant remarks, voicing the narrator's own doubts. 'Or if there's as much make-believe in history as in novels' (*Real Life*, p. 67). The narrator insists that he does not plan to write 'the real story', but rather a novel loosely based in reality, and licensed to modify its details (p. 66). As his investigation proceeds, though, he comes to despair of determining what this 'reality' was: each deposition calls into question information gathered during preceding interviews; every question elicits many answers, each of which raises new issues that are never resolved. The narrator's reflections on the difficulties of reconstructing the past challenge history's presumption of objectivity, un-mediated referentiality and truth value, all of which supposedly distinguish it from fiction: by interweaving historical subject matter and self-conscious aes-thetic discourse, 'fact' and fiction, his meditations foreground the discursivity of the object depicted even as they affirm that art is a part of and a participant in the writing of history.[3] By the end of *The Real Life of Alejandro Mayta*, then, the two meanings of '*historia*' in Spanish, 'history' and 'story' – both implicit in the novel's Spanish title, *Historia de Mayta. Novela* – have become indistin-guishable, underscoring the always already mediated nature of the past.

In this context, fiction offers hope as an alternative to truth-bearing histor-ical discourse, and may thus be used – acknowledging its limitations – to explore the past. Vargas Llosa is much more critical of fictions that do not acknowledge their constructed nature and instead present themselves as truthful. 'I have nothing against fictions', the author has claimed. 'But there are benign and malign fictions, those that enrich human experience and those that impoverish and are a source of violence.'[4] For Vargas Llosa, political ideology falls under the latter category: it claims to describe society and the forces of history, but, in his eyes, only misrepresents them. He further blames the failure of such ideologies to coincide with the objective world for render-ing their adherents unable to change their circumstances. In *The Real Life of Alejandro Mayta*, this critique is directed explicitly at Marxist ideology and socialist practice, which the author views as having furthered underdevelop-ment and injustice in Spanish America, rather than offering means of correct-ing them. Thus the narrator depicts Mayta as a utopian, Marxist idealist who is unable to put his beliefs into practice. In contrast, Vallejos is shown as trying to wed socialist praxis with a naive indigenism. He spreads socialist ideals and coordinates uprisings in the indigenous communities near Jauja, even 'while proclaiming a pro-indigenist outlook' that the narrator (focalising his thoughts through Mayta) summarises as follows: 'The real Peru was in the mountains and not along the coast, among the Indians and condors and the peaks of the Andes, not here in Lima, a foreign, lazy, anti-Peruvian city, because from the time the Spaniards had founded it, it had looked toward Europe and the United States and turned its back on Peru' (p. 19). Vallejos's plans for revolution presume a metonymic relationship between the Andes and their indigenous inhabitants: 'The day the Andes start shaking, the whole country will tremble ... When the Indians rise up, Peru will be a volcano'

(p. 12). His goal is to channel contemporary uprisings of indigenous groups into a socialist plan of action. The revolution's triumph would thus also be the triumph of communitarian indigenous activism. As the first capital of the Gobernación del Perú, Jauja was a fitting site for taking the initial steps towards the revolution that would not just emancipate the Indians, but also overthrow the foreign imperial powers governing the nation.

Like Vallejos, the narrator had once believed that Peru's indigenous populations played a key role in bringing about revolution. He reminisces that in the late 1950s, he and other 'café revolutionaries' in Paris read that several indigenous communities had appropriated land in the Andes (p. 128). He initially attributed the success of these uprisings to the involvement of revolutionaries who encouraged the Indians to take agrarian reform into their own hands, only to learn that they 'sprung up spontaneously from the peasant masses, who, spurred on by the immemorial abuse under which they lived . . . decided one day to take action' (p. 129). Characterising the uprisings as spontaneous, the narrator associates the indigenous with nature and casts the movement as non-ideological; he does, however, grant them agency and the critical role of starting the revolutionary process. Mayta's plan, in contrast, does not grant the indigenous any initiative. Instead, he views their plight as justification for planning the uprising at Jauja: they live in houses and benefit from the tools of 'civilisation' and progress, but nevertheless exist as beasts with their 'vegetable life, the same animal routine' (p. 254). It is incumbent on the intellectual, then, to enlighten them and provide a course of action (p. 254):

> Just looking around here justified what they had done and what they were going to do, didn't it? When Peruvians like this woman came to understand that they did have power, that all they had to do was become aware of it and use it, the whole pyramid of exploitation, servitude, and horror that was Peru would collapse like a rotten roof. When they understood that by rebelling they would finally begin to humanise their inhuman lives, the revolution would be unstoppable.

If Mayta's Marxism presents him with a clear hierarchy of agents of change, in Vargas Llosa's estimation it also offers him a deeply flawed approach to fomenting revolution: Mayta assumes there are specific conditions – such as intellectuals enlightening the indigenous as to their exploited condition – which, when met, will bring about the revolution, like dominoes falling in line. It is precisely this absolute faith in the capability of ideology – of socialist ideology in particular – to bring about change that Vargas Llosa challenges in his novel. Mayta has none of the practical knowledge necessary to carry out a revolution: he has never handled a gun; he does not know the languages, cultures or even topography of the Andes; and he lacks the contacts to involve the masses in the revolution planned for their benefit. Nor does he have strategies for redistributing power and resources; instead, he expects that reform will come about on its own once the revolution is underway. Even so, his confidence in his beliefs has him convinced that he, and not Vallejos, 'a well-intentioned boy lacking ideological solidity,' is better prepared to organise 'the focal point from which the revolution would radiate outward toward the rest of the nation – the flint and steel that would spark the revolutionary blaze ... [that] would set about creating the subjective conditions that would induce the workers and peasants to join the action' (pp. 83–4). But the plan fails precisely because Mayta's desire to turn ideology – his own 'fiction' – into action does not recognise when the conditions for revolution are not met. Thus he pushes ahead even though the people responsible for bringing weapons and transportation do not show up, leaving him with a few barely armed adolescent cadets and prisoners to carry out the revolution. The rebellion's failure dramatises the impracticability of Mayta's ideology, which does not recognise that reality does not always conform to human calculations. 'The plan was perfect,' an organiser declares, but he cannot explain what went wrong (p. 144).

In the end, Vallejos dies, Mayta is jailed and the rebellion seemingly fades into the dustbins of history. However, the narrator's resurrecting of the event for his research during a period of Sendero violence belies its supposed obscurity. He demonstrates that the uprising not only did not leave a legacy of reform, it actually set a precedent for the use of violence to effect change. The uprising in the novel is based on a historical rebellion – 'the first attempt at leftist insurrection in Peru'[5] – that took place in Jauja in 1962. Vargas Llosa moved the date back to 1958 for his novel, so the event would seem to be the spark that precipitated the Cuban Revolution. This sleight of hand places blame for the political crises ushered in by socialist activity in Peru and Spanish America in the 1960s and afterwards on the events at Jauja. The narrator's interweaving of the 1958 uprising with the revolutionary moment of 1983 elides the events of intervening years, juxtaposing Marxist ideals with the shortcomings of attempts to implement a socialist system; it causes past and present to appear to be cause and effect, action and repercussion.[6] 'It's hard for me to follow the thread,' the narrator writes (p. 255),

> in this labyrinth ... where the events of twenty-five years ago suddenly get confused with the air strike of a few days or weeks ago ... In the minds of the peasants there is, naturally, an association that it's cost me a lot of work to make and that very few of my compatriots see.

This collapsing of time underscores the narrator's contention that the violence unleashed by the left in the early years of the revolutionary movement culminated in the Sendero Luminoso's actions. In effect, the narrator argues that

Mayta's revolution did, after all, spread outwards from Jauja in the later incarnation of Sendero. As a result, Peru became the emblem of the trope of the 'world upside down'. The apocalyptic Peru of the novel's first nine chapters is characterised by complete disregard for the social contract: police, soldiers, revolutionaries, counter-insurgents and the invading US marines all pose threats to the social order; revolutionary violence is compounded by narco-trafficking and political crimes; and bodies are left unburied in the streets. As the narrator moves from Lima's centre to its residential neighbourhoods and outlying poor districts, he traces a path of violence and lawlessness outwards. At the same time, though, the nation has been invaded by international socialists, who have overrun Cusco and plan to take over Lima next.

Chapter 10 reveals that this scenario is the narrator's invention. And yet, while the apocalypse is no longer imminent, the garbage piles, violence and crime taking over Lima are present at all levels of narration, connecting the supposedly fictional Peru with its 'historical' counterpart. The novel, in fact, ends with the narrator declaring: 'I'll remember that a year ago I began to concoct this story the same way I'm ending it, by speaking about the garbage that's invading every neighbourhood in the capital of Peru' (p. 310). As Efraín Kristal has observed, 'Peruvian society in the first nine chapters is a degraded version of the same society as ... appears in the final chapter'.[7] The attribution of these conditions to the leftist movement likewise remains undisputed. The difference between the 'historical' Peru and the 'fictional' Peru, then, is one of degree, not kind. The revolution has come, bringing together Lima and the Andes, non-indigenous and indigenous populations alike, in a web of terror from which there is no escape – not even through fiction.

Death in the Andes

Like *The Real Life of Alejandro Mayta*, *Death in the Andes* portrays an apocalyptic Peru. The later novel, though, attributes the nation's situation to the dissemination of indigenous traditions as well as Sendero terrorism. The novel's protagonist, Lituma, is a recurrent character in Vargas Llosa's fiction. First seen in *Los jefes* ('The Leaders') (1959[8]), he appears in *The Real Life of Alejandro Mayta* as one of the officers who capture Mayta and his fellow rebels. In *Death in the Andes*, Lituma is stationed with a subordinate, Tomás Carreño, in the fictional Andean mining town of Naccos, keeping tabs on the construction of a road. However, while the men ostensibly represent official Peruvian authority, frequent Sendero attacks leave them with little doubt as to who truly controls the region. Lituma's sense of himself as an outsider (he is from the coastal city of Piura) and his recurring feeling that the mountains and their inhabitants are unintelligible to him further underscore his sense of helplessness.

Misha Kokotovic identifies four lines of narrative in the novel: Lituma's investigation of the disappearances of three men from the town; five brutal Sendero attacks; interviews with and the history of Adriana and Dionisio, the couple who own the local bar and who seem to be implicated in the disappearances; and Carreño's narration of a failed love affair.[9] Kokotovic's breakdown of the novel's structure is illuminating. Each of the five chapters in Part One has three sections that narrate, respectively, Lituma's investigations, a Sendero attack and an episode of Tomás's love story. Likewise, each of the four chapters in Part Two has three sections. Here, though, the second section focuses on Adriana and Dionisio rather than Sendero – a structural parallel that suggests a thematic one. The epilogue presents the culmination of each man's quest: Tomás's love story reaches a happy ending, while Lituma finds answers that only thwart his pursuit of justice.[10]

Vargas Llosa finished writing *Death in the Andes* before Abimael Guzmán, Sendero's leader, was captured, and before the violence plaguing Peru since the early 1980s subsided. The novel was also written in the wake of the internal coup of April 1992, when President Alberto Fujimori dissolved Congress, regional governments and the constitution, and gave the armed forces free rein to pursue terrorists in order to restore order to the country and its government. In articles from this period, Vargas Llosa excoriated the actions of Sendero and the president alike, claiming that the violence, fear and social chaos that both had engendered had set the nation on a course towards destruction. In one of these essays, he explicitly characterises the deterioration as a descent to a level of savagery from whence the human race had, supposedly, evolved. 'Today', he writes:

> there are Peruvians who believe that by blowing up buildings and homes and destroying families ... injustices are redressed and the condition of the poor is improved. This no longer has anything to do with politics. It is the triumph of the irrational, the return to a primary state of savagery that man left behind millions of years ago in order to conquer reason, common sense, the primordial values of survival and coexistence, in a word, to become human.[11]

He further argues that with the internal coup, Fujimori has replaced a legitimate government with 'a form of barbarism similar to the one espoused by those who fight it with assassinations and terrorist outrages', with the result that the confrontation between the law and the forces of violence has become a 'battle between ... two incarnations of savagery' (p. 146). Vargas Llosa's argument is at least partly rooted in nineteenth-century anthropological paradigms for social evolution, which posited that societies evolve from a state of savagery through one of barbarism to arrive at the *telos* of civilisation; another source is Domingo Faustino Sarmiento's *Facundo: Civilisation and Barbarism* (1845).[12] Progress is the driving force behind these Western-oriented models, which are predicated on the establishment of institutions and rules and the privileging of rationality over instinct as a means of restraining violent behaviour and protecting the social order. Democracy, which Vargas Llosa views as a hallmark of civilisation, has been one of the worst casualties in the battle with forces – both political and cultural – representing humanity's 'atavistic' impulses.

In *Death in the Andes*, Sendero terrorism has eroded both the rule of law and reason itself: characters remark that neither the terrorist attacks nor the killings of innocent people have any logical explanation. Sendero's brutality is matched by that of the counter-insurgency, while other government mechanisms seeking to restore order are impotent. The community of Naccos is likewise presented as outside of civilisation and beyond the reach of reason and progress. Kristal has argued that the failure of the mining industry in the town is, for Vargas Llosa, 'emblematic of the impediments to progress and civilisation in the Andean region'.[13] Gareth Williams, in turn, has observed that the road to Naccos

> is an obvious symbol of modern national integration, progress, and interregional communication . . . Without doubt it is taken here from the foundational texts of indigenism such as Arguedas' *Yawar fiesta* . . . in which the Indian's construction of a road announces indigenous collectivism as a dominant and constructive force within the nation. In *Death in the Andes*, however, the road is the central symbol of a failed national project and of perpetual underdevelopment.[14]

'Were they making any progress on that highway?' Lituma wonders. At times, he 'had the impression it was moving backward instead . . . [and after every stoppage,] Lituma always thought that instead of picking up where they had left off, the labourers retraced their steps' (p. 78).

Even as the doomed road represents Peru's failure to achieve progress through infrastructural development, Vargas Llosa uses it to demonstrate his views on how the persistence of indigenous beliefs prevents the nation from becoming 'civilised'. Where constructions of indigenous populations in *The Real Life of Alejandro Mayta* are sometimes filtered through an indigenist lens, *Death in the Andes* renders the indigenous as 'Other' and barbaric. (It is telling that Lituma describes the *sierra* as 'hell', p. 58, and the highlanders with an orientalist touch as having a 'stellar impenetrability', p. 197.) The novel's use of Greek tragedy to frame discussions of indigenous superstitions and their consequences underscores their characterisation as violent and irrational. Most pointedly, the leitmotif of the world upside-down that permeates *The Real Life of Alejandro Mayta* is reworked here as a conflict between the Apollonian and the Dionysian that further filters Peru's struggle through Sarmiento's time-worn paradigm of civilisation versus barbarism.[15] Vargas Llosa's Dionisio draws on the myth of Dionysus, the son of Zeus and a mortal woman who becomes the god of nature, irrational states, sexual energy, liquids such as wine and reproductive fluids, and Carnival in the Bakhtinian sense of a celebration in which the normal social order is inverted. As a bartender who plies his customers with alcohol, encouraging them to 'visit your animal' – that is, to heed their impulses – Vargas Llosa's character represents the eruption of instinct-driven behaviour and irrationality, whose release threatens society's stability. Together with his wife, he is directly responsible for catalysing the behaviour that results in the sacrifices at Naccos by urging allegiance to superstitions that have been eradicated in 'civilised places' (p. 86).

The novel casts the violence engendered by the couple as a resurgence of primal instincts at the individual level, and, at that of the collectivity, of a 'primitive', irrational belief system. Thus Dionysian impulses both mirror and collaborate with the political forces propelling Peru towards what Vargas Llosa views as prior stages of social evolution. The 'structural equivalence' that the novel establishes between Sendero Luminoso and Adriana and Dionisio, by devoting parallel sections of the chapters to the revolutionary group's attacks and the couple's story, serves to highlight this collusion. So, too, does 'Lituma's investigation, which links the two and identifies both as expressions of an atavistic indigenous barbarism'.[16]

Even as Vargas Llosa excoriates Sendero and Fujimori's government forces for plunging the nation into chaos, he also criticises contemporary Andean indigenous populations for what he considers to be their perpetuation of violent practices derived from pre-Columbian cultural traditions. 'I wonder', one character remarks, 'if what's going on in Peru isn't a resurrection of all that buried violence. As if it had been hidden somewhere, and suddenly, for some reason, it all surfaced again' (p. 153). It is no accident that the three Sendero executions depicted in the novel are matched by the trinity of disappearances that Lituma investigates, responsibility for which is ultimately ascribed to the townspeople of Naccos. 'The world falling apart, executions, disappearances, devils, mukis, pishtacos', Lituma muses, locating the violence of Sendero, indigenous superstitions, and the sacrifices at Naccos on a single, apocalyptic plane (p. 88). As Kristal has observed, there is a link between Vargas Llosa's investigation into the 1983 massacre of eight journalists by the Iquichano in Uchuraccay and the attitude towards indigenous populations that informs *Death in the Andes*.[17] According to Enrique Mayer, the commission – headed by Vargas Llosa – that investigated the massacre ascribed some blame to inherited traditions, buying into a fallacy that points towards 'historical evidence of cruelty, bloodthirstiness, and ritual involvement with violent acts using pre-Hispanic iconography, historical text, and hearsay as proof of the "inherent violent nature of the Indian", a psychological or racially inherited trait'.[18] The novel repeatedly characterises superstitions as irrational beliefs associated with societies that are less 'advanced' on a scale of social evolution. For example, when mountain spirits such as the *apu* are first proposed as possible suspects in the townspeople's disappearances, Lituma dismisses them, declaring that 'In civilised places, nobody believes things like that anymore' (p. 86). Nevertheless, these superstitions have spread to such 'civilised' places as Lima, Chiclayo and Ferreñafe, transporting the 'savage' instinct of the mountains to the metropolis.

Lituma ultimately attributes the deaths at Naccos to belief in the *apu*. When he learns of the pre-Conquest practice of offering human sacrifices to placate these spirits – 'barbaric things' that one character explicitly says are 'not what we call civilised' (p. 153) – for land destroyed by the construction of roads, he concludes that Naccos's victims had died in an atavistic resurgence of the practice triggered by the construction of the highway. Like the narrator of *The Real Life of Alejandro Mayta*, then, Lituma traces the violence of the present back to the nation's past and pinpoints the mountains as the site from which the chaos of terrorism radiates. However, where the earlier novel holds the various socialist groups in Peru responsible for Spanish America's current political predicament, *Death in the Andes* blames the indigenous traditions of the past for the nation's political situation: 'So that's what history was good for ... it had never occurred to Lituma that studying the customs of the ancient Peruvians might help him understand what was going on now in Naccos' (p. 175). Lituma finds the behaviour of the townspeople, who are of indigenous heritage, even more troubling because their assimilation into Western 'civilisation' – their espousal of Christianity, education and knowledge of the city, one of the emblems par excellence of civilisation – is hindered by the continued vitality of indigenous beliefs. Lituma asks himself (p. 176):

> How was it possible that the labourers, many of whom had adopted modern ways and at least completed primary school, who had seen the cities, listened to the radio, went to the movies, dressed like civilised men – how could they behave like naked, savage cannibals? You could understand if they were Indians from the barrens who had never set foot in a school and still lived like their great-great-grandfathers, but with guys like these who played cards, who had been baptised: how could it be?

This characterisation of the plight of the indigenous populations in a modern and modernising nation revisits the central theme of Vargas Llosa's *The Storyteller* (*El hablador*, 1987[19]); it is also a topic that the author has grappled with in his non-fiction and, of course, his 1990 presidential campaign. Vargas Llosa's platform sought to modernise Peru through the implementation of neoliberal market policies that, he hoped, would narrow social and economic inequalities. His strategy marked a radical break with those of earlier intellectuals such as José Carlos Mariátegui and José María Arguedas, for whom socialism represented a political system compatible with – and therefore allowing the preservation of – indigenous social organisation. For Vargas Llosa, globalisation, with its homogenisation of cultural differences – in Peru's case, the acculturation of indigenous populations – was a collateral effect of modernisation that he would be willing to accept as the price of bringing about a more just and democratic society.[20] 'Perhaps the ideal', he wrote in 1990:

> the preservation of the primitive cultures of America – is a utopia incompatible with this other and more urgent goal – the establishment of societies in which social and economic inequalities among citizens be reduced to human, reasonable limits ... If forced to choose between the preservation of Indian cultures and their complete assimilation, with great sadness I would choose modernisation of the Indian population, because there are priorities; and the first priority is, of course, to fight hunger and misery ... [W]here there is such an economic and social gap [between traditional indigenous societies and modern societies], modernisation is possible only with the sacrifice of the Indian cultures.[21]

For Vargas Llosa, the deracination of Peru's indigenous populations by changing social and economic circumstances is compounded by Sendero violence, which, he asserts, has inflicted 'mortal blows on what remained of traditional Andean society and helped to destroy the barriers that kept it apart from modern Peru'.[22] The resulting migration of indigenous people from the Andes to Lima and other cities resulted in their 'de-indianisation'; the move also left them further adrift, for they were unable to become fully integrated into their new communities (pp. 329, 331, 335). In *Death in the Andes*, Naccos, while not a metropolis, is nevertheless a site of flux inhabited by migrant workers from throughout the sierra who have come to build the road and thereby participate in national progress. Instead, they are left stranded by the modernisation project in an environment that Vargas Llosa depicts as bringing out their latent and supposedly irrational and 'primitive' nature.

Ultimately, the reader is left to wonder whether the novel's assessment of the townspeople's actions is bleaker than that of Sendero terrorism. As Kristal has observed, in the author's previous novels:

> violence always had an explanation or a rationalisation ... In *Death in the Andes*, some participate in the most depraved acts of murder and cannibalism for no apparent reason at all. The brutal massacre of the three people is therefore more disturbing and perverse than the killings by the Shining Path guerrillas, who justify violence as a means toward military and political aims.[23]

The townspeople who were sacrificed had survived the brutality of the terrorists and the counterinsurgency, only to be killed at Naccos 'to get in good with the terrucos' (p. 273). But this sacrifice, which is to placate both human and supernatural forces, fails: a landslide buries the road, resulting in the suspension of the construction project and the dispersal of the town. The impotence of national modernisation projects and of indigenous beliefs is thus underscored. 'All the horrible things', one worker laments, 'and we're worse off than before' (p. 267). The sacrifices are for naught, and there is no justice: that of the terrorists is brutal, and the people of Naccos face none – other than, perhaps, that of their own consciences.

In *Death in the Andes*, the apocalyptic Peru invented by the narrator of *The Real Life of Alejandro Mayta* becomes literal. The rain constantly pouring down is 'Noah's flood' (p. 173), and the landslide that it precipitates and that buries the road is itself 'the end of the world' (p. 177). Although Lituma proclaims after surviving the avalanche that he has been reborn (p. 195),[24] his rebirth is intranscendent, leaving him trapped in a world desperately lacking the promise of a new covenant: he solves the mystery, but realises that there is no rational explanation for the killings, just truths about the human capacity for evil that he wishes had remained hidden. His own powers of reason have only served to demonstrate reason's absence as a force guiding human behaviour. Thus the novel turns the detective story – a genre whose goal is to make sense of events, and whose successful outcome is predicated on the assumption that events are governed by a logical chain of causality for which a rational explanation may be reconstructed – on its head. And as the murder mystery in Vargas Llosa's novel is itself, as Mary Berg has pointed out, an investigation into the state of the nation, his attack on the genre may be read as a metonymy of his depiction of a nation where reason and other tools of civilisation have ceased to hold sway.[25] The only way out of the geographical, political and cultural labyrinth that the novel offers is through the resolution of the love plot. Tomás, who speaks Quechua and was raised in the Andes – though he 'seemed like a criollo'[26]– is reunited with his lover, who, like Lituma, is from Piura, where the novel suggests that the couple will return.[27] If the future of this character of indigenous background is brighter than that of Lituma, it is only because he is, in effect, leaving the Andes and its problems behind for the more 'civilised' coastal city.

Despite the ten years separating them, *The Real Life of Alejandro Mayta* and *Death in the Andes* display striking similarities in theme and stylistic techniques in their shared exploration of political violence and revolution. Both novels short-circuit the chronological progression connecting a present that is marked by the violence of Sendero and a moment in the Peruvian past. In *Death in the Andes*, the mountains are a site of extreme political violence wrought by terrorists and counter-revolutionaries alike, the culmination of the violence unleashed in *The Real Life of Alejandro Mayta*; the Andes also become a region in which indigenous beliefs and superstitions cast as irrational and barbaric thrive, and from which they spread to the nation's urban centres in a parallel trajectory to that of the Sendero violence. Both novels are also structured as frustrated investigations: while the narrator of the earlier novel finds no answers to his questions, but gains hope from writing, Lituma does get answers, but wishes that he had not. The apocalyptic Peru of *The Real Life of Alejandro Mayta* is swept away in the later novel to reveal a nation that is only slightly less apocalyptic. In both cases, the nation's situation is firmly rooted in its past, whether the socialist activism of the recent past or the indigenous culture that is its patrimony. In both cases, too, it is difficult to envision an exit from the labyrinths of the past of the Andes and their relationships to the nation that are posited here.

NOTES

1. Mario Vargas Llosa. *Historia de Mayta*. Barcelona: Seix Barral, 1984. Further inline citations refer to *The Real Life of Alejandro Mayta*. Trans. Alfred Mac Adam. New York: Aventura (Vintage), 1986.
2. Mario Vargas Llosa. *Lituma en los Andes*. Barcelona: Planeta, 1993. Further inline citations refer to *Death in the Andes*. Trans. Edith Grossman. New York: Farrar, Straus and Giroux, 1996.
3. See Linda Hutcheon. *Poetics of Postmodernism*. New York: Routledge, 1988. See especially pp. 105–57 for a discussion of what she labels historiographic metafiction.
4. Mario Vargas Llosa. *Making Waves*. Ed. and trans. John King. New York: Penguin, 1998, p. 300.
5. Efraín Kristal. *Temptation of the Word: The Novels of Mario Vargas Llosa*. Nashville, Tenn.: Vanderbilt University Press, 1998, p. 140.
6. See Hollis Huston. 'Revolutionary Change in *One Hundred Years of Solitude* and *The Real Life of Alejandro Mayta*'. *Latin American Literary Review*, 15(29), January–June 1987, p. 113. Roger Zapata. 'Las trampas de la ficción en la *Historia de Mayta*'. In Raquel Chang-Rodríguez and Gabriella de Beer (eds.). *La historia en la literatura iberoamericana. Memorias del XXVI Congreso del Instituto Internacional de Literatura Iberoamericana*. New York: Ediciones del Norte, 1989, pp. 192–3.
7. Kristal, *Temptation*, p. 145.
8. Mario Vargas Llosa. *Los jefes*. Barcelona: Editorial Rocas, 1959.
9. Misha Kokotovic. 'Vargas Llosa in the Andes: The Racial Discourse of Neoliberalism'. *Confluencias*, 15(2), spring 2000, p. 158.
10. Ibid.
11. Mario Vargas Llosa. *Desafíos a la libertad*. Mexico City: Aguilar, 1994, p. 144. (Translation Deborah Cohn.)
12. By choosing disputed teleological models of social evolution, and by describing the nation's situation as a 'regression' to a prior stage of social evolution, Vargas Llosa is, of course, advancing an extremely controversial argument.

13. Kristal, *Temptation*, p. 190.
14. Gareth Williams, *The Other Side of the Popular: Neoliberalism and Subalternity in Latin America*. Durham, NC: Duke University Press, 2002, p. 344, n. 18.
15. Ibid., p. 238.
16. Kokotovic, 'Vargas Llosa', p. 158.
17. Kristal, *Temptation*, pp. 188–93.
18. Enrique Mayer. 'Peru in Deep Trouble: Mario Vargas Llosa's "Inquest in the Andes" Reexamined'. *Cultural Anthropology*, 6(4), November 1991, p. 473.
19. Mario Vargas Llosa. *El hablador*. Barcelona: Seix Barral, 1987.
20. Francisco Lasarte. 'Mario Vargas Llosa en el laberinto. Mito y modernización en *Lituma en los Andes*'. In Luz Rodríguez-Carranza and Marilene Nagle (eds.). *Reescrituras*. Amsterdam: Rodopi, 2004, p. 105.
21. Mario Vargas Llosa. 'Questions of Conquest'. *Harper's*, 281(1687), December 1990, pp. 52–3.
22. Mario Vargas Llosa. *La utopía arcaica. José María Arguedas y las ficciones del indigenismo*. Mexico City: Fondo de Cultura Económica, 1996, p. 329. (Translation Deborah Cohn.)
23. Kristal, *Temptation*, p. 195.
24. In the original Spanish, Lituma declares that 'He nacido de nuevo' ('I have been born again'), which seems more to the point than the English translation of 'I was given a new lease on life'. (Spanish original in *Lituma en los Andes*, p. 225.)
25. Mary G. Berg. 'Narrative Multiplicity in Vargas Llosa's *Lituma en los Andes*'. In Claire J. Paolini (ed.). *La Chispa '95: Selected Proceedings. The Sixteenth Louisiana Conference on Hispanic Languages and Literatures*. New Orleans: Tulane University, 1995, p. 27.
26. This is my translation of the Spanish 'parecía un criollo', as here, too, the English translation, 'Tomás seemed more like a mestizo', is less precise.
27. Kokotovic, 'Vargas Llosa', p. 162.

8

ROY C. BOLAND

The erotic novels

In Praise of the Stepmother and *The Notebooks of Don Rigoberto*

Sexual themes figure prominently in all of Vargas Llosa's novels. In many of his essays and in some of his creative writings, he has been influenced by Georges Bataille's views on the erotic. However, the erotic is not only of aesthetic interest to him; it also has moral and even political implications. As he indicates in an epigraph for an illustrated book, *Erotic Drawings*: 'Eroticism has its own moral justification because it says that pleasure is enough for me; it is a statement of the individual's sovereignty.'[1] That being said, as a writer of erotic narrative fiction, he is primarily identified with two novels, *In Praise of the Stepmother* (*Elogio de la madrastra*, 1988[2]) and its sequel, *The Notebooks of Don Rigoberto* (*Los cuadernos de Don Rigoberto*, 1997[3]).[4]

Differences and similarities

Although they are intended to be read as companion pieces, obvious differences separate the two works. *The Stepmother* consists of 149 pages divided into fourteen chapters and an epilogue, with six chapters each incorporating a colour reproduction of a famous painting. The novel operates on two principal levels of reality: the 'actual', which consists of an objective, third-person narration of episodes occurring in a household in contemporary Lima; and the 'mythical', in which the paintings seem to come alive and address the reader in the first person.[5] *The Notebooks* consists of 304 pages divided into nine chapters and an epilogue, with each chapter structured symmetrically into four sections, except for Chapter 2, which includes a fifth section as a follow-up to its second section. The novel moves sequentially between these sections, which correspond to four narrative layers: the 'actual', which continues the plot of *The Stepmother*; the pseudo-essayistic, consisting of unsent letters in which Don Rigoberto unleashes a barrage of arguments against collectivism, which he regards as his nemesis; the imaginary, in which Don Rigoberto conjures up erotic fantasies involving his estranged wife; and the pseudo-epistolary, which includes a series of kitsch love letters that Fonchito sends anonymously to Don Rigoberto and Doña Lucrecia in the hope of bringing about their reconciliation. An artistic layer, which runs through the whole novel, is also evident via Don Rigoberto's compulsive viewing of life through the prism of art and Fonchito's obsession with the life and work of the Austrian painter, Egon Schiele (1890–1918). Each chapter ends with a sketch based on one of Schiele's paintings.

Notwithstanding their differences, the two novels are linked by a dizzying network of cross-references. In each case, the melodramatic plot revolves around the Oedipal trials and tribulations of a wealthy Peruvian family: Don Rigoberto (fifty-year-old husband and father), Doña Lucrecia (forty-year-old wife and stepmother) and Fonchito (adolescent son and stepson). A fourth character is Justiniana, an attractive family servant who progresses from being a witness to the psychosexual saga in *The Stepmother* to an active participant in *The Notebooks*. The first novel tells the story of the temptation of Doña Lucrecia by Fonchito, her fall occasioned by his preternatural beauty and cunning, and Don Rigoberto's descent into a state of abulia when he learns of his cuckolding. In *The Notebooks* the story continues, with Fonchito turning into a precocious go-between, who uses his wiles and charm to bring about a reconciliation between his estranged father and stepmother.

Over the course of both novels the protagonists multiply into many avatars inspired by Don Rigoberto's collection of art and literature. Words, ideas, symbols and conceits from the first novel are regularly appropriated and elaborated in the second. For instance, Don Rigoberto's occasional reflections on freedom, the supremacy of the individual and quest for sovereignty in *The Stepmother* are blown up in the pseudo-essayistic sections of *The Notebooks* into torrential diatribes against ecologists, feminists, sportsmen, Rotarians, nationalists, pornographers, bureaucrats and others whom he considers to be enemies of individualism. His cursory mention of Ingres's 'crowded *Turkish Bath*' in *The Stepmother* (p. 123) becomes a one-paragraph criticism of the aesthetic problems and political implications of the painter's depiction of a 'crowd of nudes' in *The Notebooks* (p. 211). His one-line vision of an Angora cat in *The Stepmother* (p. 65) is transformed into a full-blown fantasy, 'The Night of the Cats', taking up an entire section in *The Notebooks* (pp. 19–29). A fleeting scene in *The Stepmother* depicting a mythical imp called Foncín, drinking water from a stream into which a goddess called Diana Lucrecia has urinated (p. 49), is expanded into an ornate fantasy in *The Notebooks* about a castrated playboy whose overwhelming obsession is to hear Doña Lucrecia urinate (pp. 135–51). The chapter in *The Stepmother* based on Jacob Jordaens' painting of the steatopygous Queen of Lydia (pp. 13–22) is converted in the second novel into a tortuous fantasy about an old professor rejuvenated by the vision of a colleague's voluptuous bottom (pp. 172–84).

In keeping with Don Rigoberto's sneering agnosticism, both novels delight in barbed allusions to Catholic beliefs and doctrine that some readers may even consider blasphemous.[6] Ironic references to a 'happy family', which the reader knows to be in turmoil, may be construed as a mockery of the Holy Family (*The Stepmother*, p. 115; *The Notebooks*, p. 283). The iconoclastic identification of the Virgin Mary with the hedonistic Doña Lucrecia is a key motif in both novels (*The Stepmother*, pp. 135–40; *The Notebooks*, p. 204), but nowhere is such irreverence more evident than in Don Rigoberto's vision of the Eucharist as he worships his wife's breasts (*The Stepmother*, pp. 25–6). Correspondences extend to repetitions or variations of the same words, sayings or devices for dramatic or comical effect. A particular use of synaesthesia – interpreting one sense by another, such as the smell of touch – crosses from novel to novel with a twist. Whereas Don Rigoberto's preternatural olfactory sense in *The Stepmother* allows him to touch his wife erotically through the perfume of honeysuckle (pp. 101–2), in the sequel the synaesthesia is more elaborate, with Don Rigoberto seeing his wife via the aroma painted by Gustav Klimt in his masterpieces *Goldfish* and *Danae* (p. 137).

The proverb ¡*Quien se ríe a solas, de sus maldades se acuerda!* (He who laughs by himself is recalling his perversities)[7] recurs in *The Stepmother* (p. 29) and *The Notebooks* (p. 159). Likewise, the onomatopoeic 'chas, chas' (snip, snip)[8] is uttered with the same sense of pleasure in *The Stepmother* (p. 97) as in *The Notebooks*. (p. 16) Sometimes, however, there are subtle changes in the transfer of some words or phrases from the first to the second novel, which might intrigue the curious reader. For instance, the word order of the proverb above has been inverted from 'se ríe a solas' (laughs by himself) in *The Stepmother* to 'a solas se ríe' (by himself laughs) in *The Notebooks*. By the same token, the two syllables of the onomatopoeic 'chas, chas' in the first novel have become the monosyllabic 'chaschás' in the second. Are these changes incidental, the result of typographical errors, or are they intended to signify subtle shifts from *The Stepmother* to *The Notebooks*?

The recurrence of words, phrases and allusions, often with slight, provocative changes between the two works, hints at Vargas Llosa's strategy of employing intertextual play to 'tease us out of thought', an interpretation reinforced by an allusion to John Keats's 'Ode to a Grecian Urn', one of Don Rigoberto's favourite poems, from which he quotes twice in the second novel (pp. 181, 242). Vargas Llosa's strategy is informed by the idea that game-playing informs most realms of life (Huizinga), as well as the proposal that perhaps the most serious aspects of life can *only* be explored through play (Bataille). In *The Stepmother* and *The Notebooks*, Vargas Llosa's intertextuality is playfully employed to forge suggestive alliances, especially between literature and art, in order to release moral and social constraints upon the exploration of meaning. Vargas Llosa engages in a textual-visual interplay of false doublings, wordplay, literary hoaxes, puzzles, allusions and other techniques to explore themes as searching as the gaze, intimacy and subjectivity. By coaxing the reader into accepting the coexistence of multiple meanings and interpretations, aesthetic freedom prevails over restrictive frameworks of individual or social morality.

Intertextual play and eroticism

The Stepmother and *The Notebooks* comprise intertextual carnivals teeming with references to Western and Oriental cultures. The vast storehouse of knowledge reflects Don Rigoberto's encyclopaedic mind, which feeds on a collection of 400 books and 100 works of art, which he revisits constantly according to his changing tastes and criteria. Thus, Chapter 6 of *The Stepmother* is built on an intricate network of references that include the Olympic Games, Catholicism, the Crescent Moon, Indian Buddhism, the poetry of Quevedo, the Chivalric novel *Amadís de Gaula*, and the unicorn (pp. 53–67). The meaning of each reference is clarified and enriched by its relationship to the rest of the novel, which constitutes an organic unity symbolised by the 'Swiss watch' to which Don Rigoberto compares his regularly functioning stomach at the beginning of the chapter (p. 54).

The Notebooks has a farther-ranging intertextuality, encompassing figures from the extremes of popular and high culture, with Tarzan, Zorro, Cantinflas and Carlos Gardel rubbing shoulders with Plato, Saint Augustine, Cervantes and Mahler. One line reverberates with references to Ayn Rand, Roger Vailland, Cardinal Bernis, Azorín, Casanova and the Marquis de Sade, with each name forming part of an interlocking chain of meaning that sheds light on some of the novel's principal themes (p. 135). In this intertextual festival, the small gallery of paintings in *The Stepmother* expands in *The Notebooks* into an immense museum incorporating works from ancient Greece to the contemporary world. For example, the drama of a scene taking place in Don Rigoberto's feverish brain is conveyed by glosses on works by Van Gogh, Botticelli, Emil Nolde, Praxiteles, Renoir, Rubens, Titian, Courbet, Ingres, Urculo and Japanese prints of the Meiji period – names included in breathless succession in less than one page (pp. 179–80). Confronted by such plurality of references, the reader might see some connections between Vargas Llosa's writing as weaving, and the post-structuralist bent for 'an inexhaustible tissue or galaxy of signifiers, a seamless weave of codes and fragments of codes through which the critic may cut his own errant path'.[9]

Huizinga and Bataille: the ludic and the libertine

Within the array of multilayered intertextuality, the ideas of two writers stand out, giving shape and tension to the novels: the Dutch cultural historian, Johan Huizinga (1872–1945), whose famous book, *Homo Ludens* (1938), analyses the role of play in Western culture, and Georges Bataille (1897–1962), the French anthropologist and novelist who elaborates a philosophy of eroticism in such works as *La Part maudite* (*The Accursed Share*, 1949), *L'Erotisme* (*Eroticism*, 1957), *La Littérature et le Mal* (*Literature and Evil*, 1957) and *Les Larmes d'Eros* (*The Tears of Eros*, 1961).

Huizinga is cited glowingly in Vargas Llosa's novels. In *The Stepmother* he is described as a 'genius' who intuited the notion that all areas of life (language, art, literature, war, sports, law, religion, commerce, philosophy) spring from 'the irresistible human propensity for game playing' (p. 99), whereas in *The Notebooks* he is lionised as 'the great Johan Huizinga' (p. 231), whose book holds the 'key' to Don Rigoberto's and Doña Lucrecia's happiness (p. 159).

Although Vargas Llosa has written extensively on Bataille,[10] he does not cite him by name in either novel. However, not only is *The Stepmother* influenced by Bataille's novel, *Ma Mère* (*My Mother*, *Madame Edwarda* and *The Dead Man*, 1966), but Bataille's vocabulary abounds in Vargas Llosa's erotic novels, with such terms as transgression, desire, pleasure, pain, life, death, excess, instinct, violence, abyss, precipice, God, angel, demon, good, evil, perversion, ecstasy, heaven, hell, danger, shame, light, dark, clean, dirty, vice, virtue, and so on.[11] In *The Stepmother*, Vargas Llosa transmogrifies the image of a man 'with his sex erect' from the first page of Bataille's *The Tears of Eros* into Don Rigoberto's 'human staff, rising and pulsing' (p. 9), and into his vision of himself as a 'belligerent ... wondrous ... unicorn' (p. 67). In *The Notebooks*, Bataille's phallic image undergoes various transformations, most notably in Don Rigoberto's exhibitionist fantasies.

Vargas Llosa reconciles Bataille's libertinism and Huizinga's ludic world-view via the notion that eroticism involves private games that the participants play at their own risk (*The Stepmother*, p. 34; *The Notebooks*, p. 231). His fusion of Huizinga and Bataille has special relevance for the reader. With their 'exuberant dance' of language and textures, *The Stepmother* and *The Notebooks* invite the reader to enter Don Rigoberto's and Doña Lucrecia's boudoir, where the bed becomes 'the magic space' described in *Homo Ludens*, and reading turns into a 'chic, playful exercise', similar to the erotic pleasure of *jouissance*.[12] Thus, as in *jouissance*, reading Vargas Llosa's novels becomes 'erotic play', if not 'bliss'.[13]

The erotic realm in Vargas Llosa's novels has multiple dimensions, but undoubtedly the salient one comes from his reading of Bataille's vision of pleasure, excess, transgression, sovereignty and death. According to Bataille's principle of 'the unity of contraries', a human being can use the most depraved activities as a vehicle to attain an ecstatic state comparable to mysticism. In Bataille's universe, human nature is an indivisible amalgam of Good (reason, order, law, discipline and all the controls, taboos and prohibitions that permit men and women to live in social harmony) and Evil (the negative, irrational, rebellious, destructive instincts and passions that humans need to keep under control if civilisation is not to be undermined or destroyed). For individuals to experience the highest degree of freedom, which Bataille calls 'sovereignty', they must give full rein to their *part maudite* (accursed share), transgress the limits of Good and embrace Evil, the supreme manifestation of which is eroticism, an extreme form of pleasure that Bataille defines as 'the approval of life even in death'.[14]

Bataille's paradox is that, as in the macabre kingdom of the Marquis de Sade, eroticism can draw blood, cause harm or even lead to death. Moreover, if everybody practised such unbridled eroticism, communal life could be seriously disrupted and civilisation could even descend into carnage. Faced with this dilemma, Bataille struck a precarious balance between sociability and the individual's quest for sovereignty, by proposing that individuals should negotiate private strategies for controlling the dark forces within them. One such strategy was to use literature – and other activities related to the mind and the imagination – as a release for their transgressive urges.

Bataille's influence is particularly evident in the portrayal of the protagonists of Vargas Llosa's erotic novels and in the reconciliation of the scabrous and spiritual dimensions of their lives. Fonchito is depicted as a cherub with horns who personifies Bataille's unity of contraries. He represents good and evil, innocence and perversion, virtue and vice, purity and filth, candour and cunning, light and shadow, the corrupter and the corrupted. Doña Lucrecia's perception of him in *The Stepmother* (p. 112) captures his beguiling duality:

> He stuck his tongue out at her and made a face as he observed her with that liquid blue gaze beneath whose innocent crystal-clear surface *Doña* Lucrecia sometimes seemed to divine something perverse, like those tentacled creatures that dwell in the depths of ocean paradises.

In *The Notebooks* she paints a picture of a homunculus defying human or divine explanations: 'I never know if I am with a child or a dirty, perverted old man hiding behind the face of the infant Jesus . . . Because there's a grown man and a boy inside you. An angel and a devil' (pp. 124–25, 160). Fonchito is presented ambivalently as an innocent victim of Doña Lucrecia's desires (fuelled by Don Rigoberto's experiments) or as a conniving seducer. Vargas Llosa has also written a children's story, *Fonchito y la luna* ('Fonchito and the moon', 2010), which highlights the boy's spontaneity and resourcefulness, as he contrives an ingenious way to persuade a girl to give him an innocent kiss.[15]

Don Rigoberto embodies an individual's quest for sovereignty in private, while respecting social norms in public. In both novels Don Rigoberto recalls his idealistic past as a Catholic activist, when he 'dreamed of changing the world' and establishing a 'collectivist utopia of the spirit' that would unite all people in a 'Christian Republic' (*The Stepmother*, p. 54; *The Notebooks*, p. 167). When the scales are removed from his eyes by the wondrous contradictions of human beings, Don Rigoberto repudiates the impossible dream of a social utopia and seeks to create a private utopia based on the pursuit of pleasure. He proceeds to divide his life into two watertight compartments that coincide with Bataille's notion of Good and Evil. Good is represented by his public role as a successful, law-abiding director of an insurance company. Evil is his private face as a 'libertarian hedonist' (*The Notebooks*, p. 66), for whom every part of his own body and his wife's body, every one of their bodily functions, constitutes erogenous possibilities that can transport him to 'Paradise' and turn him into 'a god' (*The Stepmother*, p. 98). Don Rigoberto believes that a sovereign individual should be able to indulge any erotic whim, irrespective of how repulsive, and, like Bataille, identifies eroticism solely with pleasure, dissociating it from the 'imbecility' of reproduction (p. 100).

Since his survival as a respectable businessman depends on not allowing his private demons to intrude into the public arena, Don Rigoberto's erotic activities occur in three domains: in the bathroom, where he practises his daily ritualistic ablutions; in the bedroom, where he enjoys conjugal relations; and, most importantly, in the realm of his imagination. In this regard, Don Rigoberto emulates Bataille – and many of the artists and writers mentioned in the novels – by using his imagination as an escape valve for all the pleasurable bad thoughts and forbidden images 'that could otherwise endanger the basis for peaceful coexistence among human beings'.[16]

The portrayal of Doña Lucrecia also owes a debt to Bataille, but with one crucial difference. Whereas her husband maintains his quest for sovereignty within the bounds of his imagination, her quest crosses the boundary into the real world, where she infringes 'the bounds of the permissible' by permitting 'dirty, scabrous thoughts' to turn into transgressive behaviour, culminating in sexual relations with her stepson (*The Stepmother*, pp. 34–5). In *The Notebooks*, while retrospectively trying to comprehend her transformation from a good wife and mother into an incestuous adulteress, she draws an image immediately recognised by readers familiar with Bataille: 'ever since she was a girl, *Doña* Lucrecia had felt a fascination for standing on the edge of the cliff and looking down into the abyss, for keeping her balance on the railing at the side of the bridge' (p. 127). Unable to maintain the perilous balance between Good and Evil, Doña Lucrecia plunges into the abyss, which paradoxically raises her to mystical heights, where her blood feels as if it has been 'transubstantiated' into wine and she experiences an 'intense dangerous rapture' that she identifies with Bataille's term of 'sovereignty' (*The Stepmother*, pp. 34, 110). Such bliss brings with it the destruction of her marriage: Don Rigoberto expels her 'like a dog' from the family home, while he turns into 'a lost soul ... at death's door' (p. 143). Thus the first novel contains a warning implicit in Bataille's writings: that the price of sovereignty – that is, the experience of absolute, individual freedom – is calamity.

Eroticism: ethics and aesthetics

Vargas Llosa's engagement with Bataille's ideas represents the most significant intellectual layer in his erotic novels, which take up the dictum that 'Sex is good for thought' propagated by eighteenth-century libertine writers, among them the Marquis de Sade, Diderot, Mirabeau, Andrea de Nerciat, John Cleland and Restif de la Bretonne, whose works Don Rigoberto keeps under lock and key[17] (*The Stepmother*, pp. 123, 131). Vargas Llosa has recalled the intellectual excitement with which he first read these writers in Guillaume Apollinaire's collection of erotica, *The Masters of Love* (*Maîtres de l'amour*, 1909).[18] However, the erotic vision in *The Stepmother* and *The Notebooks* goes beyond sex and thought. In a variation of his theory of the 'totalising novel', Vargas Llosa projects the erotic as an all-encompassing experience, embracing the sexual, the mystical, the historical, the psychological, the magical and every other subjective and objective layer of reality.[19]

In *The Notebooks*, Don Rigoberto quotes John Keats's verse, 'Beauty is truth, truth beauty' (pp. 181, 242), to highlight what he considers the two salient layers of eroticism: ethics and aesthetics. Ethics for Don Rigoberto means 'truth', which he identifies with his love for Doña Lucrecia – a love to which he remains faithful under all circumstances and to which he is willing to sacrifice everything. In a twist on Keats's verse, in Vargas Llosa's novels the truth can also be ugly, as occurs in *The Notebooks* when Doña Lucrecia reveals the awful truth of her affair with Fonchito (p. 296). Nevertheless, the fact that she loves him deeply enough to tell him the truth ennobles her in the eyes of Don Rigoberto, who pledges eternal love to her: 'I'll never hate you, I love you. My darling, my dear wife' (p. 296).

As important as the ethical principle is to Don Rigoberto, '*everything* that matters is, in the long run, aesthetic' (*The Notebooks*, p. 228). A matter of individual attitude or a state of mind, the aesthetic transforms what others might find distasteful into something beautiful. Accordingly, a man in love like Don Rigoberto will perceive beauty in his wife's bodily functions, even in 'the languid stretching of her serpentine intestine' (*The Stepmother*, p. 28). In a letter to an imaginary 'Reader of *Playboy*' in *The Notebooks*, Don Rigoberto goes to great pains to distinguish between eroticism, which he champions, and pornography, which he dismisses as the cheapening and degradation of physical love: 'Pornography strips eroticism of its artistic content, favours the organic over the spiritual and mental, as if the central protagonists of desire and pleasure were phalluses and vulvas' (p. 228). In his eyes, eroticism is identified with all the physical and spiritual manifestations of beauty, a concept that he relates to the freedom, the creativity, the imagination, the originality, the mystery, the poetry and the rituals that a man or woman in love can bring to the quest for pleasure (*The Notebooks*, p. 227).

Ekphrasis: the interaction between the verbal and the visual

Mario Vargas Llosa's long-standing interest in the symbiotic relationship between literature and art provided the inspiration for *The Stepmother* and *The Notebooks*, where 'he consummates a creative pact . . . in which the two worlds of painting and writing come together to constitute an alternative reality'.[20] Although the interplay between the verbal and the visual varies from the first to the second novel, both draw the reader into an engaging, sometimes perplexing game, involving life, art, literature and erotic desire.

In *The Stepmother*, six paintings are transformed into chapters, which function as ekphrasis: they verbally enact episodes inspired by the paintings. In turn, the meaning of each painting is redefined in light of its ekphrastic text.[21] The cover of the original Spanish edition includes a detail of another painting that plays a crucial role in the story: Agnolo Bronzino's *Allegory of Love* (1545), whose representation of Venus being kissed and fondled by Cupid, her son, is a forewarning of the dangerous liaison between Doña Lucrecia and Fonchito. As the novel unfolds, it becomes increasingly apparent that there is an intriguing dialectic between the paintings and the ekphrastic text. The interplay between the words and the paintings turns the reader into a viewer challenged to find a strategy for deciphering the complex yet subtle web of issues woven into Vargas Llosa's interartistic experiment.

The interaction between the ekphrastic text and the first painting, *Candaules, King of Lidia, showing his wife to Prime Minister Gyges* (1648) by Jacob Jordaens, reveals the elaborate manner in which the narrative technique operates throughout the novel. The painting is dominated by the Queen's monumental bottom being viewed by Candaules and Gyges from behind a curtain. The ekphrasis is a fantasy conjured up by Don Rigoberto, who identifies with Candaules, from whose point of view the story is narrated, while Doña Lucrecia is identified with the Queen. Although he expresses love and veneration for his wife, Candaules/Rigoberto also refers to her as his most 'exquisite possession', thereby underlining that he looks upon her as an object whose function is to obey his sexual whims (p. 16).

The second painting, François Boucher's *Diana at the Bath* (1742), inspires Doña Lucrecia's 'voluptuous dream', in which she appears as a Sybaritic goddess called Diana Lucrecia, while Justiniana is a nymph who caters to her mistress's erotic fancies (p. 44). Hiding in a shady grove, a faun-like creature called Foncín (a variation of the name Fonchito), spies on the frolicsome women. Through Doña Lucrecia's dream, the reader/viewer can peer into her embattled psyche. The dream's contradictory images of Foncín/Fonchito – human and divine, innocent child and little goatherd with an erect penis – reflects her confusion regarding her stepson's nature. The dream also illuminates one of the novel's principal dilemmas: does Doña Lucrecia seduce Fonchito, or is it the other way round? The reader/viewer need not be an expert in dream analysis to interpret the scenes in which the goddess and nymph perform a 'floor-show' to tantalise Foncín (pp. 48–50). In a particularly telling image, the goddess is described as a 'rattlesnake' mesmerising a 'hummingbird' identified with Foncín (p. 47). Accordingly, when, in her waking life, Doña Lucrecia disports herself 'obscenely' in the bathroom in full view of Fonchito (p. 45), and then when she has carnal knowledge of him (p. 107), it may be concluded that she is a seductress fulfilling her forbidden desires.

The third painting, Titian's *Venus with Cupid and an Organist* (1548), inspires an ekphrastic fantasy narrated by Cupid, whose physical features (tiny, delicate, rosy) and contradictory nature (chaste and salacious) identify him with Fonchito, while the Venus reclining in an alluring pose is Doña Lucrecia. Although it is the Cupid/Fonchito nestling on her shoulder who speaks ardent words to excite his mother, the fantasy does not emanate from him, but from Don Rigoberto, the invisible 'master' who stage-manages the erotic scenario to prepare his wife for a night of passion with him (p. 70). However, the reader/viewer is confronted by another figure who does not seem to fit the Rigoberto/Lucrecia/Fonchito triangle: an organist staring intently in the direction of Venus/Lucrecia's pelvis. This apparent incongruity can be clarified by reference to Jacob Jordaens' painting, in which Fonchito's character is split into two. Likewise, in Titian's painting, Fonchito's lustful, manipulative side is represented by Cupid, while his pure, virginal side is embodied in the young musician who gazes at the mound of Venus without fully apprehending its erotic significance. This fantasy may be related to one of the most perverse aspects in Don Rigoberto's waking life, when he whets his sexual appetite by imagining that Fonchito is discovering the joys of sex through his stepmother (pp. 9, 33). The shadow of Oedipus hovers disconcertingly over the novel's subjective and objective layers.

The fourth painting, Francis Bacon's *Head I* (1948), evokes a fantasy by Don Rigoberto in which he identifies with a 'monster' that recounts a gamut of polymorphous perversions (pp. 91–2). While this fantasy may represent the apotheosis of Don Rigoberto's self-indulgent sexuality, at another level it may be read as an allegory of Georges Bataille's notion of the equilibrium between Good and Evil. The Head and its repulsive sexual practices symbolise Evil, which may be pursued with impunity inside the glass cage within which the monster is contained. For greater security, the Head is attached to its enclosure by a wire and steel bracket. These restraints symbolise Good, which is also manifested by the aesthetic discipline evident in the composition of the painting and the ekphrastic text. The message inherent in the dialectic between image and word echoes Bataille's warning that so long as Evil is carried out within well-defined parameters, individual transgression may coexist with civilisation; but if Evil breaks out of the cage, the inevitable result will be conflict and misery, as happens when Doña Lucrecia is unable to control her illicit desires. The painting also contains a playful irony, for while the monster believes that his cage is impenetrable to outside eyes, the reader/viewer can see him and relate the existential dilemma he embodies to the situation of the novel's protagonists.

The fifth painting, *Road to Mendieta 10* (1977), by Fernando de Szyszlo, leads the reader/viewer into the most elaborate ekphrasis, as conveyed by the chapter's title, 'Labyrinth of Love'. Since it is narrated by a woman sacrificed by a high priest in a pre-Hispanic ritual, the fantasy may be identified with Doña Lucrecia, but since it is shared with Don Rigoberto, it could be mutual. To complicate the perspective, the ekphrasis echoes the voice of Fonchito, who, in the previous chapter, has interpreted Szyszlo's painting as a 'dirty picture' of Doña Lucrecia. Another interpretation is that the painting is a projection of Doña Lucrecia's desire to experience absolute pleasure: the death-like experience that she identifies by Georges Bataille's term of 'sovereignty' (p. 116). A suggestive line – 'Now you would like to dissolve me in a theory' – in which the victim addresses a 'libertine' who ravishes and eviscerates her, evokes another possible interpretation: that the 'Labyrinth of Love' comprises an allegory of Bataille's 'theory' of transgression and excess (p. 119). In the theoretical realm of the imagination, the most abominable sexual aberrations are possible, but as Doña Lucrecia's experience demonstrates, when put into practice, unbridled desire can lead to all-too-real trauma and pain.

The final painting, Fra Angelico's *Annunciation* (1437), inspires an ambiguous compensatory fantasy by Don Rigoberto after he gives up his erotic practices. After reading an essay by Fonchito recounting the boy's affair with Doña Lucrecia, Don Rigoberto's utopian dream bursts 'like a soap bubble' (p. 134). Deciding there and then to abjure all carnality, he imagines that he has been transformed into the Archangel Gabriel and Doña Lucrecia into the Virgin Mary. However, as the reader/viewer contemplates the miracle depicted in the painting, the eye falls on the belly that the maiden seems to be protecting from the angel's gaze. By connecting this image to the story of the cherubic Lucifer called Fonchito, the reader/viewer wonders whether the Virgin Mary could be protecting herself from a demon seed implanted in her body. The last painting, therefore, contains a supreme irony: that the Virgin Mary, a fully-clothed, chaste female, is the most naked – that is, exposed, threatened and vulnerable – of all of Doña Lucrecia's avatars in *The Stepmother*.

An intertextual reference to Kenneth Clark's *The Nude* (1956), a book Don Rigoberto has read with interest, provides a clue for identifying one of the paramount issues linking word and image in this novel: the vulnerability of the female body when exposed to the eye of the male reader/viewer (*The Stepmother*, p. 123). According to Clark, an unclothed female is 'nude' when she is balanced, prosperous and confident, and 'naked' when she feels on display, threatened or embarrassed.[22] The depiction of Doña Lucrecia in various states of undress confronts the reader/viewer with a troubling question: does the way one looks (gazes, glances, stares, gawks, ogles) at her influence whether she feels nude or naked? Significantly, the word '*mirar*' (to look) and its derivatives recur throughout the novel, and the way in which the figures in the paintings look at each other, or at the viewer, is an important motif. Moreover, since the paintings are related to Don Rigoberto's and Doña Lucrecia's fantasies or dreams, they provide a window for looking into their psyches and perceiving the demons that inhabit them.

In the epilogue to *The Notebooks*, after the family has been reunited, Don Rigoberto similarly addresses this central theme: 'Schiele! . . . a pornographer . . . this misbegotten hack' (p. 288). Don Rigoberto has a jaundiced opinion of Egon Schiele because of the malign influence that the life and work of the Austrian artist have had on Fonchito. Is there, however, any difference between the sexual obsessions depicted in Schiele's paintings and those described in *The Stepmother* and *The Notebooks*? Schiele creates works of art with images and Vargas Llosa with words. There is no substantive reason to condemn one to a greater extent than the other for the expression of similar gestures in different media. Far from being pornographers or hacks, however, both are artists, whose 'all-encompassing, merciless eye' corresponds with that of the 'buzzard' or 'bird-of-prey' with which Schiele is identified in *The Notebooks* (p. 123). This is an image akin to the one

Vargas Llosa has used throughout his career to refer to the novelist: 'a vulture' who feeds on carrion – the ugliest, most monstrous aspects of humanity, including sexual and erotic experience – to create literature.[23] In this light, Vargas Llosa's novels and Egon Schiele's paintings embrace the erotic as an aspect of life that cannot be swept under the carpet in an exploration of the human condition.

NOTES

1. *Erotic Drawings*. Rochester: Grange Books, 2005, p. 3. No author or editor named.
2. Mario Vargas Llosa. *Elogio de la madrastra*. Barcelona: Tusquets, 1988. Further in-line citations refer to *In Praise of the Stepmother*. Trans. Helen Lane. New York: Farrar, Straus and Giroux, 1990.
3. Mario Vargas Llosa. *Los cuadernos de Don Rigoberto*. Madrid: Alfaguara, 1997. Further in-line citations refer to *The Notebooks of Don Rigoberto*. Trans. Edith Grossman. London: Faber and Faber, 1998.
4. For a perceptive commentary on the erotic designs of the front covers, see Robert W. Gaston. 'Pictorial Representation and Ekphrasis in *Elogio de la madrastra*'. *Antípodas*, 8–9, 1996–7, pp. 216–29.
5. I use the distinction between 'actual' and 'mythical' made by Anthony Burgess in his provocative review of *In Praise of the Stepmother*: 'On Wednesday He Does His Ears'. *The New York Times*, 14 October 1990 (www.nytimes.com/books/98/06/28/specials/llosa-stepmother.html), accessed 29 June 2011.
6. For more on Mario Vargas Llosa's use of satire at the expense of the Catholic Church, see Roy C. Boland. 'Pantaleón y las visitadoras: A Novelistic Theory Put into Practice'. *Revista de Estudios Hispánicos*, 16(1), 1982, pp. 15–33.
7. The English translation changes from 'He who laughs by himself is recalling his perversities' in *The Stepmother* to 'He who laughs alone remembers evil things he's done' in *The Notebooks*.
8. In English, the translation changes from 'snip, snip' in *The Stepmother* to the less resonant 'whisper' in *The Notebooks*.
9. See Terry Eagleton. *Literary Theory: An Introduction*. Minneapolis: Minnesota Press, 1996, p. 119.
10. Two of Vargas Llosa's best-known publications on Bataille are 'El placer glacial' ('Glacial pleasure'), a prologue to *Historia del ojo*. Barcelona: Tusquets, 1978, the Spanish translation of Bataille's novel *L'Histoire de l'oeil* (*The Story of the Eye*, 1928); and the essay 'Bataille o el rescate del mal' ('Bataille or the Redemption of Evil') in *Contra viento y marea*. Vol. II (1972–83). Barcelona: Seix Barral, 1986, pp. 9–29. An abbreviated translation of this essay is found in Mario Vargas Llosa. *Making Waves*. Ed. and trans. John King. London: Faber and Faber, 1996.
11. For an informative and penetrating analysis of Bataille's influence on Vargas Llosa, see Efraín Kristal. *Temptation of the Word: The Novels of Mario Vargas Llosa*. Nashville, Tenn.: Vanderbilt University Press, 1998, pp. 115–17, 169–81.
12. For *jouissance* and erotic play in language, see Eagleton, *Literary Theory*, pp. 72–117.
13. Ibid., p. 72.

14. Vargas Llosa, *Making Waves*, p. 118.
15. Mario Vargas Llosa. *Fonchito y la luna*. Madrid: Alfaguara, 2010.
16. Kristal, *Temptation*, p. 181.
17. See José Miguel Oviedo. 'La carrera de un libertino'. *Cuadernos Hispanoamericanos*, 574, 1998, pp. 29–39.
18. Mario Vargas Llosa. *El pez en el agua. Memorias*. Barcelona: Seix Barral, 1993. *A Fish in the Water: A Memoir*. Trans. Helen Lane. London: Faber and Faber, 1994, pp. 331–2.
19. For an explanation of his conception of reality, see Mario Vargas Llosa. 'La novela'. In Norma Klahn and Wilfrido H. Corral (eds.). *Los novelistas como críticos*. Mexico City: Fondo de Cultura Económica, 1991, pp. 351–3.
20. Roy C. Boland. 'Mario Vargas Llosa: Literature, Art and Goya's Ghost'. *Mester*, 29, 2000, pp. 93–115.
21. See Rosemary Geisdorfer Feal and Carlos Feal. *Painting on the Page: Interartistic Approaches to Modern Hispanic Texts*. State University of New York Press, 1995, pp. 10–16, 197–235.
22. Kenneth Clark. *The Nude*. New York: Pantheon, 1956, p. 327.
23. See Vargas Llosa, 'La novela', p. 354; and Boland, 'Goya's Ghost'.

9

CLIVE GRIFFIN

The dictator novel

The Feast of the Goat

Vargas Llosa has characterised himself as a 'novelist intoxicated by reality, fascinated by the history being forged around us and by the past which still weighs so heavily upon the present'.[1] This is an instructive description of the author of *The Feast of the Goat* (*La fiesta del Chivo*, 2000[2]), a realist novel depicting historical events: the assassination in 1961 of the dictator Rafael Leónidas Trujillo Molina and the legacy of his regime, which was still very evident in the Dominican Republic in the 1990s, when some of its scenes are set.

Trujillo, known as 'el Chivo', both owing to his reputation as an indefatigable stud and because of the word's association with the Devil, ruled that country in person or by proxy from 1930 until his death. He was one of the most cynical, sanguinary and absurdly histrionic of twentieth-century dictators, creating a police state, terrorising his subjects through a network of thugs and informers, and accumulating political, legal, military and economic power that turned the Dominican Republic into his and his grasping family's private fiefdom. Even more sinister was the control his propaganda machine and cult of personality enabled this lethal megalomaniac to exert over the minds of his subjects. Trujillo was the creature of the USA, trained by the Marines and ruling with the support of successive administrations in Washington, which he was careful to cultivate by presenting himself as a bulwark against communism while bankrolling American politicians and opinion-formers. However, by the early 1960s, the reckless actions of his security services abroad (in particular, their attempt on the life of Rómulo Betancourt, president of Venezuela), the brutal repression of dissent at home, the opposition of a previously supine Catholic Church, economic problems, and the antagonism of other Caribbean and Latin American countries in a new international context resulting from the Cuban Revolution (1959), persuaded the USA that he had become a liability.

Trujillo's long reign, commonly referred to as the 'Era', embodied much of what, by the time he wrote *The Feast of the Goat*, Vargas Llosa had come to see as the evils of both left-wing and right-wing dictatorships: the belief that some countries need a 'strong man' to govern them, militarism with its attendant machismo, authoritarianism, the arbitrariness of the law, state criminality, cronyism, censorship, nationalism and, in many cases, racism. The novel is a reconstruction of Trujillo's rise to power, a description of his regime and its effects on individuals' lives, and an account of the dictator's death and its bloody aftermath as the assassins and their accomplices are hunted down, tortured and murdered. At the same time it examines the 'Era' through the lens of the present, showing how Trujillo's ghost still stalks his country, something Vargas Llosa experienced at first-hand while living in the Dominican Republic, in 1975 and again in the 1990s. He has outlined his approach:

> When it comes to writing historical fiction, I have little time for what one might call 'archaeological' novels, that is, novels which seek to do no more than recreate or reconstruct the past as it was. No, I prefer to view the past from the perspective of the present, in order to see how it has helped shape the present and assess the degree to which it continues to affect it.[3]

The Feast of the Goat is a political thriller and forms part of a long tradition of depicting Latin American dictatorships in fiction. Although it is an ambitious work in which a great amount of historical research is interwoven with fiction to create a gripping plot, it is more readily accessible than Vargas Llosa's more complex early novels. It proved an instant bestseller which readily lent itself to adaptation for the cinema, and a filmed version was directed by Luis Llosa in 2005. At the same time, it has urgent and important things to say about the horrors of dictatorship, and does so through a cunningly crafted structure in which three interlaced strands make up much of the plot. Such interlacing is characteristic of much of the author's fiction, and ultimately derives from his admiration for the subtle effects achieved by William Faulkner's manipulation of time in his novels and stories. In *The Feast of the Goat*, however, the cross-cutting between plot lines is simpler than in Vargas Llosa's earlier works, such as *Conversation in The Cathedral* (*Conversación en La Catedral*, 1969[4]), with which it nevertheless invites comparison, because both explore the corrosive consequences of dictatorship for individual lives, and do so with an intensity lacking in many of his later novels. The principal strands of *The Feast of the Goat* switch from one period in the Dominican Republic's history to another, not only creating almost unbearable suspense, but also allowing Vargas Llosa to infuse the novel with the sort of suggestive patterns and ironies that are a hallmark of his writing.

There are three principal strands. First, Trujillo's activities on 30 May 1961, on the evening of which he will be assassinated (Chapters 2, 5, 8, 11, 14, 18). The dictator's mind wanders back to previous events in his career, some of which have led to the myriad problems in which his regime is mired, a predicament mirrored by his personal degeneration into incontinence and impotence.

The second strand is composed of the imagined thoughts of four of Trujillo's assassins, who are real historical figures and who mounted the ambush into which he fell that same evening (Chapters 3, 6, 9, 12, 15). They, in turn, rehearse how they came to hate the dictator whom they had previously served. Tension builds as they lie in wait to do the seemingly impossible: kill the all-powerful Trujillo. Many Latin American readers would already know the fate that befell the dictator, but Vargas Llosa nevertheless contrives to maintain suspense, as plotters and readers await his end. In the third strand (Chapters 1, 4, 7, 10, 13, 16, 24), we follow another single day, thirty-five years later, on which a fictional character, Urania Cabral, returns to the Dominican Republic, having fled into exile in the USA at the age of fourteen. A successful lawyer, she visits her father Agustín Cabral, once a member of the dictator's inner circle, but now a forgotten and decrepit victim of a stroke. In the course of that day she dwells on the past of her native country and on her own personal history. For the first time since her flight, she meets her estranged cousin, aunt and niece, and she relives the terrible personal experience that led to her exile in 1961. Again, suspense is built up: readers sense from the very first chapter that Urania is the wounded product of adolescent trauma, but can only guess, as the author provides them with a series of false leads, the exact nature of that trauma. It is not until the last chapter of the book that she reveals the sexual abuse she suffered at the aged dictator's hands, and the role her father played in it. *The Feast of the Goat* is the first of Vargas Llosa's novels in which a woman is the central figure. Urania is a credible, disturbing and ultimately unfathomable character, but she also symbolises the dictator's violation of the Dominican Republic, all Trujillo's subjects who were the victims of his abuse of power, and especially the women, who were particularly vulnerable to the machista depredations of the dictator and his family. Trujillo's brutish intrusion into her body and the degradation he forced her to suffer parallel the dictator's irruption into the most intimate aspects of his subjects' lives. Urania's continuing and long-unvoiced terror, so many years after his death, similarly mirrors the legacy of dread and silence sown by his dictatorship. The weight of the past on the present forms the weft and warp of *The Feast of the Goat*; at the same time, the three plot threads interweave the private (or personal) and the public (or political), illustrating how each affects the other.

Vargas Llosa researched Trujillo's regime over many years, and it is not difficult to appreciate why the despot's assassination and the events leading up to it proved such an attractive subject to him. His own youthful experience and hatred of military dictatorship in Peru – fictionalised in *The Time of the Hero* (*La ciudad y los perros*, 1963[5]) and *Conversation in The Cathedral* – is brought to bear on an emblematic military dictator at an especially important period, both in modern Latin American history and in Vargas Llosa's political development: Trujillo was killed during the heady early days of the Cuban Revolution – of which Vargas Llosa was at the time an enthusiastic supporter – and only a month after the revolutionary forces routed an American-backed invasion of Cuba at the Bay of Pigs which aimed to topple Fidel Castro. It was a time of euphoria for the Latin American left.

Vargas Llosa's declared ambition in his fictional reconstruction of this period is to create the illusion of reality. Indeed, he largely avoids depicting the most extravagant excesses of Trujillo's regime for fear that they might prove implausible. Plausibility is a major concern for the historical novelist of realist bent, who has to furnish the reader with background information without breaking that illusion. Most readers require the information, but at the same time they are reluctant to be lectured at in novels. His solution to this dilemma is the creation of Urania Cabral. She is one of the principal vehicles through which historical information is imparted to the reader and judgement passed on it, her store of knowledge being explained by her role as an amateur researcher, from the safe distance of her New York home, into Dominican history. To this extent she is an alter ego of the novelist, employing her forensic skills to investigate what is known about the 'Era', and recreating imaginatively what cannot be recuperated from historical sources, while, owing to her long absence from her homeland, sharing with him an outsider's view. On her return to the Dominican Republic, Urania views the past through the lens of the present. However, the welter of historical detail is, like the novel's insistence on local colour, sometimes awkwardly inserted into her thoughts, threatening the illusion of reality for which Vargas Llosa strives.

He claims that his novel is faithful to what actually happened or, where reliable information about events is lacking, to what might have happened. This caveat allows him considerable leeway, but he does generally get his facts right. This did not prevent some Dominican readers from being infuriated by the novel's account of the general collusion with Trujillo, and even by its portrait of the heroic but flawed individuals who assassinated him, leading to a polemic that resulted in a long-overdue debate among Dominicans about the dictatorship. However, Vargas Llosa is not writing history and is critical of readers who judge fictional accounts against verifiable fact. In *The Feast of the Goat* he does not hesitate to modify the past for his own ends – for example, having General Pupo Román imprisoned immediately after Trujillo's funeral, whereas his arrest actually took place some days later; the two events are compressed in Chapter 20 in order to increase the novel's pace and suspense. More radically, Vargas Llosa invents some of *The Feast of the Goat*'s characters, and imagines the conversations and thoughts of historical figures like Trujillo, as he tries to understand how the dictator rationalised and justified his actions. While history unfolds chronologically, the author organises his novel non-chronologically. For instance, we are given access to some of Trujillo's imagined thoughts and plans *after* we have witnessed his assassination, which takes place in Chapter 12, the mid-point of the novel. As much of the plot up to this point has consisted of his killers lying in wait for the dictator, Vargas Llosa risks dissipating the carefully wrought tension. However, he is not only a past master in structuring his novels, but often makes his structures carry meaning. In this case, the 'survival' of Trujillo into the second half of the novel dramatises the extraordinary power he wielded over his countrymen's lives and minds, even after his assassination. It also makes it clear that the despot's death, a public event, is not the climax of the novel; we have to wait a long time – until the revelation of the causes of Urania's trauma in Chapter 24 – for that climax, and it is then that we realise that the most important consequence of the dictator's regime is its devastating effect on the private lives and psyches of his subjects.

The novel not only manipulates history, it invites us to meditate on how much we can discover about the past, especially that of a dictator who controlled all sources of information. Many aspects of Trujillo's rule are known only through uncorroborated anecdote and rumour (what Vargas Llosa repeatedly calls the 'human tom-tom'); this is mirrored in *The Feast of the Goat* by events being narrated from different perspectives, each of which is coloured by the consciousness through which it is filtered, and by characters' unreliable memory. Thus in Chapter 12, when he realises that Trujillo has been killed, Antonio de la Maza exclaims, 'He's dead, damn it!' Yet three chapters later, Pedro Livio Cedeño's recall of that same moment is different: 'he heard an exultant Antonio de la Maza – "This buzzard won't eat another chicken" *or something like that*' (pp. 226, 283; emphasis added). We do not know which – if either – account is accurate, and that is surely the point.

Urania probes the squalor of private lives under the dictatorship, but many of her questions remain unanswered. She demands to know from her disabled father whether her mother had been solicited by Trujillo, as so many of his ministers' wives were. Agustín Cabral is the only person who could have provided a reply, but his stroke has deprived him of the power of speech and, possibly, understanding. During the course of the novel, Vargas Llosa tantalises the reader, hinting that Señora Cabral may indeed have been one of Trujillo's sexual victims: we are casually informed that she died in an accident (a car crash being one of the deaths often faked for those who had offended or proved an embarrassment to the dictator); Trujillo's pimp, Manuel Alfonso, sizes up the adolescent Urania as a potential bed-fellow for his master, chillingly remarking how she is growing to look like her mother; and Urania wears her mother's earrings to her assignation with the dictator at his country estate, where the prospect of sleeping with the daughters of former lovers gives him a particular erotic thrill. But these hints remain just that. Urania and the reader receive no reply to her burning question, and the visit in Chapter 4 by Trujillo to Señora Cabral when her husband is away from home turns out to be merely the product of Urania's imagination, shot through with her own terror. The mute Agustín Cabral is an emblem of the inaccessibility of the regime's darkest secrets.

Nor are we given the answer to a question affecting the public life of the nation: how much did Joaquín Balaguer, who had served the regime since the 1930s, know about the plot to kill Trujillo? He was the principal beneficiary of the assassination, going on to rule the Dominican Republic for much of the second half of the twentieth century. Chapter 22 is a compelling dramatisation of this self-effacing but Machiavellian politician's manipulation of the dictator's heirs, which results in his wresting control of the Republic from the Trujillo clan. The reader senses that only a novelist who, like Vargas Llosa, has had first-hand experience of the unsavoury reality of politics could have written such a convincing account of wheeler-dealing at the top. Balaguer emerges as an intriguing and enigmatic figure; Trujillo's son Ramfis tortures the plotters in an attempt to discover whether Balaguer was involved, but no proof is forthcoming. Vargas Llosa again drops hints, but mirrors the uncertainty about Balaguer's role in the conspiracy, which is one of the unresolved mysteries of Dominican history. However, his seizure of power is not in doubt, and is subtly underlined by *The Feast of the Goat*'s structure. After Chapter 16 and the pivotal discussion between Agustín Cabral and Manuel Alfonso about the sacrifice of Urania to Trujillo, the regular permutation of the three narrative threads ceases; much of the last third of the novel depicts the chaotic aftermath of Trujillo's death, and this is reflected in a looser structure. We follow the assassins' fate in a series of chapters, striking for their brevity, while by far the longest chapter in this section (and, indeed, in the whole novel) depicts Balaguer's seizure of power. He takes over the novel as he does the country, and the sidelining of the men who freed the Dominican Republic from Trujillo is mirrored by their waning importance in the novel's structure. It is only in Chapter 24, when the action returns largely to 1996, that Balaguer will be eclipsed, just as he was in reality at that time.

The Feast of the Goat is not, then, an attempt to provide an objective history of the Trujillo period. It is a recreation and questioning of it that is coloured by Vargas Llosa's political views of the late 1990s. Despite its teeming cast, his account of the 'Era' is largely the story of a handful of influential families and individuals: the Trujillos from San Cristóbal, the De la Mazas from Moca, and so on. One reason why Trujillo may have been an attractive subject for Vargas Llosa is that he was not assassinated for ideological reasons by utopian revolutionaries, but as the result of a group of individuals' personal grievances.

Political ideologies or social forces do not lie behind the conspiracy, and the assassins repeatedly admit their lack of interest in politics. Likewise, it is striking that ordinary Dominicans hardly impinge on the narrative; when they are occasionally glimpsed, they are usually treated with disdain. They are described as animals; when they see Trujillo taking his walk through the city, they lean out of their cars and trucks to shout sycophantically, 'Long live the Chief!'; thousands queue in paroxysms of grief after his death to pay their last respects to a dictator who had despised, abused and exploited them; and they rush to inform on his assassins, although they will soon be revering them as patriotic heroes.

There are various possible reasons for the assassins' lack of political ideology and for the novel's treatment of ordinary people. By 1960 it had become apparent to the US government that supporting Trujillo was no longer in its own interest. President Eisenhower had recognised that any move against the left-wing Castro, whom he saw as the real threat in America's 'own backyard', would be unacceptable to US public opinion while his administration continued to support a right-wing dictator in the Caribbean. However, the Americans were also concerned that Trujillo might suffer the same fate that had recently befallen the Cuban dictator Fulgencio Batista: to be overthrown by left-wing revolutionaries. The CIA was therefore willing to back only non-leftist plotters in the Dominican Republic, and Trujillo's assassins, who received some minimal support from that organisation (the CIA's involvement is very marginal to the novel), fitted the bill. Vargas Llosa's account of the assassins' indifference to politics is, then, historically accurate; at the same time, it reflects his belief that dictatorships eradicate political culture.[6] More importantly, however, brave men motivated not by ideology, but by the need to expiate their guilt and shame at their connivance with Trujillo, by outrage at the way the regime has brutalised them and, in the case of Salvador Estrella Sadhalá, by religious principle, were bound to appeal to the Vargas Llosa of the 1990s, who had long since become disenchanted with the Cuban Revolution and sceptical of utopian ideologies such as Marxism. His portrayal of the assassins' motives is redolent of his own opinions in the 1990s, and is laden with irony because he is describing a period, the 1960s, normally associated with the rise in Latin America of revolutionary ideology, which the author shared at the time. In its treatment of ordinary Dominicans, *The Feast of the Goat* could again faithfully reflect history: under a dictatorship, where ordinary people have no political voice, they are marginalised. Just as Trujillo and his family despise the mass of Dominicans in whose name they claim to rule, so the novel can, in turn, affect to despise them. However, such disdain also reflects the author's current opinions: what are important are the decisions and actions taken by individuals, and this belief is accompanied by his distrust of any grand theory of the importance of social forces in history.

In *The Feast of the Goat* Vargas Llosa treats historical events with literary licence, on the one hand in order to enhance the fiction, on the other to convey his own opinions. It is a novel that, through taking liberties with history, seeks to embody deeper 'truths'. Vargas Llosa refers to this as 'the truth of lies'. He maintains that fiction inevitably falsifies: it distorts the even flow of historical time; it transforms experience into something very different: language; and it reshapes the chaos of reality into an order the reader can understand. But through such falsification, fiction can reveal more profound 'truths'.[7] I shall outline four of Vargas Llosa's 'truths' embodied in *The Feast of the Goat*.

First, the novel suggests that history does not follow a predetermined or logical course. Events are presented not as the inevitable outcome of rational causes, but as the result of such causality combining with chance and irrationality. For example, on the night of his assassination, all is prepared for Trujillo to go out to his country estate, the Casa de Caoba, where an appetising schoolgirl awaits him. However, at the last minute he decides, on a whim, to stay in the capital and sleep instead with a woman he knows called Moni. It transpires, however, that Moni has – or says she has – her period. Revolted by this revelation (Vargas Llosa's Trujillo, like his son Ramfis, does not much like women, despite a history of rampant sexuality), he reverts to his original plan, sets off for the Casa de Caoba and falls into the fatal ambush. The assassins all have good reasons to want to kill the despot, and these come together with the domestic and international situation, which favours the elimination of the dictator. However, Moni's period was fortuitous. Indeed, Vargas Llosa's Trujillo had an assignation arranged for him at the Casa de Caoba that night in order to put behind him the humiliation he had recently suffered there when he had been unable to deflower Urania because of a chance reoccurrence of his prostate problem. For a man who used sex as an instrument of power, and whose reputation as a stud was an essential element in his cult of personality, this had been a devastating blow; his obsession with sexual failure made him curiously inattentive to important matters of state, one of which was his own security. Urania was therefore indirectly, unwittingly and ironically, one element in a skein of chance and rational causes leading the dictator to his death.

A second 'truth' emerges from the scene in Chapter 11, in which, on the day of his assassination, Trujillo regales a captive audience with a melodramatic account of a pivotal moment in the consolidation of his regime: his order of October 1937 that thousands of Haitian immigrants be massacred. His embroidered version of the past is cross-cut with flashbacks to what actually led him to take that decision. As so often in his novels, Vargas Llosa's cross-cutting technique exposes a shocking truth: Trujillo had not been the decisive 'strong man' he portrays himself as many years later, but a procrastinator. Indeed, the novel constantly demythifies the Trujillo created by the regime's cult of personality, showing the tawdry reality it concealed. More specifically, this episode reveals that the dictator had to be galvanised into action by the young Agustín Cabral and Henry Chirinos. Their racist and nationalistic arguments for the elimination of Haitians from the Republic (proudly outlined to the child Urania by her father early in the first chapter of the novel) were not only subsequently internalised by Trujillo – in much the same way that he comes to believe the pious nonsense propagated by Joaquín Balaguer that Trujillo's reign was ordained by God – but are systematically deconstructed by Vargas Llosa. The novel reveals that the nationalist image promoted by the regime of a white, Hispanic, Catholic, modern, rational, cultured and civilised Dominican Republic, defined in opposition to a black, African, pagan, superstitious, backward and barbaric Haiti, with which it shares the island of Hispaniola, is a lie, but this lie nevertheless formed the ideological basis of his rule. Cabral and Chirinos are both honey-tongued lawyers, who confect specious arguments in order to provide an intellectual underpinning for Trujillo's regime, to persuade the dictator, and to justify his excesses to others. These two men embody an important truth for Vargas Llosa: at the heart of the darkness of this dictatorship lurks the abject intellectual. He suggests that the despot comes to power and is sustained in it thanks to the complicity not only of the mass of his fellow-countrymen, but, more especially, of those whose intelligence and education should have led them to take a stand against him. It also suggests that if Trujillo was a monster, it was others who made him so.

In *The Feast of the Goat*, Vargas Llosa's Trujillo is not only a particular dictator of a particular country, but represents dictatorship more generally (the novel alludes to many despots: Batista, Duvalier, Franco, Hitler, Pérez Jiménez, Perón, Rojas Pinilla), and the depiction of those who served Trujillo suggests a 'truth' about the self-seeking or craven intellectual that is a leitmotif running through much of his later critical and autobiographical writing, particularly influenced by his experience as a candidate for the Peruvian presidency.[8] Two more modern Latin American leaders in particular, whom Vargas Llosa considered dictators, were on his mind while he was writing this novel. After his victory over the novelist in the presidential election of 1990, Alberto Fujimori had undermined Peruvian democracy in a coup d'état backed by the military. Fidel Castro, long Vargas Llosa's bête noire, had recently come to power in Cuba at the time when most of *The Feast of the Goat* is set, and was still ruling with an iron fist forty years later; the young Vargas Llosa had at first admired him, but later came to see him as the embodiment of the *caudillismo* that has plagued so much of Latin American history. Fujimori lies behind the figure of Henry Chirinos, Vargas Llosa settling a personal score by modelling this despicable character on Senator Enrique Chirinos Soto, a supporter in the novelist's presidential campaign, who deserted him and subsequently devised legalistic arguments to justify Fujimori's coup. Some Peruvian readers of *The Feast of the Goat* were shocked to discover that the character Abbes García was closely based on Trujillo's intelligence chief of that name, and not a lightly disguised portrait of the corrupt Vladimiro Montesinos who fulfilled a similar role under Fujimori. Vargas Llosa's brutal Abbes García is in turn suggestively compared in his icy ruthlessness to Castro, who, while never appearing as a character, is nevertheless a constant point of reference in *The Feast of the Goat*.

Agustín Cabral's slavish service to the dictator conveys a third 'truth': the urge to self-abasement to which, the novel suggests, intellectuals are particularly prone. Through the second-person singular narrator, who often maintains a sort of interior dialogue with Urania – a character so traumatised that she has turned in on herself, and whose conversations appropriately take place inside her own head – Vargas Llosa asks what drove members of the Dominican elite to devote themselves to Trujillo (p. 63):

> what you've never understood is how the best-educated Dominicans, the intellectuals of the country, the lawyers, doctors, engineers, often graduates of very good universities in the United States or Europe, sensitive, cultivated men of experience, wide reading, ideas, presumably possessing a highly developed sense of the ridiculous, men of feeling and scruples, could allow themselves to be ... savagely abused.

Urania's reply to her own question, as she addresses her aged father, touches on the dark, irrational motivations that the author discerns behind human actions: 'Sometimes I think ... that you ... really liked getting dirty. That Trujillo pulled a vocation for masochism up from the bottom of your souls, that you were people who needed to be spat on and mistreated and debased in order to be fulfilled' (p. 64).[9] The allure of self-abasement would become a major theme in Vargas Llosa's later novel, *The Bad Girl* (*Travesuras de la niña mala*, 2006[10]), and is one of the many sinister forces at play in *The Feast of the Goat*, a novel of extreme violence and cruelty, which, in their turn, may appeal to his readers' own darker side.

This leads to the fourth and most urgent 'truth' conveyed through the fictional depiction of the 'Era'. None of Trujillo's assassins is an intellectual. They are men of action who escape the thrall in which he has held them; they overcome the paralysis and the seductive abnegation of responsibility that are, Vargas Llosa believes, inevitable consequences of dictatorship. The assassins reassert their freedom to take decisions, and so are in a position to liberate their country. The novel uses the term 'free will' to describe their flexing of their resolve, and its theological associations are particularly appropriate in the case of Salvador. He is a devout Catholic whose name is a happy coincidence for a man of Middle Eastern origin, who in the novel likens 'el Chivo' to the Beast of the biblical book of Revelation, and who lays down his own life for the sake of others to overcome evil, for this is a novel with evil at its core and which traces its spread throughout a society. Salvador's death at the end of Chapter 21 is one of the most poignant scenes in the novel. After he and several of his fellow-conspirators have suffered torture, which is rendered especially shocking for the reader by its matter-of-fact narration, a drunken Ramfis Trujillo takes delight in executing them. However, Salvador is not dragged to his place of execution; he manages, feet tied together, to shuffle there on his own. He exercises a sort of hobbled liberty – possibly Vargas Llosa's acknowledgement that the duty to use our free will is easier to advocate than to fulfil. Salvador cannot escape Ramfis's revenge, but he dies with dignity, while his murderer, the psychopathic playboy, rapist and torturer, who has been indulged by his father and allowed complete freedom of action without responsibility, is a despicable, and in some ways pathetic, product of the spiritual wasteland created by the dictator.

Salvador and his fellow-plotters accept their responsibility to slough off their fear and helplessness. They determine to kill Trujillo, and that decision has enormous public consequences. The obverse of the coin is Agustín Cabral's abnegation of responsibility in a private context, and Vargas Llosa's condemnation of him lies at the heart of the novel's ethical purpose. One of the key moments of the novel is the excruciating and wonderfully written scene in Chapter 16, where Trujillo's pimp, Manuel Alfonso, suggests how Cabral can regain the dictator's favour, and faces Urania's father with a decision about whether to sacrifice her to Trujillo. Manuel Alfonso's proposal that her virginity be traded for Cabral's rehabilitation is so unspeakable that initially it is suppressed by Vargas Llosa from their conversation, leaving the reader to deduce it. However, Cabral is aware that what is involved is nothing less than a betrayal, and it is no coincidence that he thinks he hears a cock crowing as Manuel Alfonso speaks. What is so immoral in this scene is not that Cabral agrees to the pimp's plan, but that he fails to reject it, and then supinely allows events to take their course. The moral depths he plumbs become even more apparent when he tries to pass the responsibility for the decision to attend Trujillo's 'party' for two on to his young daughter, even though Urania cannot know what she is deciding about.

This is the most chilling example in the novel of the refusal to exercise, and the denial of another's, free will. Vargas Llosa records its terrible consequences for daughter and father. There is a chance that Cabral will regain Trujillo's favour if he accepts the radical humiliation of allowing his daughter to be deflowered by his master. However, far from producing the result intimated by Manuel Alfonso, Trujillo's own humiliation when he fails to achieve an erection in Urania's terrifying sexual encounter with him (in his frustrated rage he tears her hymen with his fingers) means that her father will never now be rehabilitated. Ironically, the dictator will in any case soon be dead. It has all been a waste: Urania is put in mortal danger and is psychologically scarred for life. Vargas Llosa has frequently mentioned the scars his relations with his own father left on him; in *The Feast of the Goat*, Urania is a victim of both her own father and the man who styled himself the 'Father of the New Nation'. Neither behaves responsibly as either a literal or a figurative parent. Trujillo despises his family and fellow countrymen; Cabral, for his part, lays everything at the dictator's feet, thereby losing the only thing worth having: his daughter's love. Urania makes him pay dearly.

Here, then, a fictional account of a personal relationship set in a particular historical context passes a moral judgement that goes far beyond that context. Yet it also makes a more specific comment about the long-term consequences of dictatorial regimes. Urania's revenge on her father, and her treatment of her cousins and her aunt, are implacable. The reader understands and sympathises with her, but she is no less brutal for all that, as she goads the aged and defenceless Cabral. Indeed, the juxtaposition of scenes centring on Urania with those in which we are given access to Trujillo's imagined thoughts (Chapters 1 and 2, 4 and 5, 7 and 8, 10 and 11, 13 and 14) invites the reader to draw unpalatable and what might at first seem surprising parallels between two such different characters: Urania not only reproduces Trujillo's obscenities in her speech, but mirrors his cruelty. Dictatorship infects its subjects' intimate lives; it coarsens and perverts language, feelings and relations, breeding an inhumanity which long outlives it – indeed, right up to 1996, when Urania revisits her homeland for the first time.

It is not fortuitous that Vargas Llosa should have chosen that date for her return and for much of the action of the novel, for it was the year in which open elections at last offered the hope of democracy in the Dominican Republic, after Trujillo's and, later, Balaguer's tyrannies. As mentioned at the outset, here is 'history being forged around us and the past which still weighs so heavily upon the present'. For Vargas Llosa, democracy is the public exercise of freedom and responsibility. Urania's life and the lives of her generation have been devastated by dictatorship, but at the end of the novel she is able to shake off the lassitude that has beset her since returning to the Dominican Republic. This icy, feisty lawyer seemed to lose her power to decide and act when jogging in the streets of Santo Domingo soon after her arrival in the country, but once she has confronted her past and that of Trujillo by recounting her trauma to her family, her decisiveness returns: in the last chapter she is able to deal briskly with the overtures of a drunken American sex-tourist. She can now exercise her free will to make choices. The final words of the novel are 'she decides', as Urania determines to keep in touch with a new generation of Dominicans represented by her niece Marianita, to whom she has revealed the horrors of the country's despotic past that had been swept under the carpet by the older members of her family. It is too late for Urania, but in a democratic and more optimistic future, the young may at last be able to escape the legacy of dictatorship.

These are four of Vargas Llosa's deeper 'truths' conveyed by this historical novel. However, it is not quite so simple, and I am left with two questions. First, *The Feast of the Goat* takes an ethical stand. It condemns some characters: Chirinos, for example, is caricatured morally and physically as unscrupulous, unkempt and repulsively obese (even his house is described as being fat). The slippery second-person singular narrator, who ostensibly, as Vargas Llosa himself argues, articulates Urania's interior dialogues, often serves as the sort of authorial mouthpiece largely absent from his early novels, in which he aspired to disappear in a web of competing voices.[11] Are the author's opinions communicated so unequivocally, then, that readers are allowed little of the freedom that the novel otherwise advocates? Second, how comfortably does this infusing of the novel with the author's political and philosophical opinions, accompanied by *The Feast of the Goat*'s apparent disdain for ordinary Dominicans, sit with its promotion of democracy?

NOTES

1. Mario Vargas Llosa. *Un Demi-siècle avec Borges*. Ed. and trans. Albert Bensoussan. Paris: L'Herne, 2004, p. 7. (Translation Clive Griffin.)
2. Mario Vargas Llosa. *La fiesta del Chivo*. Madrid: Alfaguara, 2000. Further in-line citations refer to *The Feast of the Goat*. Trans. Edith Grossman. London: Faber and Faber, 2002.
3. Dominic Moran. 'Interview with Mario Vargas Llosa'. *Hispanic Research Journal*, 7(3), 2006, pp. 259–73, quote on p. 263.
4. Mario Vargas Llosa. *Conversación en La Catedral*. Barcelona: Seix Barral, 1969.
5. Mario Vargas Llosa. *La ciudad y los perros*. Barcelona: Seix Barral, 1963.
6. Moran, 'Interview with Mario Vargas Llosa', p. 271.
7. For example, Mario Vargas Llosa. 'La verdad de las mentiras'. In *La verdad de las mentiras*. 2nd edn. Madrid: Alfaguara, 2002, pp. 15–30.
8. For example, Mario Vargas Llosa. *El pez en el agua. Memorias*. Barcelona: Seix Barral, 1993. *A Fish in the Water: A Memoir*. Trans. Helen Lane. London: Faber and Faber, 1994, especially Chapter 14: 'Cut-Rate Intellectuals', pp. 301–17. Also Mario Vargas Llosa. '*La granja de los animales* (1945), George Orwell. Socialista, libertario y anticomunista'. In Vargas Llosa, *La verdad de las mentiras*, pp. 213–27.
9. Compare with Vargas Llosa's statement, 'How to explain [the] masochism of the intellectual species?' In *A Fish in the Water*, p. 303.
10. Mario Vargas Llosa. *Travesuras de la niña mala*. Madrid: Alfaguara, 2006.
11. Moran, 'Interview with Mario Vargas Llosa', pp. 260–1; Mario Vargas Llosa. *Literatura y política*. 2nd edn. Madrid: Instituto Tecnológico y de Estudios Superiores de Monterrey and Fondo de Cultura Económica de España, 2003, pp. 91–2.

10

EFRAÍN KRISTAL

From utopia to reconciliation

The Way to Paradise, *The Bad Girl* and *The Dream of the Celt*

In Vargas Llosa's literary world, unhappiness and suffering are as pervasive as the two responses with which individuals strive to prevail over their feelings of malaise: rebellion and fantasy. In the 1960s – as a committed socialist – Vargas Llosa was persuaded that human dissatisfaction was directly linked to the shortcomings of the same political and economic realities that inspire the most urgent works of literature. *Conversation in The Cathedral* (*Conversación en La Catedral*, 1969[1]), a towering achievement, depicted the ripple effects of political corruption on individuals, communities and a whole nation. In the 1980s, Vargas Llosa abandoned his socialist convictions, and became an outspoken advocate of free market democracy. He no longer argued that revolutionary violence was a legitimate means to achieve the kind of political change that would eliminate the causes of human discontent. In fact, he began to make the counter-claim, that political unrest and instability could be traced directly to the same illusion he once held: that social utopias are possible. In this decade his novels were concerned with the fragility of societies assailed by fanatics, political opportunists or well-intentioned idealists. *The War of the End of the World* (*La guerra del fin del mundo*, 1981[2]), for example, explored the propensity of humanity to idealise violence with the visions of apocalyptic religious leaders, the patriotic fervour of military professionals, or the abstractions and intimations of intellectuals who fail to comprehend war for what it is: a devastating collective experience. In the 1980s, Vargas Llosa remained optimistic that our propensities to unrest and instability could be effectively diffused. He speculated that the literary imagination could mingle elements from the realities of our imperfect lives with our most irrational drives, to give us the illusion of a fulfilment we could never achieve in the real world.

Since his defeat in the Peruvian presidential elections of 1990, a less optimistic vision has informed Vargas Llosa's writings – fictional and non-fictional alike – a growing sense that all struggles to prevail over our intractable feelings of discomfort are doomed to disappointment. Vargas Llosa continues to be an advocate of liberal democracy, and he has not shunned opportunities to express his political views, but the tone of his observations is ever more reserved. He has lost the confidence he once had in the effectiveness of political activity. He is no longer the militant who defends a political programme, but the moralist who draws attention to injustice, even as he is resigned to the imperfections of human beings, and to the proposition that evil may be impossible to eradicate. The first inkling of this pessimism in his literary works can be traced back to *Death in the Andes* (*Lituma en los Andes*, 1993[3]), when a character in the closing pages of the novel is unable to explain why he participated in a senseless massacre, but it is also evident in a thought expressed by a character in an Amazonian episode of *The Dream of the Celt* (*El sueño del celta*, 2010):[4]

> Evil, my friend is in our soul. In Europe it is easier to conceal it because it needs excuses to break out in public and collective ways. In the Amazon, on the other hand, it can show itself barefaced, and perpetrate the worst monstrosities without the subterfuges of patriotism or religion. The evil that is poisoning us is everywhere where you find human beings. Its roots are deep in our hearts.

Vargas Llosa's pessimism has given rise to a more indulgent attitude in his essays, and a feeling of greater commiseration towards intellectuals and public figures with whom he had quarrelled in the past. In his commentary on Günter Grass's confession about his brief involvement with Nazism, Vargas Llosa does not expresses himself with the polemical tone of their previous exchanges, but rather with understanding:

> Why has Günter Grass decided to speak out now? Surely to clear his conscience of something that must have tormented him, but also because he knew that his silence on this remote episode of his youth might cast a shadow over his reputation as a committed writer, who has also been regarded as the moral conscience of Germany. This is the normal conduct of a normal person who is not, and does not pretend to be, a hero or a saint.[5]

The tone of Vargas Llosa's more conciliatory essays also corresponds to an important change in how he presents the imperfections of his literary characters. The change is so significant that it is possible to speak about a third period in his trajectory as a novelist, after the moments when his literary works resonated with his optimistic views with respect to socialism in the 1960s, and liberal democracies in the 1980s. In this new period, he published four novels: *The Feast of the Goat* (*La fiesta del Chivo*, 2000[6]), *The Way to Paradise* (*El paraíso en la otra esquina*, 2003[7]), *The Bad Girl* (*Travesuras de la niña mala*, 2006[8]) and *The Dream of the Celt* (*El sueño del celta*, 2010).

Vargas Llosa no longer believes in revolutionary action, but the acumen and pain with which he had diagnosed sick and corrupt societies in the 1960s has returned in full force, as have characters who either challenge or flee from the injustices of human communities fraught with violence and abuse. Vargas Llosa remains as concerned with the mindset of those disposed to fight for their utopias, but he no longer deplores them – as he did in the 1980s – as hopeless fanatics or misguided utopians with grotesque convictions. Vargas Llosa begins to treat his fanatics, and even his revolutionary characters, with concern, compassion and empathy. His focus has shifted from the dreadful consequences of fanaticism, to an empathetic exploration of the traumas and suffering that turn some individuals into enemies of the world.

Until this latest period in his literary trajectory, Vargas Llosa's female characters were, by and large, the allies of men or the objects of their sexual desire. His most memorable female characters of the past, including Teresa in *The Time of the Hero* (*La ciudad y los perros*, 1963[9]), Lalita in *The Green House* (*La casa verde*, 1966[10]) and Jurema in *The War of the End of the World*, behaved according to patterns of female obedience and submission, while their romantic relationships served to highlight the personal dramas of Vargas Llosa's male protagonists. The most recurring female character type in Vargas Llosa's fiction was a woman who responds with resilience and vitality to untold humiliation and abuse. In the last four novels, Vargas Llosa has shifted his focus to a more sombre exploration of sexual abuse and its consequences, on individuals and even on generations to come. The theme of a woman who has repressed her sexual needs as a result of traumatic experiences links Flora from *The Way to Paradise* with Urania from *The Feast of the Goat*, and with the enigmatic female protagonist of *The Bad Girl*.

In *The Feast of the Goat*, the sexual violation of an adolescent girl is an allegory of the humiliation suffered by an entire nation at the hands of its dictator. This is the first novel about a Latin American dictator that explores the process whereby a corrupt, strong man undermines the dignity and self-worth of his closest collaborators and associates to remain in power, and one of the few Latin American political novels in which outrage at the crimes of a dictator goes hand in hand with the guilt, shame and pangs of conscience felt by victims and perpetrators alike. From this point of view, the murder of the dictator by his former collaborators is an act of catharsis. There is, however, a more significant act of catharsis in Urania's confession thirty-five years after the event, in which she reveals to her aunts and cousins that she had left her country because her father had allowed the dictator to abuse her sexually. Not all of her female relatives want to hear the details of a story that would compromise some of them, but Urania feels that a weight is lifted off her shoulders when she tells her story, and she allows herself to make peace with the children of those relatives whose moral conscience had been paralysed by the dictatorship.[11]

The Way to Paradise

The Way to Paradise is also a novel whose secret theme is the reconciliation between two generations that have suffered the consequences of trauma. Here, Vargas Llosa recreates the lives of the French activist, Flora Tristan, and her grandson, the painter Paul Gauguin. The novel's chapters neatly alternate between a fictional account of 1844, the last year of Flora Tristan's life, during which she embarked on a campaign in provincial French cities to gain adherents to a political programme that would unite women and workers in a peaceful, bloodless revolution; and a recreation of Gauguin's Tahiti period (1891–1903), during which the painter hoped to revive a holistic sense of physical, spiritual and religious inquiry in modern art. The narrative moves skilfully back and forth in time and space, to offer glimpses, insights and anecdotes about the pasts of the two protagonists, as they strive, and fail, to achieve their aspirations in various regions of the globe. In these flashbacks, Vargas Llosa gives pride of place to the period Flora Tristan spent in Peru with her father's family in Arequipa – Vargas Llosa's own birthplace.[12]

Vargas Llosa's narrator oscillates between a third-person descriptive mode and a second-person singular voice, engaged in an intimate, ambiguous dialogue with his protagonists' consciousness: at times the narrator appears to raise his own unresolved questions regarding his characters' aspirations. There are even moments in which the narrator encourages his characters to revisit some of their own experiences, with hindsight and a historical perspective that belong to him rather than to them. It is this second-person narrative voice – empathetic and keenly aware of his protagonists' formative moments – that allows for the seamless movement between different periods in the lives of 'Florita' and 'Koké', the endearing nicknames the narrator uses to address his protagonists.

In the chapters devoted to Flora Tristan, she is presented as both witness and victim of abuses against women. The French authorities do not recognise her mother's marriage to a Spanish citizen from Peru. On that basis, they confiscate her property when her husband dies, and confer to Flora the legal status of an illegitimate daughter deprived of inheritance rights. Flora marries a vindictive sexual abuser who forces himself upon her and their young daughters. He is treated lightly by the French legal system, which favours the rights of husbands over their wives, and by lawyers and judges, who find it expedient to side with the accused in cases of rape and incest.

Transgressive sexuality has always been at the heart of Vargas Llosa's literary concerns. He has been interested in exploring sexual violence, sexual relations that offend public morality even as they offer fulfilment to his characters, and sexuality as a force that undermines the social bonds by which his characters wish to live. Since *Who Killed Palomino Molero?* (*¿Quién mató a Palomino Molero?*, 1986[13]), he has been concerned with the theme of incestuous sexual abuse. In *The Feast of the Goat*, the sexual abuse of a seemingly loving father, who makes a present of his daughter's virginity to a dictator, takes on the dimension of a political allegory of a nation abused by a corrupt political regime. In both *The Feast of the Goat* and *The Way to Paradise*, sexual abuse is emblematic of the mistreatment of women by patriarchal society. Urania Cabral feels horror at the thought of a sexual encounter after the dictator forced himself on her; and in every chapter of *The Way to Paradise*, the narrator underscores Flora Tristan's revulsion at the thought of an intimate encounter with a man. But even her propensities towards a fulfilling relationship with a woman she loves are hindered by the pretext that romance is incompatible with her political commitment on behalf of women's rights and other righteous causes, as when she abandons her lover (p. 306):

> Didn't you regret abandoning sweet Olympia that way, Florita? No. It was your duty to do what you did. Redeeming the exploited, uniting workers, achieving equality for women, bringing justice to the victims of this imperfect world – these things were more important than the marvellous egotism of love, the supreme indifference to one's fellows that was produced by pleasure. The only feeling you had room for in your life now was love for humanity.

Flora Tristan's wanderings to promote her political ideals are presented as a noble enterprise, but also as her way of coping with the consequences of the sexual abuse she and her daughters suffered.

As with all his literary characters inspired by historical characters, Vargas Llosa's Flora Tristan is a literary creation inspired by historical documentation and by the inventions of his own imagination. Vargas Llosa reworks Tristan's diaries, letters and even manuscripts, in order to fashion his character, and was especially interested in a diary Flora Tristan kept during her trips through France to gain supporters to her political cause. She had intended to write a book from the notes, but died before she was able to undertake the project. A careful reading of the diary shows that Vargas Llosa transformed Flora's notes to suit his literary purposes. Vargas Llosa eliminates many fundamental traits of the activist that can be gleaned from her observations: her religiosity, her theories about love as a necessary means to gain clarity in political matters, her nationalistic fervour, her paternalistic attitude towards the working class, the physiological categories with which she considered that some humans were inferior for hereditary or biological reasons, and her authoritarian and anti-democratic impulses. Vargas Llosa also invents aspects of the character, including her troubled relationship to sexuality, and directly transforms episodes from her diary.[14] For example, during a visit to a French province, Flora records a meeting with M. Escudié, a man who wanted to join her cause, but who is unable to do so: 'he has the honest desire to serve the exploited classes and understands that herein lies the life and the future of humanity, but his flesh, precipitates him towards vice and he is therefore not useful to our cause'.[15] In the novel, Vargas Llosa transforms Tristan's regret about the inadequacies of a political supporter into an episode in which an unwholesome interlocutor makes suggestive comments premised on the realisation that, underneath her apparent prudishness, Flora is struggling with her repressed sexuality: 'Flora felt that her legs were trembling. She did what she could to change the direction of their conversation, fearful that Escudié, rushing her in that direction would open the gateways to her secret hell, those lewd and salacious depths in which, to judge from her pupils tinged with vileness, were harbouring many demons' (p. 405).

In *The Way to Paradise*, Paul Gauguin's sexual experimentation is presented as a point of contrast to Flora's sexual restraint. For the painter, as he appears in the novel, sexuality is experienced as a boon rather than a bane, at least at first sight. He considers his sexuality to be at the core of his creative drive. He comes of age artistically as he loosens his bourgeois mores, embraces his bisexuality and becomes fascinated by the possibility of other sexual orientations. That being said, he is willing to abandon anyone with whom he has been sexually involved for the sake of his art, whether it be his Danish wife, whom he leaves to fend for herself in Europe, or the teenage girls in Tahiti, who lived with him, served him and with whom he had children. As the narrative voice indicates on several occasions, love, for Gauguin, was an insurmountable obstacle to his mission as an artist: 'you had come to the conclusion that love for artists should be exclusively physical and sensual, as it was for primitive peoples, it should not involve the emotions of the soul' (p. 221).

The limited remorse Gauguin feels when he abandons women might be linked to the hidden anger he felt towards Aline Gauguin, his own mother and Flora's daughter, who, in order to become the secret mistress of a businessman involved in the art world, left Gauguin in a boarding school. On the surface, *The Way to Paradise* is a novel about two kinds of utopia: an artistic one and a political one; but there is another sobering connection that unites the two tales to an even greater degree, namely, the consequences of sexual abuse. Indeed, Gauguin's posthumous reconciliation with his mother Aline – herself neglected and abandoned by her activist mother and a victim of incestuous abuse by her father – is the underlying link between the two main stories of the novel. In Flora's case, the consequences of sexual abuse generate a sense of horror towards sexuality, and in Koké's case it produces an exalted sense of sexual liberation by an individual who becomes indifferent to the consequences of his sexual prerogatives. In both cases, the vital mission of the character is linked to a personal attitude towards sexuality which precludes the possibility of love.

There are antecedents to Flora Tristan's political fervour in characters steadfastly committed to utopian ideals, like Alejandro Mayta in *The Real Life of Alejandro Mayta* (*Historia de Mayta*, 1984[16]), or Galileo Gall in *The War of the End of the World*. There are also antecedents to Paul Gauguin in characters determined to trade one sort of existence for another, like Saúl Zuratas in *The Storyteller* (*El hablador*, 1987[17]), who abandons a modern urban centre to live with an indigenous community in the Amazon. But Vargas Llosa used to treat his fanatics and eccentrics at a remove, with distance and reserve, sometimes with a measure of irony or even contempt. In *The Way to Paradise*, he presents his fanatical protagonists with more indulgence, greater empathy and less distance from his own artistic concerns and political experiences. Indeed, there is a clear parallel between Vargas Llosa's fictional account of Flora Tristan's courageous, but failed attempt to launch a political movement in the novel and his autobiographical account, *A Fish in the Water* (*El pez en el agua*, 1993[18]), of his own unsuccessful effort to establish a stable and lasting political party during the Peruvian presidential campaign of 1990. So too, Vargas Llosa's depiction of Gauguin resonates with his recent view that the painstaking achievements that an artist might attain on canvas or in a novel – sometimes as a result of considerable personal sacrifice – are poignant reminders of what can never be attained in the realm of everyday life.

Like his Flora Tristan, Vargas Llosa's Gauguin is also a literary creation. Vargas Llosa transforms the biography of the painter, and even details of well-known paintings by Gauguin, to fit his literary ends. The theme of the inherent connection between the sexuality and the creativity of the painter, for example, is not stressed in Gauguin's autobiographical writings, and Gauguin's artistic aims, in the novel, are more apposite to Vargas Llosa's own views about art than to Gauguin's. Gauguin would often write that he was not pleased with his mastery of artistic technique, even when he felt satisfied with the promise of a painting, as in *Vision after the Sermon*, one of his seminal works:

> I've just painted a religious painting, very poorly executed, but I was interested in what I was doing, and I like it. For me the landscape in the painting featuring the struggle between Jacob and the angel exists only in the imagination of those individuals who pray after having heard a sermon.[19]

The discussion of the same painting in the novel takes on a different emphasis that corresponds more precisely to Vargas Llosa's own artistic interests. The emphasis is not on the capacity of a painter to capture an inner vision, but on the creation of a new reality that erases the boundaries between the subjective and the objective. Vargas Llosa's narrative reads like a correction of Gauguin's assessment of the painting (*The Way to Paradise*, p. 286):

> The true miracle of the painting was not the apparition of those biblical characters in the mind of those humble peasant women. The miracle was to have been able in that canvass to have finished with prosaic realism and to have captured a new reality in which the objective and the subjective, the real and the supernatural are confused, become indivisible.

The same discrepancy between Gauguin's vision as reflected in his autobiographical writings and Vargas Llosa's Gauguin can be noticed in the description of some of the Tahitian paintings mentioned in the novel. Vargas Llosa's fictional treatment of Gauguin's *Nevermore* is a case in point. The painting represents Pau'ura, Gauguin's companion during his second and final sojourn in Tahiti (1895–1903). In Gauguin's account, *Nevermore* is poorly painted, but succeeds in conveying both a savage luxuriousness and a resigned sadness as it transforms the 'raven' of Edgar Allen Poe's famous poem into a local Tahitian bird. In his literary treatment of the painting, Vargas Llosa makes a statement that has less to do with Gauguin's understanding of his own work, and more with Vargas Llosa's recent reflections on the ultimate helplessness of human beings against the cruel forces of the irrational (p. 155):

> The reclining woman accepted her limitations, knowing herself to be powerless before the secret, cruel forces that descend suddenly upon human beings to destroy them.

With the exception, perhaps, of his largest canvas, *Where do we come from? Who are we? Where are we going?* (1897), Gauguin did not speak of his paintings as masterpieces. Gauguin was painfully aware of his limitations; but he was also certain and proud that he had cleared artistic ground for other artists to follow. Vargas Llosa's Gauguin is more confident about his artistic powers, about his ability to produce masterpieces of various kinds, and about his ability to blur the lines between reality and fantasy, and none of these views correspond to the autobiographical writings of the painter.

The Way to Paradise is of course not an essay of art criticism, but a work of fiction in which Vargas Llosa wilfully veered away from Gauguin's autobiographical writings to engage his own artistic vision: his new-found conviction that the perfection an artist might achieve in a work of art is a reminder of that which can never be attained in the real world. This thought has little to do with his convictions of the 1960s that the socialist revolution could resolve the very problems that literature can diagnose, and it is also a clear departure from his literary manifestos of the 1980s, including the preliminary essay of *La verdad de las mentiras* ('The truth of lies') (1990)[20]. In the 1980s, Vargas Llosa had argued that the literary and erotic imagination could be a temporary, but satisfying compensation to our most irrational drives. It is worth noting, however, that along his literary trajectory his fictions have sometimes corrected his own ideas about art, and that his most recent fictions have been slowly unravelling that proposition. In *The Way to Paradise*, as we have noted, a persuasive work of literature is no longer understood as a compensation, but as an example of what can never be achieved in the here and now; and *The Bad Girl* makes a comparable counter-statement with respect to Vargas Llosa's previous ideas about the erotic as a compensation for the insufficiencies of life.

The Bad Girl

The Bad Girl has many humorous touches, but it is also a novel tinged with a sense of compassionate ruefulness. In this novel, Vargas Llosa is closer to the uncompromising realism of his admired Russian writers, most notably Tolstoy, than to his Flaubertian explorations of self-deceit. Ricardo Somocurcio, the protagonist of the novel, is not a great artist, but an interpreter and a translator. Nevertheless, his life is a parallel to Vargas Llosa's own. They were born around the same date, they lived more or less in the same cities around the same years, and their lives – whether they liked it or not – were both deeply intertwined with the vicissitudes of Peruvian history. Indeed, the novel includes a running commentary on the major political and historical events in Peru from the 1950s until the late 1980s, stopping short of Vargas Llosa's own political campaign for the Peruvian presidency. The main relationship in the novel, between Ricardo Somocurcio and a mysterious woman, the 'bad girl', is Vargas Llosa's most searching allegory about his own relationship to Peru. Within the typology of Vargas Llosa's fictional characters, Ricardo is a reincarnation of sorts of Santiago Zavala, due to his impotent empathy with the misery of his fellow Peruvians. And, on account of her sense of pride and need to rebel, the bad girl is a female reincarnation of Jaguar from *The Time of the Hero*. Like Santiago Zavala, Ricardo

Somocurcio is keenly aware of the social injustices of Peru. He observes 'the hell that Peru is for the poor' (p. 79) and expresses his understanding for the 'millions of Indigenous peoples who have arrived in the cities from the Andes, fleeing hunger and violence' (p. 292); and, like Santiago Zavala, he can only trade his observations for feelings of malaise and frustration. Like Jaguar, the bad girl becomes cruel because, as the narrator intimates, 'she was convinced that life was a jungle where only the worst would triumph' (p. 131). Ricardo is not himself politically engaged, but he aids and abets a Latin American revolutionary leader in Paris, a communist who is preparing to participate in a subversive campaign in Peru, because he has developed a personal friendship with him. Ricardo's literary sensibilities are closer to those of Ivan Bunin, the fiercely anti-Bolshevik Russian Nobel Prize winner, who wrote a biography of Anton Chekov and updated his master's literary themes in apolitical stories that were more suited to the realities of the early twentieth century. In the novel, Ricardo is the Spanish translator of both Bunin and Chekhov, and Vargas Llosa's novel is an homage to those two masters of Russian literature, with whom he establishes a dialogue to develop one of the novel's central themes: the sense of realism that arises from the understanding that human aspirations and achievements are impermanent and precarious. For the humorous elements of the novel, Vargas Llosa drew on the kitsch of the popular Mexican cinema of the 1940s that has always informed the popular and melodramatic touches in his narrative fiction.

Thirty years ago, with *Aunt Julia and the Scriptwriter* (*La tía Julia y el escribidor*, 1977[21]), Vargas Llosa created the first of a series of novels, including *The Storyteller* and *In Praise of the Stepmother* (*Elogio de la madrastra*, 1988[22]), in which chapters devoted to the drab everyday reality of his characters alternate with chapters rehearsing the compensatory nature of the imagination. This pattern was a tribute to Gustave Flaubert's *Temptation of Saint Anthony*, in which the colourless reality of a religious hermit alternates with scenes informed by the wild powers of the human imagination. In these novels, Vargas Llosa was keen to create a counterpoint between the mediocrity of everyday life and the compensations of the literary or the erotic imagination, an impulse consistent with his essays on the social role of art of that period.

In *The Bad Girl*, the line used to demarcate drab existence from the imagination in Vargas Llosa's novels of the 1980s has not just blurred, but disappeared altogether.[23] Indeed, the female protagonist of the novel, the bad girl, is as much a realistic character of the novel as she is the product of a dream. She appears and disappears from Ricardo's life in the most extraordinary circumstances, and is unable to differentiate, as the narrator once puts it, 'the world in which she lived from that in which she said she lived' (p. 175).

Every time she appears in the novel she enters the world of Ricardo Somocurcio's drab reality as if she were a woman of flesh and blood, but she is also a fantasy, a literary creation that has stepped into the world of the living, as in Julio Cortázar's stories, in which the world of fiction and the world of the everyday are connected as the two sides of the Moebius strip.[24] A consummate master of narrative fiction, Vargas Llosa is able to present his character with sufficient ambiguities, mysteries and ellipsis so that each chapter of the novel can be read as either a fantasy or a reality. In a brilliant twist on Gabriel García Márquez's *One Hundred Years of Solitude* (*Cien años de soledad*, 1967), each chapter of the novel moves chronologically according to the history of Peru, from 1950 until the late 1980s, and to the chronological life of Ricardo Somocurcio; but time also appears to be standing still, as each chapter tells exactly the same story, or rather a variation on the same theme, as the repetition of an obsession. In each chapter, the bad girl appears in the life of Ricardo; in each chapter she is the object of his erotic drives; in each chapter the erotic is contrasted with an encounter with the death or the agony of a character. As in a musical composition, in which a hopeful, light-hearted theme is composed against a more sombre one, reflecting the gravity of a human struggle, repetition undermines the illusion, as the lighter theme cannot bear the weight of the more serious one. Indeed, the theme of the compensatory imagination weakens as it is dissected and its underlying sources are revealed. The great revelation in the novel is the past of the bad girl. She was a Peruvian girl of indigenous origins, the daughter of Andean immigrants to Lima, who grew up in sordid poverty. When Ricardo discovers the bad girl's Peruvian roots, his focus on her as the object of his erotic fantasies is transformed into feelings of compassion for her suffering: 'I imagined her, as a little girl, living in the promiscuity and squalor of those precarious card-board shacks built on the shores of the river Rimac' (p. 322). The revelation is moving, but it is also sobering and overarching: sobering, in that the novel becomes a meditation on the effects of trauma; and overarching, in that this theme offers a key to Vargas Llosa's entire oeuvre.

For many years, Mario Vargas Llosa argued that the literary imagination is a compensation for the insufficiencies of life. His character, the bad girl, can be read as a correction, even as a counter-statement to his own doctrine, one that emerges from his own literary imagination. As a girl, the bad girl has suffered severe trauma associated with sexual violence, and, as a result, the narrator understands her need to escape into a world of fiction: 'To live that fiction gave her reasons to feel more secure, less threatened, than to live in the realm of truth. For everybody it is more difficult to live in truth than it is to live in a world of lies. But this is all the more so in her situation. It will take a lot for her to get accustomed to truth' (p. 267). The commentary is expanded on, in the novel, by a specialist in torture and trauma: 'She and all those who lived trapped in a world of fantasies that they create in order to abolish the realities of life, know and don't know what they are doing. The borderline between the two things becomes eclipsed for a while and then it reappears' (p. 268).

In Vargas Llosa's meditations on José María Arguedas, he insists that the various contradictions and tensions in his countryman's novels have their source in childhood traumas. Arguedas's literary imagination – in which sexuality is invariably presented as sin and his narrative voice is seeking what Arguedas himself called 'the purifying fire' – according to Vargas Llosa, has its source in traumatic experiences Arguedas suffered as a boy. Arguedas's literary imagination is presented, by Vargas Llosa, as a compensation for a sense of outrage that runs deeper than the vicissitudes of Arguedas's lifelong commitment and devotion to the rights and the culture of the Peruvian indigenous peoples, his attempts to link those commitments to socialist political movements and his anthropological contradictions.

Vargas Llosa has occasionally intimated that traumatic experiences drove him to create alternative realities, and that this impulse drew him to become a writer of fictions. His most poignant confession has been his recollection of the feeling that he had lost his innocence, when his father, whom he thought was dead and whom he had idealised, returned to his life as a despotic and abusive paternal figure. For years, Vargas Llosa has insisted on the dangerous, irrational forces that drive an individual to invent alternative realities as a response to realities that leave much to be desired, but in *The Bad Girl*, the compensations of the literary imagination and of the erotic experience prove insufficient, and their insufficiencies are commensurate with a degree of suffering that make them pale in comparison to experiences that are all too real. This novel is as sexually explicit as any Vargas Llosa has written, but its sexuality is tinged with pain and sadness. As sexuality and the erotic imagination cease to be the main driving forces of the relationship between the novel's main protagonists, Vargas Llosa begins to explore a new theme: love. The development of this theme in the novel involves the awareness by the protagonists that a trauma in the distant past is the obstacle to a loving relationship between them. The novel's protagonists come to the difficult but mature realisation that the compensations of fantasy and of the erotic may be subterfuges aimed at protecting damaged human beings from emotions that may be more painful, because more real, and therefore more redemptive. As in the short stories by Anton Chekhov, which Ricardo Somocurcio translated into Spanish, the true complexities of life are never resolved with ease, and we are in no position to begin to understand them without the painful realism of love.

If *The Bad Girl* is the first novel by Vargas Llosa that explores the possibilities of love, *The Dream of the Celt* is the first novel in which a bond of friendship develops among characters, a jailer and a prisoner who hold profoundly different convictions. *The Dream of the Celt* is also a tragic version of *The Bad Girl*. In both novels, characters, who keep reinventing themselves, voyage from a utopic world of fantasy to a harsh confrontation with reality. However, as opposed to *The Bad Girl*, which ends with the possibility of love and the affirmation of life by a character who is facing death, *The Dream of the Celt* ends with Casement's private, stoic feeling that life is not worth living. The character who feels betrayed in life and in love, and dissatisfied with the compensations of friendship, arrives at a fatalistic acceptance of death. In this sense, Vargas Llosa's last two novels share the feeling that the sources of human dissatisfaction will not be resolved by rebellion or through fantasy. These novels have characters who oscillate between spiritual longing and fatalism, and who are open to love and to reconciliation when they come to terms with the fragility of humanity.

The Dream of the Celt

The Dream of the Celt was inspired by the life of Roger Casement. The novel might also be loosely inspired by a Jorge Luis Borges story, 'Theme of the Traitor and the Hero' ('Tema del traidor y del héroe', 1944), in which an Irishman is remembered as a hero because his people want to remember him as such, even though he was deeply flawed. The historical Roger Casement was an Irishman who served Britain in the consular services of the Empire in Africa and in the Amazon region of Peru. Unable to maintain the impartiality expected of consuls and diplomats, he became a human rights activist, denouncing the exploitation of indigenous peoples in Africa and South America, and, on returning to Europe, turned against the British Empire to devote the rest of his life to the project of Irish independence. He conspired with the Germans against Britain during the First World War, as he had hoped that a German triumph might be a boon for the project of Irish independence. Casement was captured by the British secret services and during the legal proceedings against him a set of personal diaries emerged, which he refused to accept as his own, detailing his life as a homosexual man. Casement was executed at Pentonville Prison in London in 1916, while the war was still raging. In Vargas Llosa's novel, Casement is transformed into a man who embraces a number of utopias and fantasies, and who reinvents himself several times as each of the dreams he embraces becomes undone: the imperial dream, the dream that human rights activism can change society, the dream of Irish nationalism, and the dream of the afterlife.

Vargas Llosa became interested in the life of Roger Casement – and thought the Irishman a worthy subject for a novel – while exploring the possibility of a writing project based on the life of King Leopold II of Belgium. Leopold's colonial territories included the Congo, which had been visited by Joseph Conrad and had inspired *The Heart of Darkness*.[25] Vargas Llosa had transposed aspects of Conrad's African novel in *The Green House*, most notably the character of Fushía, who was created by a fusion of a real-life character and Conrad's protagonist. Like Kurtz, Fushía is a foreigner who creates a fiefdom of indigenous peoples, and like Kurtz, he is removed from the heart of the jungle on a fateful boat trip on a major river by a navigator who feels compassion for a fallen man, guilty of unleashing horrific aspects of humanity in himself and others. Vargas Llosa must have been fascinated to learn that Casement and Conrad shared a room together for several weeks in the Congo, and that Casement's account of the atrocities in Africa must have played a role in Conrad's conception of the setting for his classic novel. And it must have surprised Vargas Llosa even more to learn that, after his twenty-year stay in Africa, Casement was posted to the Peruvian Amazon region. There, he met and denounced notorious exploiters of *caucho*, or rubber trees, including Julio Arana, who is mentioned by name and looms large in *The Green House*. Indeed, the end of Casement's five-year posting in the Amazon region (1906–11) corresponds, in Vargas Llosa's earlier novel, to the legendary establishment of the first 'Green House', a house of prostitution whose founder's personal life was shocking to those who had acquiesced to its existence. The mix of a sexuality that shocks the local sensibility and the denunciation of human rights abuses also feature in Casement's biography. In 1911, Casement drafted a scathing report on the violations of human rights in the Amazon, while secretly keeping a diary chronicling his sexual exploits, including many with young boys. In some senses, the Amazon sections of *The Dream of the Celt*, set in the period of the heyday of the *caucho* boom, offer a pre-history to *The Green House*, set in the boom's decline.

The Dream of the Celt offered Vargas Llosa the opportunity to revisit the theme of transgression from a perspective consistent with his new conciliatory mood. The narrative frame of the novel is the relationship, established in its opening lines, between Casement and his prison guard, a man who has as much contempt for the Irish patriot-turned-spy as the Irish patriot has for the British Empire he had served as a diplomat for the greater part of his life. Like Manuel Puig's *The Kiss of the Spider Woman* (*El beso de la mujer araña*, 1976) – a novel Vargas Llosa admired – the prison setting brings men holding opposing views about politics and sexuality together, as if the development of human bonds tempers their commitment to causes, or their adherence to prejudices. In *The Dream of the Celt*, the two men come to realise that they share an underlying sense of fatalism that belies their convictions and spiritual longings. In Puig's novel, the dream factory of cinema slowly brings the two opposite characters together; in *The Dream of the Celt*, their feelings of despondency serve a similar purpose.

The Dream of the Celt is divided into three sections: 'The Congo', 'The Amazon' and 'Ireland'. In a recursive pattern, each section alternates between Casement's experiences in prison as he awaits the appeals that might prolong or save his life, and the story of his life, giving pride of place to his experiences in Africa, Latin America and Europe, when he became an Irish nationalist. The scenes in prison focus on Casement's personal apprehensions, on the letters and visits he receives from friends who are working on his behalf, and, most importantly, on the relationship that slowly develops between himself and his jailer. Ordered to keep his interactions with Casement to a minimum, the prison guard was initially happy to do so.

In the African and Latin American sections of the novel, the reader follows Casement's development from a distant observer to a compassionate man who takes it upon himself to denounce crimes against humanity in areas where voracious greed and the enjoyment of violence have trumped any attempt at lawfulness. In one of the novel's turning points, Casement realises that his awareness of human rights violations have made him more suscep-tible to an unhappy life, which leads him to conclude that 'there is no bloody beast who is worse than the human being' (p. 98). One of the high points of the novel, a section that merits inclusion in an anthology of Latin American literature, is devoted to the whip: the tool and symbol of those who yield unjust power and who circumvent the law. The pages devoted to the whip poignantly unite the African and Amazonian sections of the novel. The second turning point of the novel, commensurate with Vargas Llosa's own sense of disenchantment with organised politics, is Casement's realisation that his attempts to fight for human rights in Africa and Latin America were quixotic. His findings are countered by the ruses of the exploiters and the machinations of governments who manipulate human rights violations of their rivals to advance their own political ends, or met with the incredulity of those who might otherwise sympathise, or with the indifference of those who have the power to intervene. On the other hand, as one dream is shattered, another is born: 'there in the Congo, living with injustice and violence he has discovered the great lie of colonialism and began to feel "Irish", that is to say a citizen of a country occupied and exploited by an empire which had bled Ireland and taken away its soul' (pp. 119–20). Casement's new appreciation of Ireland will also lead to a rediscovery of Catholicism. Vargas Llosa writes, 'As if reaching out to Catholicism was a natural consequence of all that he had done or had tried to do in these last years, including his mistakes and failures' (p. 125). In turn, Casement's Catholicism intensifies as his dream of nationalism is undermined.

Vargas Llosa devotes a considerable number of pages to Casement's homosexuality: his fascination with the shape of the male body, his sexual repression as a young man in Europe, and his sexual awakening in Africa and Latin America. An important concern of the novel is inspired by a document, the discovery of Casement's *Black Diaries*, which appear to offer a detailed account of his homosexual life. These diaries consolidated the fall of Casement's reputation among his enemies, and were initially considered a fabrication by his defenders. In the novel's epilogue, Vargas Llosa (or a narrative voice close to his own) indicates that he is persuaded that the *Black Diaries* were drafted by Casement himself, but that much of what is there is 'exaggeration and fiction, that he wrote any number of things because he would have liked, but was not able, to live them' (p. 449). Whether or not the real diaries include many exaggerations and fictions, the authorial voice in the novel assumes that this was the case. In the novel, Casement is a gay man who had few sexual encounters, but imagined he had many, and recorded the exaggerations in his diaries. It is instructive to see how Vargas Llosa used the real diaries to create his character, by comparing one of its entries to its transformation in the novel. The entry dated Wednesday, 30 August, which Casement wrote in Barbados on his return from the Amazon to Europe reads:

> To Hastings Bath 7.50 and several and then nice fair hair boy, blue pants and thick and stiff. To bath together 11.30. He then glorious form and limbs and it ... Latter lovely and huge one too. Only 11 years old on 17th July. Bath buds present.[26]

In *The Dream of the Celt*, the eleven-year-old boy is transformed into a seventeen-year-old teenager, who rejects Casement's advances, and Vargas Llosa's recreation of the entry reflects the older man's sexual frustrations (p. 298):

> When he returned to his hotel, taken with excitement, he wrote in his diary, with the vulgar and telegraphic language he used for the most intimate episodes: 'Public baths. Son of a cleric. Very beautiful. Long phallus, delicate, that became stiff in my hands. I took it in my mouth. Happiness for two minutes.' He masturbated and took another bath, meticulously scrubbing himself with soap, while he attempted to avert the sadness and the feeling of loneliness that used to overtake him in these situations.

Vargas Llosa's recreations use more graphic language and narrative embellishments than the annotations in the *Black Diaries*, but the diaries are more disturbing, given the terse accounts of sexual encounters with under-age boys in Africa and Latin America.

In the novel, Casement's only sexual relationship that develops into a romance is with a young Norwegian man, who eventually betrays him to the English secret services. One of Casement's motifs is his acknowledgement that sexuality ('the sexual demon', p. 315) is not love, and is at odds with his religious urgings, as when he goes through periods of sexual abstinence because 'his head was full of religious preoccupations' (p. 320).

Unlike the historical Casement, whose last writings expressed his heartfelt commitment to the Irish cause until the end ('Surely it is the most glorious cause in history', Casement wrote in a document shortly before his death[27]), Vargas Llosa's Casement slowly abandons all of his commitments and convictions: the dedication with which he had served Great Britain as a diplomat, the passion with which he had defended human rights in Africa and the Amazon, his adherence to Germany during the Great War, and his dedication to the cause of Irish independence. His nationalistic zeal begins to wane when he questions the in-fighting of those committed to the cause, and when he realises that in the Ulster rebellion, some nationalist leaders had hoped to sacrifice the lives of militants in the hope that their martyrdom would serve the cause in the future. At the end of his life, Vargas Llosa's Casement is concerned about his deteriorating physical and mental health, and it is not even clear if he has vestiges of the religious longings that had engaged him towards the end of his life. When he is asked if he would like to say something before his execution by hanging, he whispers the word 'Ireland' without much conviction, appearing grateful to his executioner, who recommends that he hold his breath if he wants death to come to him a little faster.

In the end, his closest human bond is with the jailer who guarded him. They come together stripped of convictions, with a shared sense of emptiness. Life lost its meaning for Casement's jailer when his son died fighting the Germans, for whom Casement had been a spy. He confesses that he has been on the verge of suicide (p. 277):

> If I have not killed myself, it is because my religion forbids it. But it is not out of the question that I do it. If I'm unable to defeat this sadness, this feeling of emptiness that says to me that nothing matters, I'll do it. A man ought to live as long as life matters. Otherwise he should not live.

It is poignant that as Casement is awaiting execution, it is he who consoles the jailer.

As the novel closes, the reader is left with a strong impression that, unlike the historical Casement, who is persuaded of his nationalist causes to the very end, Vargas Llosa's Casement is a nihilist who tried to embrace a series of causes to which, ultimately, he was not truly committed, because he was unable to establish meaningful human bonds that might have given meaning to his life. In the end, Casement's conversion to Catholicism is no different to any of his other experiences in Africa and the Amazon as a human rights activist, or in Europe as an Irish nationalist or spy: they are roles he longs to play, but which he cannot fully embrace. After his 'conversion' to Catholicism before his execution, he has no interest in any further discussion with the priests or any interest in exploring whatever spiritual longings he may have had. According to some sources, the historical Casement's final words were, 'Lord Jesus, receive my soul',[28] but even if this particular account is apocryphal, it is clear that Vargas Llosa reworked the existing sources to create a character who does not correspond exactly to them: his Roger Casement is as much a Vargas Llosa character as his Gauguin or his Flora Tristan.

Vargas Llosa's most recent novels share in the assumption that the sources of human dissatisfaction with the here and now are intractable; that evil is a real presence, generating a need for reconciliation among flawed human beings, an opening to love; and that transgression and rebellion are preconditions for spiritual intimations. It is an open question whether the spiritual sense of longing expressed by Paul Gauguin in *The Way to Paradise* or Roger Casement in *The Dream of the Celt* will be further developed in Vargas Llosa's fiction. It is clear, on the other hand, that the feelings of spiritual longing or of fatalism that grip Vargas Llosa's most recent characters resonate with a Catholic worldview according to which the fulfilment of humanity is not reserved for the kingdom of this world. It is also clear that the power of Vargas Llosa's fiction lies in his consummate ability to keep his readers unsettled by the imperfections of our world and riveted by the literary imagination, whether or not it can compensate for the insufficiencies of the here and now.

NOTES

1. Mario Vargas Llosa. *Conversación en La Catedral*. Barcelona: Seix Barral, 1969.
2. Mario Vargas Llosa. *La guerra del fin del mundo*. Barcelona: Seix Barral, 1981.
3. Mario Vargas Llosa. *Lituma en los Andes*. Barcelona: Planeta, 1983.
4. Mario Vargas Llosa. *El sueño del celta*. Madrid: Alfaguara, 2010, p. 298. (Translation Efraín Kristal.) *The Dream of the Celt*. Trans. Edith Grossman, New York: Farrar, Straus and Giroux, 2012.
5. Mario Vargas Llosa. 'Günter Grass en la picota'. *El País*, 27 August 2006.
6. Mario Vargas Llosa. *La fiesta del Chivo*. Madrid: Alfaguara, 2000.
7. Mario Vargas Llosa. *El paraíso en la otra esquina*. Madrid: Alfaguara, 2003. Further in-line citations refer to *The Way to Paradise*. Trans. Natasha Wimmer. New York: Farrar, Straus and Giroux, 2003.

8. Mario Vargas Llosa. *Travesuras de la niña mala*. Madrid: Alfaguara, 2006. All translations in this chapter are by Efraín Kristal.
9. Mario Vargas Llosa. *La ciudad y los perros*. Barcelona: Seix Barral, 1963.
10. Mario Vargas Llosa. *La casa verde*. Barcelona: Seix Barral, 1966.
11. For a detailed analysis of *The Feast of the Goat*, see Clive Griffin's chapter in this book.
12. Several years after Tristan's death, the same family members welcomed her daughter, Aline Gauguin, and her son Paul, for a seven-year stay in Lima.
13. Mario Vargas Llosa. *¿Quién mató a Palomino Molero?* Barcelona: Seix Barral, 1986.
14. The theme of a woman who has repressed her sexual needs as a result of traumatic experiences links Flora to Urania from *The Feast of the Goat*, and both with the eponymous protagonist of Jorge Luis Borges's short story, 'Emma Zunz' (1948).
15. Flora Tristan. *Le tour de France. Journal 1843–1844. Tome 2*. Paris: Indigo & Coté-femmes éditions, p. 45. (Translation Efraín Kristal.)
16. Mario Vargas Llosa. *Historia de Mayta*. Barcelona: Seix Barral, 1984.
17. Mario Vargas Llosa. *El hablador*. Barcelona: Seix Barral, 1987.
18. Mario Vargas Llosa. *El pez en el agua. Memorias*. Barcelona: Seix Barral, 1993.
19. Letter to Vincent van Gogh with sketch of *Vision after the Sermon* dated 22 September 1888. In Belinda Thomson (ed.). *Gauguin by Himself*. London: Little, Brown, 1993, p. 66.
20. Mario Vargas Llosa. *La verdad de las mentiras. Ensayos sobre la novela moderna*. Barcelona: Seix Barral, 1990.
21. Mario Vargas Llosa. *La tía Julia y el escribidor*. Barcelona: Seix Barral, 1977.
22. Mario Vargas Llosa. *Elogio de la madrastra*. Barcelona: Tusquets, 1988.
23. It is worth noting that this is the aesthetic ideal that Vargas Llosa's Gauguin aspires to in *The Way to Paradise*.
24. As, for example, in Cortázar's short story, 'The Continuity of Parks' ('Continuidad de los parques', 1956). In Julio Cortázar. *Blow-Up and Other Stories*. Trans. Paul Blackburn. New York: Pantheon, 2004.
25. See Vargas Llosa's essay on *The Heart of Darkness* in which he discusses Casement and his role in the gestation of Conrad's novel: 'Las raíces de lo humano'. In Vargas Llosa, *La verdad de las mentiras*.
26. Jeffrey Dudgeon. *Roger Casement. The* Black Diaries. *With a Study of his Background, Sexuality, and Irish Political Life*. Belfast Press, 2002, p. 307.
27. Ibid., p. 2.
28. Ibid., p. 8.

11

JOHN KING

The essays

When you set out for Ithaka
Ask that your way be long,
Full of adventure, full of instruction.
C. P. Cavafy, 'Ithaka'[1]

Mario Vargas Llosa is the most widely discussed – and debated – public intellectual in the Spanish-speaking world; his commentaries are read across the globe.[2] To many he has become – in a phrase that he used with intentional irony to describe his long-term ideological sparring partner, Günter Grass – 'the 'conscience' of an era, for he is a writer 'who has opinions on and debates everything'.[3] He has been commenting on politics since the early 1960s, though his conviction that a writer of fiction can play a decisive role in the political arena waned considerably after his own failed candidacy for the Peruvian presidency in 1990. His publications, on politics and on broader cultural issues, are more extensive than his works of fiction, and are so inextricably linked to his intellectual biography that they are best understood in the context of developments and changes in his views about politics, the arts and culture. Indeed, his collections of essays often include open letters and documents that attest to his ongoing participation in public affairs in Peru and elsewhere.

He first gained employment as a sixteen-year-old cub journalist in Lima for *La Crónica* newspaper, in early 1952, while still at secondary school. In his evocation of Peru in his Nobel Prize Lecture in December 2010, he talked with affection of his early days in the dusty newspaper offices, remarking that journalism, along with literature, had been a constant throughout his life that allowed him to 'live more fully, know the world better, meet people from all walks of life, excellent, good, bad and execrable people'.[4] Journalism was initially an economic necessity: he would work in French radio and television as a reporter while he wrote his early novels in Paris from 1959 to 1966. But even when the success of his novels made it possible for him to make a living from his creative writing, he continued contributing to newspapers and magazines, and, most consistently, since the early 1990s, for the Spanish newspaper *El País*: his fortnightly column, 'Piedra de Toque' ('Touchstone'), is currently syndicated throughout Latin America. These columns have allowed him the space to debate issues of current concern, and offer a platform for his ideas. The articles have also often mapped the journeys taken on extensive research trips for his novels, from Brazil to Polynesia to the Congo, though his curiosity would also take him to visit some of the world's most troubled spots, including Iraq, the Gaza Strip, Afghanistan and Darfur. Selections of these articles and essays have been collected in eight books.[5]

He has also written consistently about the craft and the practice of fiction in a series of publications – a further nine book-length studies – that would outstrip the efforts of all but the most prolific and dedicated academic scholar. When he moved to London from Paris in 1966, he worked for a time – once again, as an economic necessity – at Queen Mary College London, and later at King's College London, until his literary agent, Carmen Balcells, persuaded him to give up teaching and write full-time. This prompted a further move to Barcelona, in 1970, where Gabriel García Márquez, José Donoso and other Latin American writers were devoting their lives to writing. Yet his full-time writing career would often find him returning to the academic world, teaching for a term, lecturing at universities across the globe. The phone call that announced him winning the Nobel Prize on 7 October 2010, found him awake in New York at 5.46 in the morning, taking advantage of jet lag to prepare for a class at Princeton on the literary techniques of the Cuban writer Alejo Carpentier. Several books have been based on classes given at different universities, though he has always asserted that he is not an 'academic' critic, that his books are informed by his own personal readings. Indeed a recurring theme in his work is his rejection of critics whose theoretical abstractions divorce literature from pressing human concerns, especially when they ignore the delights of direct engagements with literary texts. He has no patience for the views inspired by Roland Barthes and Michel Foucault, among others, according to which the conscious or unconscious motivations of an author are irrelevant to the study of literature.

Many of his major essays on different writers were first rehearsed as lectures at symposia and writer congresses throughout the world. From the 1960s, Vargas Llosa, along with Carlos Fuentes, José Donoso and other Latin American 'Boom' novelists, would constantly lecture and write about his own literary practices, as well as those of friends and colleagues. Vargas Llosa's first major published book of criticism is a detailed account of Gabriel García Márquez's early novels and short stories. He would later publish books in which he explored how Gustave Flaubert, José María Arguedas, Victor Hugo and Juan Carlos Onetti developed their craft: their techniques and obsessions are charted in dialogue with his own novelistic concerns. The illustrations at the end of this chapter – lecture notes prepared for a class at Columbia University in 1975 – show how his books on García Márquez,

Arguedas and Onetti are part of a wider vision of the Latin American novel that he would develop and modify throughout his life.

Vargas Llosa's books about a single author offer searching insights into the writers he is analysing, but they are also a privileged vantage point from which to consider his views about literature, revealing elements of continuity, but also important changes, over the years. In his early socialist period, when writing about García Márquez in *Historia de un deicidio* ('García Márquez: history of a deicide') (1971[6]), he was persuaded that literature had a political role to play, that it was inspired by a sense of frustration with a social reality that could be changed for the better. As he became disenchanted with socialism, he shifted to a view of literature as a source of consolation: many of the essays that make up the first edition of his anthology *La verdad de las mentiras* ('The truth of lies') (1990[7]) were written at his most active moment in politics, 1987–90, when he was involved in setting up a new political party in Peru and eventually running for president. Reading the baroque Spanish poet Luis de Góngora, or writing about Henry Miller or Alberto Moravia, the Italian novelist, would allow him some respite from his immersion in that very different world of rallies and touring, endless speeches, attempts on his life and death threats.[8]

Vargas Llosa's concerns as an essayist are not confined to literature and politics. Art critic, cinema buff, music lover, football fan, bullfight aficionado: all of Vargas Llosa's many facets find their way into his non-fiction writing. From the 1960s, he began writing 'chronicles' for journals such as *Primera Plana* in Argentina and *Caretas* in Peru, where amused observations can be found alongside more serious explorations of politics and culture. He has continued to write in this vein to the present day. Some of his most memorable articles are descriptions of people and places, usually autobiographical, usually self-deprecating, as when he describes the transformation of his son Gonzalo into a sixteen-year-old Rastafarian while boarding at an English public school; his phobias about rats and mice; his fear of flying; and his visit to the dog cemetery in Paris to visit the grave of Rin Tin Tin. Since the early 1970s, he has devoted a considerable amount of attention to the visual arts, which have become increasingly central to his later novels and plays. He has published essays on artists Fernando Botero, George Grosz and the Peruvian Fernando de Szyszlo, and on the institutional spaces of culture.

In order to trace the main landmarks of this intellectual odyssey, a journey through different geographical locations and ever-changing cultural and political landscapes, the chapter is divided into two sections: politics and literature/art. Vargas Llosa's writing on literature and art is more concerned with the irrational wellsprings of a work of art, which he often depicts as the 'demons' of creation. In his political writing, on the other hand, he focuses most often on situations in which freedom is under threat. His sense of moral indignation about the curtailment of the rights of individuals to act, speak or think without coercion or censorship has underpinned his political views, even as they have shifted over the years. The movement described in this chapter, therefore, is both inward and outward. Our starting point is the outward movement towards politics.

Politics

The first articles published by Vargas Llosa in book anthologies date from 1962, placing him firmly in the exuberant initial aftermath of the Cuban Revolution. However, his memoir, *A Fish in the Water* (*El pez en el agua. Memorias*, 1993[9]), as well as his articles published in the 1950s, reveal a firm commitment to socialism and revolutionary ideas from as early as his days as a student at the University of San Marcos from 1953. In *A Fish in the Water*, writing with ironic distance in the early 1990s, he would entitle his chapter on student life 'Comrade Alberto', following his very brief flirtation with the underground communist party in Peru during the Odría dictatorship (1948–56). A later chapter would be entitled 'The Brave Little Sartrean', a nickname given him by fellow students in 1954, signalling an engagement with the work of Sartre that would be ongoing throughout the late 1950s and 1960s. In an article written three days after the award of the Nobel Prize, he describes the moments between receiving the phone call from the Swedish Academy and the official announcement of the prize fourteen minutes later, during which he recalled certain key moments from his earliest readings and writings: 'I thought about my friends from adolescence, Lucho Loayza and Abelardo Oquendo . . . and the ferocious discussions that we sometimes had as to who was more important, Borges or Sartre. I argued for Sartre and they supported Borges, and they were, of course, right. It was then that they gave me the nickname "the brave little Sartrean" (which delighted me)'.[10]

One of his earliest published articles was an assessment of the Peruvian Marxist intellectual, José Mariátegui (1894–1930), in particular his 1928 book, *Seven Interpretive Essays on Peruvian Reality* (*Siete ensayos de interpretación de la realidad peruana*).[11] His appreciation of the freshness and originality of Mariátegui's thought would remain constant even in the 1990s, when he would compare Mariátegui favourably against the 'cut-rate' Peruvian intellectuals that he encountered during his electoral campaign.[12] Equipped with readings of Mariátegui and Sartre, among others, Vargas Llosa had been prepared to embrace the early promise of the Cuban Revolution. His first trip to Cuba took place in 1962, in the aftermath of the Missile Crisis, establishing a pattern that would be repeated constantly throughout his life of writing travel reports from familiar or unfamiliar places in which analysis of important contemporary concerns is buttressed by personal experience. His work in the 1960s would be shaped by commitment to the Cuban Revolution. When he received the Rómulo Gallegos Prize for *The Green House* (*La casa verde*, 1966[13]) in 1967, he gave a vibrant account of the political function of literature in a lecture entitled 'Literature is Fire'. Given the extraordinary poverty, inequalities and exploitation in Latin America, he argued, the Cuban model offered the way forward, and the writer of fiction would be at the vanguard of social change: 'Warn them [contemporary societies] that literature is fire, that it means nonconformity and rebellion, that the *raison d'être* of a writer is protest, disagreement and criticism.'[14]

The image of Cuba was tarnished in his mind when Castro approved the Soviet invasion of Czechoslovakia in 1968, which Vargas Llosa termed an imperialist aggression and a dishonour to the land of Lenin. Fidel's words in support of the military intervention, he said, were as incomprehensible and unjust as the noise of the tanks entering Prague. The question of who had power over words took centre stage in early 1971, when Cuban poet Heberto Padilla was subjected to a rather shameful show trial, during which he made an abject personal recantation of his 'antirevolutionary' writing. This perturbed a number of intellectuals from Latin America, North America and Europe, who signed two open letters to the Cuban regime complaining about Padilla's shoddy treatment. Castro replied in a furious manner, branding his critics as bourgeois intellectuals, lackeys of imperialism and CIA agents. Vargas Llosa, who had helped draft the letters to Castro, also wrote to the director of Cuba's official cultural journal, *Casa de las Américas*, Haydée Santamaría, resigning from its organising committee: 'I know that this letter might be greeted with invective', he wrote, 'but it will be no worse than what I have received from reactionary elements for having defended Cuba'.[15] And invective he did receive, perhaps much more than he had imagined, as the Cubans and the pro-Cuban left closed ranks and moved onto the offensive.

But Vargas Llosa's political writing thrives on polemic. He would become embroiled in a number of heated debates with other writers in the early to mid-1970s, as he tried to organise his feelings about Cuba, and about socialism. While he came under strong attack in the early 1970s, he would never shy away from vigorous rebuttal, either instigating or responding to debates. In a book review published in December 1974, he would state that the Cuban Revolution had been the most significant event in his life, the first tangible proof that true socialism might be a possibility in Latin America. But he had gradually came to the conclusion that the Cuban model would not guarantee intellectual freedom. He still finds himself saying, between clenched teeth: "'I'm with socialism.'" But I say it now without the hopes, the joy and the optimism that for years the word socialism inspired in me, thanks exclusively to Cuba.'[16] Socialism seemed the only option to the wave of savage military dictatorships enveloping many countries in Latin America in the mid-1970s.

But this was a view that began to change from 1975, and the shift is expressed in an essay that he wrote in May 1975 and published in December of that year: 'Albert Camus and the Morality of Limits'.[17] Whereas in the 1960s he had been attracted to Sartre's ideas of commitment, by the mid-1970s, Camus, whom Vargas Llosa had previously rejected for his 'intellectual lyricism', would now offer an ethical model. In Vargas Llosa's reading, Camus rejected totalitarianism as a social system in which the human being becomes an instrument of state power. The duty of writers and intellectuals in this less strident world is to 'remind those in power, at every moment, and by every means at their disposal, of the morality of limits'.[18]

His reading of intellectual figures and essayists such as Isaiah Berlin, Karl Popper and Jean-François Revel would help consolidate his move away from socialism. Berlin's collected work (*Russian Thinkers*, 1978; *Against the Current*, 1979) offered certain key definitions and concepts. Its influence is clear in Vargas Llosa entitling his own volumes of collected essays *Contra viento y marea* ('Against wind and tide'). For example, Berlin's concept of 'negative' liberty allows people to do what they want as long as this does not impinge on other people's freedom, whereas 'positive' liberty, the basis of socialism and communism, according to Berlin, seeks to use politics to liberate people from either inner or outer barriers or repressions. 'Negative' freedoms are best guaranteed by democracy. Vargas Llosa would often quote Berlin's insight that the core values underlying democracy – equality, freedom and justice – can contradict each other, leading to possible conflict and loss. It was because of these 'contradictory' values that Berlin came to recommend pragmatic approaches to political problems, and to reject any notion of an ideal society or ideal human behaviour, an insight that would inform Vargas Llosa's developing criticism of utopias. His reading, in 1980, of Popper's *The Open Society and its Enemies* (1962) would add further insights into what Popper describes as the idea of relative rather than absolute truths, and the progression from 'closed' to 'open' societies. Jean-François Revel's political trajectory was similar to that of Vargas Llosa: a socialist who later came to reject what he perceived as the authoritarianism of socialist parties and governments in such works as *La Tentation totalitaire* (*The Totalitarian Temptation*) (1976) and *Le Terrorisme contre la démocratie* ('Terrorism against democracy') (1987). Revel's polemical engagement and his forthright defence of liberal values would chime with Vargas Llosa's own outlook, for he was drawn to intellectuals who were men of action – like André Malraux – rather than ivory tower thinkers. Every time Vargas Llosa engaged with a new current of thought, he would explain it to himself and to others through articles, talks and book chapters.[19]

The mid-1970s would also see his return to Peru, after living in Europe for some sixteen years. Back in Peru, a military regime was in power, but one that proclaimed itself to be socially just and interested in state-directed national development. Initially under General Juan Velasco Alvarado, and in much more muted form under General Francisco Morales Bermúdez, there was widespread agrarian reform and state intervention in many aspects of the economy, and a policy of selective nationalisation of foreign enterprises. Vargas Llosa became increasingly critical of the government, especially in its control of the media, which contributed towards his weariness and wariness of populist 'progressive' military governments.

The presidential elections in May 1980 brought back the conservative Fernando Belaúnde Terry, after twelve years of military rule. This year also marked the military emergence of the Sendero Luminoso guerrilla movement, founded by philosophy lecturer Abimael Guzmán. Within a few years, this ultra-violent group – whose literature spoke of the necessary 'quota' of blood sacrifice for each militant – had built up bases in the south central Andes and the shanty towns of Ayacucho, Huancayo and Lima, heralding a decade of what became known as '*Manchay tiempo*', the Time of Fear. Sendero received countrywide attention with the press and television coverage of the massacre, early in 1983, of eight journalists and their guide by villagers in Uchuraccay, north-west of the capital of Ayacucho, an area in which Sendero conducted operations. The government set up a commission of prominent Peruvians to investigate the killings, with Vargas Llosa as a member. Its report was hotly contested, especially by those incredulous that the perpetrators of the massacre were not members of the Peruvian armed forces, but rather local villagers caught in the crossfire of the dirty war. Vargas Llosa's account of this incident, 'Massacre in the Andes', ranks among his most powerful examples of investigative journalism, revealing the destructive nature of insurgent movements in the region, and the equally brutal government reprisals in an analysis that would underpin his fiction of the 1980s and early 1990s.[20] In another journalistic report, he offered an even-handed account of a month spent touring revolutionary Nicaragua in 1985, and would argue that Nicaragua seemed to be following its own independent path, and that it should look to rein in further revolutionary activity and implement democratic reforms.

When the president succeeding Belaúnde Terry, Alan García, sought to reverse IMF stabilisation policies in Peru by imposing a fixed exchange rate, import controls and his own level of debt repayment, finally announcing, in 1987, that he would nationalise all banks and financial institutions in Peru, Vargas Llosa wrote an article in opposition, 'Towards a totalitarian Peru', which became a rallying cry. He became involved in heading a process that would lead to the founding of a new political party, Libertad, and culminate in him running for president in the 1990 elections, as the candidate for FREDEMO, a coalition that included Libertad and two other political parties on the centre-right. His account of these three years, interspersed with memories of his school and university years (1947–59), is found in *A Fish in the Water*, published after Alberto Fujimori had won the 1990 elections, and, two years later, on 2 April 1992, with army support, had suspended the constitution and abolished the Congress. The memoir is analysed elsewhere in this volume. Its postscript is illustrative of his future intent. He states that, after 2 April 1992, he felt obliged once again to pluck up his courage, 'so as to overcome the visceral disgust that political action had left in my memory, to condemn, in articles and interviews, what seemed to me to be a tragedy for Peru: the disappearance of legality and the return of the era of strongmen'.[21]

He would find a fortnightly platform to air his views on Peru and on all manner of different topics in the Spanish newspaper, *El País*. From the early 1990s, his column, 'Touchstone', would be syndicated throughout the Spanish-speaking world and allow him to maintain a very visible presence as a public intellectual: writing about politics without the straightjacket of being a politician, and also writing about any interesting aspect of culture that his nomadic existence might lead him to. Unlike his longer essays and more elaborate monographs, which involve a considerable amount of research, the pieces in 'Touchstone' avoid footnotes and scholarly references and focus on a single guiding idea, which is most often introduced with a sense of urgency, when he is addressing a moral or a political issue, or a sense of intrigue and wonder, as when he is exploring cultural or artistic matters.

The political concerns expressed in 'Touchstone' cover Latin America and the wider world, with a recurring emphasis on the dangers of nationalism and populism, and a qualified embrace of globalisation. He has written passionate articles against dictators and populist leaders, including essays in praise of Spanish judge Balthazar Garzón's attempts to extradite the Chilean dictator Augusto Pinochet, to stand trial for violations of human rights, and he has also embraced the Egyptian uprising that brought down the regime of Hosni Mubarak.[22] During and after a trip to China in June 2011, he would point out the inequalities and human rights violations that accompanied the extra-ordinary economic growth of China in recent years.[23] That being said, Peru remained a focus, in particular, his regular appraisal of the regime and then the decline and imprisonment of Alberto Fujimori, along with his sinister henchman, Vladimiro Montesinos, who kept a video record of all the politicians, businessmen, judges, bankers and media personnel that he bribed throughout the 1990s. The fragile return to democracy in Peru would always be subject to potential setback, as when Antauro Humala (the retired military officer and brother of the current President, Ollanta Humala) occupied a police station in the Andes in 2005, demanding the resignation of the president, Toledo. It was Ollanta Humala who stood for presidential election in 2006, prompting Vargas Llosa to support the other presidential candidate, none other than his former political enemy, Alan García, as the lesser of two evils. Alluding to the opening line of one of his most famous novels, *Conversation in The Cathedral* (*Conversación en La Catedral*, 1969[24]), Vargas Llosa would write with exasperation in 2005: '"When did Peru screw up, Zavalita?" Are you still asking that same question, you moron? Peru is a country that screws up every day.'[25] These mordant interventions have remained constant. On 13 September 2010, Vargas Llosa published an open letter to Alan García, resigning from a commission to establish a Museum of Memory in Lima, in protest against government decree 1097 that seemed to offer amnesty to individuals, including members of the armed forces, involved in human rights abuses during the Fujimori regime. García would backtrack on this decree in the face of Vargas Llosa's protest.

It was during the 2011 Peruvian election campaign that Vargas Llosa would once again support a presidential candidate who had previously been a political opponent. In the first round of votes, he was outspoken against the candidacies of both Keiko Fujimori, the daughter of the imprisoned ex-president, and also Ollanta Humala, whom he had vigorously opposed in 2006. But when the second round of voting saw these two candidates pitted against each other, he would offer very public support to Ollanta Humala, in order to block what he viewed would be a return to the 'fascistic' principles of Fujimori, replayed by his daughter. He argued that Humala had reconsidered his earlier populist policies and was intent on establishing a centre-left government, in the style of Lula in Brazil, a government that would not tamper with liberal economic policies. In a close ballot, Humala won the election on 5 June 2011, and commentators agreed that Vargas Llosa's intervention had clearly helped this victory.[26]

In Vargas Llosa's eyes, authoritarianism still stalked Latin America, often under the guise of populist nationalism. Fidel Castro has been a source of his ire since the 1980s, as an example of a dictator, but in the first decade of the twenty-first century, Vargas Llosa would begin to speak out more stridently against populist leaders who came to power through democratic processes. The vigorous, oil-rich Hugo Chávez in Venezuela, and, to a lesser degree, Evo Morales in Bolivia and the Kirchners in Argentina, would embroil him in heated discussions about race and nation in a number of articles. Still no stranger to polemic, in 1990, Vargas Llosa described the ruling party in Mexico, the PRI, as presiding over a 'perfect dictatorship', much to the annoyance of fellow intellectual and writer Octavio Paz, who had reached an uneasy truce with the PRI. It was a phrase that gained common currency throughout Latin America. Through the 1990s, as the PRI lost its monopoly position, this 'dictatorship' would become less 'perfect', with open elections fought in 2000. Overall the repeated plea of Vargas Llosa was for modest, democratic regimes, on the Chilean model, where the boring (in a good way) political system established since 1990 had helped restore stability post-Pinochet to such an extent that a left-of-centre president, Bachelet, could leave office with a very high approval rate and hand over to a right-of-centre president without alarm. Such a system was the best guarantee of individual freedoms.

In Vargas Llosa's analysis, nationalism is an abiding ill; it is 'the culture of the uncultured, the religion of the demagogue, and a smokescreen behind which prejudice, violence and often racism can be found lurking'.[27] For him, blinkered nationalism is a blight on a modern world that ought to promote porous boundaries and global markets. Few issues upset Vargas Llosa more than the barriers to the free movement of individuals across national boundaries. An article entitled 'Fataumata's Feet' exemplifies these concerns. It paints the picture of a Gambian migrant worker in Catalonia, subject to a xenophobic and racist arson attack that burned down her immigrant hostel and left her badly injured. Her only option was to keep moving through a hostile landscape: 'As soon as she leaves the hospital, her wise feet will set off again, without any clear destination, along the dangerous fire-strewn roads of Europe, that cradle and model of Western civilisation.'[28]

The first decade of the twenty-first century would see the writer travelling the globe, not only for research into novels he was writing – this would have him following Gauguin to the South Seas as he was preparing to write *The Way to Paradise* (*El paraíso en la otra esquina*, 2003[29]), and Roger Casement to the Congo, as he was researching his novel, *The Dream of the Celt* (*El sueño del celta*, 2010[30]) – but also as an investigative journalist, looking at contemporary hot spots in ground zero New York just days after 9/11, in Darfur, in Afghanistan, Iraq and the Gaza Strip. *Diario de Irak* ('Iraq diary') (2003[31]) offers an example of his working method. Two and a half months after the symbolic toppling of the statue of Saddam Hussein in Baghdad, and having made declarations against the invasion carried out without a proper UN mandate, Vargas Llosa visited Iraq for twelve days, managing to gain access to some of the most important political figures involved, from US Ambassador Paul Bremer, to the principal Shia Ayatollah, Mohammed

Bakr al Hakim, as well as a range of other interlocutors: students, business-men, teachers, army officials, religious clerics, people in the street and chance encounters in cafes and restaurants. Between leaving Iraq on 6 July and writing the prologue to his book two months later, three of his main sources, the Imam al Hakim, the UN special envoy Sergio Vieira de Mello and a Spanish naval official Manuel Martín-Oar, would be assassinated. To gain access to Ambassador Bremer, the Spanish head of section in Baghdad had invented (or anticipated) the award of the Nobel Prize to Vargas Llosa: 'When I explained to the disappointed US colonel [Bremer's aide-de-camp] that there was no Nobel prize winner around, and that the interview was to be with a mere novelist from Peru, he muttered in a rather demoralised attempt at humour: "If you tell the ambassador about all this confusion, he'll fire me."'[32] Amusing anecdotes, well-drawn, sympathetic character sketches, evocative descriptions of place, a narrative voice that moves effortlessly across first, second and third person, stories constructed as captions for his daughter Morgana's vivid photographs, matter-of-fact description of un-imaginable brutality cross-referencing his novel of dictatorship, *The Feast of the Goat* (*La fiesta del Chivo*, 2000[33]): these are the storytelling techniques that are deployed as successfully in Vargas Llosa's non-fiction as in his fictions. He would change his mind about the invasion during this visit, arguing that the overthrow of an extreme tyrant could be justified, as the lesser of two evils.

Two years later, once again with his daughter Morgana as photographer, he would visit Gaza. Despite being a long-term defender of the Jewish state, and the recipient of the 1995 Jerusalem Prize, he would criticise Israel's policy towards the Palestinian population in no uncertain terms. Towards the end of *Israel/Palestina. Paz o guerra santa* ('Israel/Palestine: peace or holy war') (2006), he makes what appears at first a surprising observation, declaring that the only place in the world where he can feel left-wing is in Israel, among the Israeli left that he sees as undogmatic, open, heroic and ethical: *les justes*, in Camus's terms. It was being in Israel in the mid-1970s, he argues, that helped him to rethink his attachment to the 'hemiplegic left' in Latin America.[34] Whatever political moment or movement is under scrutiny, he has sought out those he considers *les justes*. His restless criss-crossing of the globe has been in no small part instigated by a search for men and women of moral convictions.

Literature/art

Despite their ferocious polemic in the 1970s about the nature of revolutionary movements in Europe and Latin America, Vargas Llosa has been drawn to writers like Günter Grass because of the scope and ambition of their work, their attempt to embrace all facets of life and culture, and their desire to offer guidance through their essays and inspiration through their creative writings. But his current view towards these writers, including Jean-Paul Sartre and Octavio Paz, has become more circumspect, albeit tinged with a certain nostalgia, as their influence had irremediably declined in a world of specialisation and postmodern scepticism.

He has written consistently on the craft of writing and on the social function of writing, but he has moved away from Sartre's view that creative writers play a key role in the transformation of societies. Instead, he would come to argue that literary freedom can be an affront to oppressive or totalitarian regimes. That said, there are certain recurrent themes and metaphors that emerge in his analysis of literature. Literature, one way or another, is a form of insurrection or protest against the world as we find it. It reveals, and also seeks to bridge, the gap between our limited reality and our desires; between the lives we actually lead, and the possibilities we will never experience. Writing usually feeds on dissatisfaction, the way a 'vulture' feeds on carrion. Writing is inspired by inner 'demons', irrational elements, obsessions, while the rational skill of writing is there to harness these conflicting forces. Novelists, especially those Vargas Llosa most admires, aspire to 'totality': they are 'deicides' who turn their back on Creation and erect in its place, the alternative, total creation of a literary work. First and foremost, writers draw on their own lives. They are like striptease artists in reverse, starting out naked and then clothing themselves in such an array of disguises that the autobiographical elements are dispersed. In a later image, he calls a writer a *catoblepas*: a mythical creature quoted in two of his favourite authors, Flaubert and Borges, who feeds on itself, starting with its feet.[35]

This exploration of the rational and the irrational pervades his critical essays: he focuses both on writers' conscious use of literary technique and on their 'demons'. He is interested in what he calls 'the truth of the lies' of fiction, the ways in which great writers create alternative fictional worlds in which the fiction becomes more persuasive than reality itself. As he argues in his analysis of *Mrs Dalloway*, 'What gives a novel its originality – marks its difference from the real world – is the added element that the fantasy and art of the writer provides when he or she transforms objective and historical experience into fiction ... Only failed fictions reproduce reality: successful fictions abolish and transfigure reality.'[36] The writer he mentions most consistently as having a key influence on his own writing, a writer whom he first read with pen and pencil in hand, looking to work out the narrative complexities, was Faulkner. Faulkner, he would observe, wrote in English, but he was one 'of our own', because Faulkner's South was recognisably Latin American, and he could tell his ferocious tales in formally innovative ways.

Georges Bataille also stalks Vargas Llosa's literary analysis: literature's relationship to what Bataille calls Evil (obsessions, frustrations, pain and vice), its communication of essentially negative – *maudit* – experiences and the literary vocation as a quest for sovereignty. For it is through the transgression of different prohibitions that we can assert our own sovereignty. Yet, paraphrasing Bataille, Vargas Llosa argues that unrestrained freedom would undermine the foundations of society: the demons have to be checked for coexistence to be maintained. How, then, to express such desires without destroying society? Literature, in particular erotic literature, can be a site of such Dionysian transgressions. In his 2001 analysis of Conrad's *Heart of Darkness* – an essay that should be read alongside *The Dream of the Celt*, in which Vargas Llosa first mentions that someone should write a great novel about Roger Casement – he states that the novel is an exploration of the roots of humankind, 'those inner recesses of our being which harbour a desire for destructive irrationality that progress and civilisation might manage to assuage but never eradicate completely.'[37]

These recurring images and ideas, however, would be adapted to the writer's developing political views. In the Vargas Llosa of the 1960s, the 'carrion' the writer feeds on is the corrupt capitalist system, and, following this analysis, the transgressive forces of literature are allied to the cause of socialism. Fictions, drawing from the exploitation and blinding inequalities in Latin America, would 'reveal, in a direct or indirect way, through facts, dreams, testimonies, allegories, nightmares or visions, that reality is imperfectly made, that life must change'.[38] By 1974, however, in an essay on *Madame Bovary*, a text that anticipates his monograph, *The Perpetual Orgy: Flaubert and* Madame Bovary (*La orgía perpetua. Flaubert y* Madame Bovary, 1975[39]), he modifies his earlier views about the connections between literature and politics, arguing that while his favourite novels stir up in him anger and other emotions, these emotions are not necessarily conducive to political change. Creative writing remains a rebellion, but here the frame is more broadly existential. Veering away from his earlier opinions, he volunteers the idea that literature can also act as a kind of compensatory fantasy, a way of living out and working through difficulties encountered in real life, or a way of living all the lives that we can only live through fiction, condemned as we are to one solitary existence. He gives the dramatic example of feeling suicidal, when Emma Bovary came to his rescue: her 'fictitious suffering neutralised the suffering that I was experiencing'.[40] The epigraph of his monograph on Flaubert, published the following year, quotes a letter from Flaubert that provides the title for his study: 'the one way of tolerating existence is to lose oneself in literature, as in a perpetual orgy'.[41]

Given the important changes already noted in his aesthetic and political views, we might offer a tentative chronology of these developments in his literary essays, taking as signposts the books he has devoted to single authors. His study on García Márquez ('García Márquez: history of a deicide') offers an incisive, sober and minutely worked analysis of García Márquez's literary techniques, while also exploring his own views about the demonic and the deicidal in contemporary fiction. It is also a high point of optimism in the literary 'Boom', reflecting a belief that literature could gauge and denounce social ills, and that writers were at the forefront of a movement where political and literary vanguards might meld. By the time he approaches Flaubert's *Madame Bovary* in the mid-1970s, as we have seen, this optimism is tempered. Instead, literature can be viewed not just in terms of its formal complexities – and Flaubert is, for Vargas Llosa, the first modern writer in his use of narrative point of view – but also as a way of compensating for the inadequacies of life. Literature might offer a space for manageable and controlled transgression. In the first edition of his book of essays on twentieth-century literature, 'The truth of lies', he makes explicit that literature allows us this limited transgression: it allows us to stare into the abyss, like Gustav von Aschenbach in Thomas Mann's *Death in Venice*:

> An abyss teeming with violence, desires, and horrific, fevered ghosts, which we are not normally aware of except through privileged experiences which occasionally might reveal it, reminding us that, however much we might try to consign it to the shadows and wipe it from our memory, it is an integral part of human nature and remains, with its monsters and seductive sirens, as a permanent challenge to the habits and customs of civilisation.[42]

It is through literature that we can both glimpse and, for a time, live out a total sovereignty which society stifles for the sake of social existence. But of course, it is essential to differentiate between the world of literature and the world of reality, of social order; another feature of literature is that it makes for more subtle readers, who are aware of these fundamental differences. He wrote this essay at the end of a decade in which Sendero Luminoso had been hanging dead dogs on the lampposts of Lima as an obscure condemnation of a supposed Chinese reformist president deviating from a pure Maoism; at a time when he and his wife, Patricia, would go jogging surrounded by security guards, on the lookout for would-be assassins; at a moment when the opposition to his presidency would read out extracts from his recently published erotic novel, *In Praise of the Stepmother* (*Elogio de la madrastra*, 1988[43]). It was, perhaps pressingly important to Vargas Llosa to believe that transgressions were played out in literature alone, and that a literary intelligence like his own could help to create an open, well-ordered society in Peru.

After his defeat in 1990, he found it less easy to believe in the inherent perfectibility of human nature. In his next book of criticism, *La utopía arcaica*,

José María Arguedas y las ficciones del indigenismo ('The archaic utopia: José María Arguedas and the fictions of *indigenismo*') (1996[44]), he focuses on the burdens of writing literature under the pressure of measuring up to political imperatives or cultural expectations. He argues that Arguedas could write splendid novels set in the Andes that gave pride of place to the Peruvian indigenous world – *Deep Rivers* (1958) in particular – but that the pressure of having to reconcile his commitment to some indigenous 'essence' of Peruvian society and to the aims of revolutionary socialism (Vargas Llosa called this an 'archaic utopia') took its toll on some of his writings and Arguedas's own life. In writing about Arguedas in 1996, he was addressing both explicitly and implicitly the role of the 'indigenous' in Peruvian culture, notwithstanding the attacks he received for being purportedly anti-indigenous, and his own election defeat at the hands of a candidate who constantly slurred him for being 'European'. The final part of the study offers a direct attack on Fujimori and his manipulation of the popular/indigenous sectors. Arguedas, and literature itself, Vargas Llosa argued, needed to be rescued from these mired debates.

In Vargas Llosa's 2004 study, *The Temptation of the Impossible: Victor Hugo and* Les Misérables (*La tentación de lo imposible. Victor Hugo y* Los miserables[45]), there is an increasing sense that life can never measure up to the achievements of literature. He offers a revealing study of the narrator in Victor Hugo's work and talks about his deicidal ambitions. But here, 'the temptation of the impossible' is defined as the space of fiction, where readers can live out the 'impossible', sharing lives richer and more intense than those that they are confined to in the 'high security prison that is real life'. Literature is the only space where the impossible can be incorporated into the possible. By contrast, he offers only a cautious optimism about the transformative effects of literature in society and about progress in general. In a statement laced with qualifications, he writes:

> The most minimal conclusion that we can draw is that if human history is advancing, and the word progress has a meaning, and that civilization is not a mere rhetorical fabrication but a reality that is making barbarism retreat, then something of the impetus that has made all this possible must have come – and must still come – from the nostalgia and enthusiasm that we readers feel for the actions of Jean Valjean and Monseigneur Bienvenu, Fantine and Cosette, Marius and Javert, and all who join them on their journey in search of the impossible.[46]

At the very least, literature can be seen as a shared experience, a shared journey.

In his 2008 study, *El viaje a la ficción. El mundo de Juan Carlos Onetti* ('The road to fiction: Juan Carlos Onetti's world'), there is a similar dichotomy. The first chapter, almost a stand-alone essay, extols the place of literature in the development of human civilisation, but the main body of the study on Onetti points in a different direction. Onetti is seen as a supreme craftsman,[47] the first truly modern novelist in Latin America, but his attitude towards literature, and his refuge in literature, is a way of coming to terms with the futility of life. 'For Onetti, writing was not an "escape" but a way of living more intensely, a form of magic that turned failures into triumphs'. The only recompense he could hope for was that his writing allowed him to 'cheat on this awful life'.[48]

However we might map Vargas Llosa's developing ideas on the relationship between literature and life, there is no doubting that his has been a life of passionate engagement with reading and writing about literature: the finely crafted twentieth-century novels, the epic sweep of the great nineteenth-century novels, early romances of chivalry, *Don Quixote*, the development of Latin American fiction, adventure novels from Dumas to Steig Larsson's Millennium trilogy, have all been explored in monographs and articles. Framing further discussion of the writer's work, or of wider issues in society, are the houses he has visited on his constant journeys. Vargas Llosa has called himself a literary fetishist who likes to explore the spaces of writers and painters. A 2010 visit to Russia took him to Tolstoy's house in Yasnaya Polyana and the house where Dostoevsky lived in the final years of his life, and where he wrote *The Brothers Karamazov*.[49] Writers' houses often serve as museums, and Vargas Llosa has had an abiding interest in museums that has developed as he has written increasingly about art in recent years. Museums can have the same function as literary texts, for they are 'dream factories': 'We go to a museum ... to step out of real, pedestrian life and live a sumptuous unreality, to have our fantasises embodied in other people's fantasies.'[50] Museums also have a clear educational value: they are as necessary as schools and hospitals because they can both offer subtle forms of education and also 'cure' societies of prejudice, superstition and ignorance. Museums break down the barriers of provincial mentalities and offer a 'broad, generous, plural' vision of the world, they 'refine sensibilities', 'stimulate the imagination' and help foster critical, and self-critical, ways of thinking.[51]

Vargas Llosa's writings on art also explore both the rational and the irrational, the angels and the demons, in his favourite painters. He has written extensively on the Peruvian Fernando de Szyszlo, and he explores the violent, visceral mysteries of some of his work. He offers a reading of the cover image to this *Companion*, 'Camino a Mendieta 10', as depicting a sacrificial ceremony in which someone bleeds to death in both pain and pleasure, while a strange totemic male figure waits by the primitive, sacrificial altar. Szyszlo's work is seen as a blend of influences – pre-Columbian art, landscapes of Peru, the assimilation of modern Western art, cubism and surrealism – all transformed by its own 'secret heart', where experiences and teachings are fused into his particular vision. Szyszlo thus exemplifies Latin American art and culture: 'An art which, like Latin America, is buried in the night of obliterated civilisations and which rubs shoulders with the newest civilisations from all corners of the globe. It emerges at a place where all these roads intersect, eager, curious, thirsty, free from prejudice, open to all influences.'[52] Vargas Llosa offers a similar definition of Latin American art in his study of the work of the more 'rational' Colombian painter and sculptor, Fernando Botero. Botero is seen as showing a similar attraction to, and rejection of, European models in his original recreation of a Colombian world.[53] Art appreciation has been woven increasingly into the fabric of Vargas Llosa's novels. The essays reveal a constant engagement with painting, from a book-length study of the German expressionist, George Grosz, an exemplary *maudit* artist, to writing about contemporary exhibitions where, in one example among many, he derides the banality of much contemporary erotic art. At an exhibition at the Thyssen-Bornemisza Museum in Madrid in November 2009, he finds himself moving from the pleasure of Antonio Canova's sleeping *Endymion* to Sam Taylor-Wood's video of the dormant football and style icon, David Beckham – *Sleeping Beckham* – which is 'not only an anticlimax but also a dialectical leap from genuine art to frivolous art (or simple nonsense)'.[54] In such essays on contemporary culture written later in the first decade of the twenty-first century, he began to fashion a critique of 'the civilisation of the spectacle', which will be the subject of a future monograph.[55]

Conclusion

In the first chapter of his study of Onetti, entitled 'The road to fiction', Vargas Llosa offers an optimistic reading of the place of literature and storytelling in society, from the time of stories told around the fires of our earliest ancestors. That message would be at the heart of his 2010 Nobel Prize Lecture, entitled, 'In Praise of Reading and Fiction' – as passionate a statement about literature in a world of free market capitalism as his 1967 lecture 'Literature is Fire' was about literature and socialism. For Vargas Llosa, fiction is the 'guardian angel' that travels with us as 'we discover human rights, freedom, and create the sovereign individual'. In the Onetti essay, he encapsulates ideas he has been debating constantly for more than fifty years. We need to remain faithful, he argues, to the ritual of dreaming together, brought together by the words of another dreamer – storyteller, teller of tales, minstrel, troubadour, playwright or novelist – in order to exorcise our fear and escape our frustrations, achieve our hidden desires, avoid old age and conquer death, and live the love, the devotion, the cruelty and the excesses that the angels and demons that we carry with us demand, multiplying our lives in the warmth of the fire that sparks from that other, impalpable, bewitching and essential life that is fiction.[56]

It is our capacity for fiction, Vargas Llosa is saying, that makes us human, and for the Peruvian writer, politics and culture meet on the journey to and through fiction.

NOTES

1. E. Keeley and P. Sherrard (eds.). *Six Poets of Modern Greece*. London: Thames and Hudson, 1960, p. 42.
2. It is interesting, in this respect, to note that the award of the Nobel Prize received plaudits from world leaders as diverse as the King of Spain and Obama's State Department, and reticence from the Cuban and Venezuelan regimes. In the December 2010 issue of the journal, *Foreign Policy*, Vargas Llosa was placed 64 in a list of 'Top One Hundred Global Thinkers', just below the outgoing Chilean president, Michelle Bachelet.
3. Mario Vargas Llosa. 'Günter Grass en la picota'. *El País*, 27 August 2006.
4. Mario Vargas Llosa. 'In Praise of Reading and Fiction'. Nobel Lecture, 7 December 2010. See the Nobel Prize website (http://nobelprize.org/nobel_prizes/literature/laureates/2010/vargas_llosa-lecture_en.html), accessed 2 July 2011. See also Mario Vargas Llosa, *In Praise of Reading and Fiction: The Nobel Lecture*. Trans. Edith Grossman. New York: Farrar, Straus and Giroux, 2011.
5. See the Further reading section in this volume for a full list of titles.
6. Mario Vargas Llosa. *García Márquez. Historia de un deicidio*. Barcelona: Seix Barral, 1971.
7. Mario Vargas Llosa. *La verdad de las mentiras. Ensayos sobre la novela moderna*. Barcelona: Seix Barral, 1990.
8. Vargas Llosa, *La verdad de las mentiras*, 1990, expanded version. Madrid: Aguilar, 2002.
9. Mario Vargas Llosa. *El pez en el agua. Memorias*. Barcelona: Seix Barral, 1993. Further in-line citations refer to *A Fish in the Water: A Memoir*. Trans. Helen Lane. London: Faber and Faber, 1994.
10. Mario Vargas Llosa. 'Catorce minutos de reflexión'. *El País*, 11 October 2010.
11. See Efraín Kristal. *Temptation of the Word: The Novels of Mario Vargas Llosa*. Nashville, Tenn.: Vanderbilt University Press, 1998, pp. 8–11.
12. Vargas Llosa, *A Fish in the Water*, p. 306.
13. Mario Vargas Llosa. *La casa verde*. Barcelona: Seix Barral, 1966.
14. Mario Vargas Llosa. *Making Waves*. Ed. and trans. John King. London: Faber and Faber, 1996, p. 72.
15. 'Letter to Haydée Santamaría', in Vargas Llosa, *Making Waves*, p. 106.
16. Mario Vargas Llosa. 'Un francotirador tranquilo'. *Plural*, 39, December 1974, p. 77.

17. Mario Vargas Llosa. 'Albert Camus y la moral de los límites'. *Plural*, 51, December 1975. English translation in Vargas Llosa, *Making Waves*, pp. 107–16.
18. Vargas Llosa, *Making Waves*, pp. 112, 115.
19. See, for example, articles on Berlin and Popper in Mario Vargas Llosa. *Wellsprings*. Cambridge, Mass.: Harvard University Press, 2008.
20. Vargas Llosa, *Making Waves*, pp. 171–99.
21. Vargas Llosa, *A Fish in the Water*, p. 529.
22. Conscious of corruption in political regimes, he would point out that Pinochet was not just authoritarian, but also deeply corrupt, siphoning tens of millions of dollars into private bank accounts.
23. Mario Vargas Llosa. 'El aire fresco y las moscas'. *El País*, 3 July 2011. For an account of his discussions with students in Shanghai, with whom he talked about the theme of dictatorship in his writing, see 'Vargas Llosa in attack on corrupt, authoritarian rule'. *The Irish Times*, 16 June 2011.
24. Mario Vargas Llosa. *Conversación en La Catedral*. Barcelona: Seix Barral, 1969.
25. Mario Vargas Llosa. 'Payasada con sangre'. In Vargas Llosa. *Sables y utopías. Visiones de América Latina*. Madrid: Aguilar, 2009, p. 239.
26. Ollanta Humala had been anxious to realign himself as a centrist politician many months before the election. On 18 December 2010, he made a statement, published in different newspapers, that Vargas Llosa thought that he was 'maturing as a politician'. For Vargas Llosa's account of this presidential campaign, in which he sets out the measures that he hopes Humala will follow as president, see, 'La derrota del fascismo'. *El País*, 19 June 2011.
27. Mario Vargas Llosa. 'Nationalism and Utopia'. In Vargas Llosa. *Touchstones. Essays on Literature, Art and Politics*. Selected, ed. and trans. John King. London: Faber and Faber, 2007, pp. 219–44. (First published as 'El nacionalismo y la utopía'. *El País*, 2 June 1991.)
28. Mario Vargas Llosa. 'Three Character Sketches'. Trans. Romy Sutherland with John King. *Granta*, 100, winter 2007, p. 83.
29. Mario Vargas Llosa. *El paraíso en la otra esquina*. Madrid: Alfaguara, 2003.
30. Mario Vargas Llosa. *El sueño del celta*. Madrid: Alfaguara, 2010.
31. Mario Vargas Llosa. *Diario de Irak*. Madrid: Aguilar, 2003.
32. 'Iraq diary', in Vargas Llosa, *Touchstones*, pp. 313–14.
33. Mario Vargas Llosa. *La fiesta del Chivo*. Madrid: Alfaguara, 2000.
34. Mario Vargas Llosa. *Israel/Palestina. Paz o guerra santa*. Madrid: Aguilar, 2006, pp. 107–8.
35. Mario Vargas Llosa. *Cartas a un joven novelista*. Barcelona: Planeta, 1997. Further in-line citations refer to *Letters to a Young Novelist*. New York: Farrar, Straus and Giroux, 2002, pp. 16–17.
36. Vargas Llosa, *Touchstones*, pp. 51–2.
37. Ibid., p. 37.
38. Mario Vargas Llosa. 'Literature is Fire' (lecture given in 1967). In Vargas Llosa, *Making Waves*, p. 73.
39. Mario Vargas Llosa. *La orgía perpetua. Flaubert y Madame Bovary*. Barcelona: Seix Barral, 1975. Further in-line citations refer to *The Perpetual Orgy: Flaubert and Madame Bovary*. Trans. Helen Lane. New York: Farrar, Straus and Giroux, 1986.

40. Mario Vargas Llosa. 'Una pasión no correspondida'. *Plural*, 37, October 1974, p. 37.

41. *The Perpetual Orgy*, unnumbered title page.

42. This essay, dated September 1988, was first published in Vargas Llosa, *La verdad de las mentiras*. The English translation is in Vargas Llosa, *Touchstones*, p. 49.

43. Mario Vargas Llosa. *Elogio de la madrastra*. Barcelona: Tusquets, 1988.

44. Mario Vargas Llosa. *La utopía arcaica. José María Arguedas y las ficciones del indigenismo*. Mexico City: Fondo de Cultura Económica, 1996.

45. Mario Vargas Llosa. *La tentación de lo imposible. Víctor Hugo y* Los miserables. Madrid: Alfaguara, 2004. Further in-line citations refer to *The Temptation of the Impossible: Victor Hugo and* Les Misérables. Trans. John King. Princeton and Oxford: Princeton University Press, 2007.

46. Vargas Llosa, *The Temptation of the Impossible*, p. 177.

47. Mario Vargas Llosa. *El viaje a la ficción. El mundo de Juan Carlos Onetti*. Madrid: Alfaguara, 2008, p. 226.

48. Ibid. (Translation John King.)

49. In a case of life imitating art, the Peruvian Minister of Culture, Juan Ossio, declared on 20 November 2010 that Mario Vargas Llosa's birthplace in Arequipa would be turned into a museum, based on the Tolstoy house.

50. Vargas Llosa, *Touchstones*, p. 154.

51. Mario Vargas Llosa. 'El Perú no necesita museos'. *El País*, 8 March 2009.

52. Mario Vargas Llosa. 'Szyszlo in the Labyrinth'. In Vargas Llosa, *Making Waves*, p. 270.

53. Mario Vargas Llosa. 'Botero: A Sumptuous Abundance'. In Vargas Llosa, *Making Waves*, pp. 254–67.

54. Mario Vargas Llosa. 'La desaparición del erotismo'. *El País*, 1 November 2009.

55. In 2011, Vargas Llosa was preparing a book-length essay entitled *La civilización del espectaculo* ('The civilisation of the spectacle').

56. Vargas Llosa, *El viaje a la ficción*, p. 31.

Notes for a course on the Latin American novel taught in English at Columbia University (October 1975–January 1976). The notebook with the notes is held at the Mario Vargas Llosa Archive (Notebook B-1, Box 1, Folder 8), Manuscripts Division, Princeton University Library.

1) THE PROTO-NOVEL : a) THE CHRONICLES
                     b) THE BOOKS of TRAVELLERS
                     c) THE BOOKS OF RELIGION, ETC...
                     (MIRACLES, LIFE OF SAINTS, ...)

2) THE BEGUINNINGS :

A) THE IMITATIVE PERIOD =
       THE EUROPEAN MODEL = The first novels
describe what the novelists read, not the life
and reality of latin american countries.
              They imitated not only the themes, matters,
but also the language and techniques of the
european novel (spanish sometime, but principally french)
       "MARIA" by JORGE ISAAES
       (ATALA de CHATEAUBRIAND)

B) A POOR, MEDIOCRE GENRE (SECOND RATE)
   DIFFERENCES WITH POETRY AND ESSAY
       LACK OF ORIGINALITY
       POORNESS OF IMAGINATION

THE BEST NARRATORS ARE THE ESSAYISTS =

More powerful, inspiring in { DIALOGUES
PLOT
CARACTERS
DESCRIPTIONS

Works originally written as works of history or
sociologie,
that can be read now as novels.
"FACUNDO", by SARMIENTO, and
1) ⟹ ["OS SERTOES", by EUCLIDES DA CUNHA]

C) THE FOLKLORISTIC PERIOD
A) reaction against the imitaters
b) Discovery of the OWN REALITY { NATURAL = geografhy

SOCIALLY = INJUNTICE

c) SOCIAL CONCIOUSNESS = DENONCIATION OF
LATIFUNDIA, TIRANY, IMPERIALISM, ECONOMICAL
EXPLOITATION OF PEASANTS, RACIALISM, ETS

IT is MOST IMPORTANT AS HISTORICAL, SOCIOLOGICAL
AND POLITICALLY DOCUMENTS THAN AS ESTHETICAL
ACHIEVEMENT

SOME EXAMPLES

1) "AVES SIN NIDO" (Clorinda Matto de Turner)
   "HUASIPUNGO" (Jorge Icaza)
   "LA VORAGINE" (Eustacio Rivera)
   "DOÑA BARBARA" (Romulo Gallegos)
   "LOS DE ABAJO" (MARIANO AZUELA)
   "DON SEGUNDO SOMBRA" (GUIRALDES)
   → "EL SEÑOR PRESIDENTE" (MIGUEL ANGEL ASTURIAS)

3) THE COMING OF AGE (Novel of Creation)

1) A GREAT DIVERSITY AND VARIETY = Now it is impossible to reunite all the novels that are been written in one current or tendence because there are many currents, a great diversity of styles, techniques and subjets or themes.

2) THE DIFFERENCES ARE NOT NATIONAL, BUT CROSS THE COUNTRIES
   INSIDE ONE COUNTRY COEXISTENT MANY FORMS AND KINDS OF NARRATORS AND NOVELISTS (ARGUEDAS AND RULFO, for INSTANCE)
A) A REALISTIC LITERATURE (THE SAME PROBLEMS THAN THE INDIGENIST NOVEL)

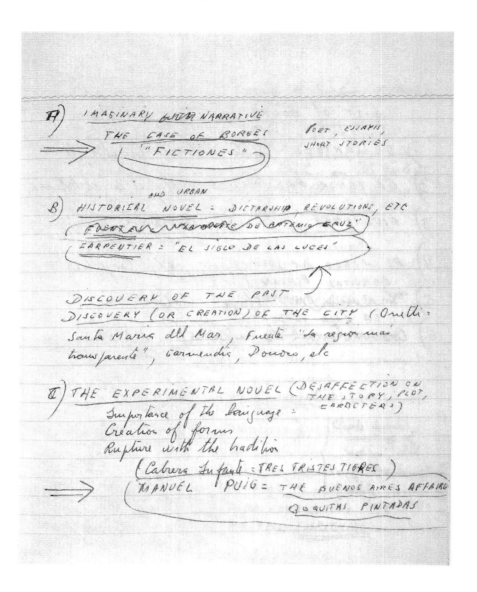

A) IMAGINARY ~~AND THE~~ NARRATIVE
    THE CASE OF BORGES   POET, ESSAYIS,
        "FICTIONES"   SHORT STORIES

                AND URBAN
B) HISTORICAL NOVEL = DICTARSHIP REVOLUTIONS, ETC
    FUENTES ~~IXBA~~ ~~MUERTE~~ DE ARTEMIO CRUZ"
    CARPENTIER = "EL SIGLO DE LAS LUCES"

DISCOVERY OF THE PAST
DISCOVERY (OR CREATION) OF THE CITY (Onetti =
Santa Maria del Mar, Fuente "La región más
transparente", Garmendia, Donoso, etc

C) THE EXPERIMENTAL NOVEL (DESAFFECTION ON
        Importance of the language =   THE STORY, PLOT,
    Creation of forms   CARACTERS)
    Rupture with the tradition
        (Cabrera Infante = TRES TRISTES TIGRES)
        (MANUEL PUIG = THE BUENOS AIRES AFFAIRG
                        BOQUITAS PINTADAS

LIST of BOOKS

1) OS SERTOES   de Euclides da Cunha

2) EL SEÑOR PRESIDENTE , Miguel Angel Asturias

3) FICCIONES ,   Jorge Luis Borges

4) EL SIGLO DE LAS LUCES , y Ejo Carpentier
   BOQUITAS PINTADAS

5) ~~The Buenos Aires Affair~~ , Manuel Puis
   LA CASA VERDE
6) ~~Conversation with the Cathedral~~ " MVLL

12

KELLY AUSTIN

The memoir

A Fish in the Water

The drafts of *A Fish in the Water* (*El pez en el agua*[1]) in the Mario Vargas Llosa Papers at Princeton University Library bear witness to a creative, literary process in the work of autobiography: organising a life into language and genre. The preliminary drafts catalogued as 'First Draft Version A' and 'First Draft Version B' (over 200 pages each) closely follow Vargas Llosa's run for the Peruvian presidency, which he lost to Alberto Fujimori in 1990. Between his 'Second Draft', with the indication that it was completed in November 1991, during his residency at an institute for advanced studies in Berlin, and the completed book, with the indication that it was completed at Princeton in February 1993, he had composed at least four other drafts.[2] The final version alternates between two kinds of chapters. The even chapters, closely related to the content of original drafts, amount to a political memoir of his failed political campaign. The odd chapters are a coming-of-age autobiography that chronicles Vargas Llosa's formative years, while the political chapters shed light on the private story of an individual who became a political figure. The coming-of-age narrative evokes aspects of the *Bildungsroman*. The pattern of alternating chapters resembles Vargas Llosa's most recurrent literary technique from *Aunt Julia and the Scriptwriter* (*La tía Julia y el escribidor*, 1977[3]) until *The Dream of the Celt* (*El sueño del celta*, 2010[4]), in which he alternates narratives that correspond to different periods in the lives of his characters, or to different literary registers. In short, there was a considerable amount of literary thinking brought to bear in the gestation of this book.

The counterpointing of Vargas Llosa's formative years with his political campaign is far from disparate or arbitrary. The juxtaposition of registers of the formative novel and the political memoir, corresponding to two distinct moments in Vargas Llosa's life (his adolescent years and his political campaign), produces certain literary delights, not least of which is the creation of apparent dissimilarity, only to suggest a concomitant symmetry, even unity. As Roy Boland points out:

to give coherence to the book, Vargas Llosa takes advantage of one of his favourite novelistic techniques: the 'communicating vessels', consisting in telling two apparently disparate episodes or scenes within a single narrative. If *A Fish in the Water* were submitted to the type of analysis that is normally applied to his novels, one would arrive at the conclusion that the two plots – the personal and the political – develop symmetrically. The creative progression can be explained thus: the memory or memoir of the writer is transformed into a mirror that, on reflecting two fragments of his life separated by time and space, links or grounds them in a surprising way. As a result, throughout the narrative there is a constant counterpoint between the two stories and histories.[5]

Boland identifies the rub of reading *A Fish in the Water*. First, he suggests that only 'if' we read it with the literary analysis that we might apply to his novels do we come to the resulting aesthetic understanding of the juxtaposition of the chapters. And he intimates that this reading leads us to the perhaps necessary, but paradoxical, conundrum of reading the memoir and memory (in Spanish the word '*memoria*' is used for both) in an unorthodox fashion that places the reader at a crossroads between history and storytelling (in Spanish the word '*historia*' is used for both). It is my contention that the resulting text produces a series of what Vargas Llosa himself has called *cajas chinas* ('Chinese boxes'), a literary technique in which stories serve as containers for other stories. In the case of *A Fish in the Water*, the procedure can fascinate as much as it can frustrate: it self-consciously raises and manipulates the reader's awareness of the mutability and, at the exact same moment, the persistence of genre expectations. The narrative accounts for the process whereby a storyteller gains the raw material for the narrative of a life, which at times feeds into his novels, and which ultimately turns its back on life and towards storytelling. Finally, in concert with these processes, Vargas Llosa reasserts his vision, according to which both creative writing and the telling of an individual's life can have a positive impact in the political arena and on ethical relations, among individuals and the community at large. His biography confronts, frustrates and faces up to the authority of fanaticism and dogmatism and, above all, their totalitarian and dictatorial expressions.

As Vargas Llosa fashions his memoir, he is ever mindful to forefront that this reconstruction of memory is both enabled and plagued by the power of its form, by writing itself. He pieces together a less than comprehensive collection of accounts of his life, whose fidelity to both truth and genre expectations (autobiography and campaign memoir) leads both writer and reader on a circuitous journey that ends not merely with a return to writing, but to a homecoming of sorts, where home is writing, specifically writing as Vargas Llosa's own (political) self-fashioning. As Vargas Llosa intimates in *A Fish in the Water* (p. 388):

I have used many of my memories of Radio Panamericana in my novel, *Aunt Julia and the Scriptwriter*, where they are jumbled together with other memories and flights of fancy. Today I have doubts about what separates one sort from another, and it is possible that certain invented ones have crept in among the true ones here, but I suppose that too may go by the name of autobiography.

While Vargas Llosa talks of his 'use' of memories in the aesthetic construction of this novel (and others), he also points to his equal 'use' of 'flights of fancy' ('*fantasía*') in the fashioning of autobiography. The implication of memory is that the stories it harbours of life may sometimes be true, invented or both. All may go by the name of autobiography. For Vargas Llosa, memory – as it is written, recollected and ultimately called autobiography – is premised on a profound, human fallibility in its relation to truths that, in turn, come face to face with his ethical admission of 'doubts'.

Vargas Llosa tackles the criticism that the inventions in his autobiography are misleading. He maintains in *A Fish in the Water* that he was 'fascinated by novelistic technique' in the service of a 'work's verisimilitude', suggesting that poetic licence is not an obstacle to the kernel of autobiographical truth (p. 340). And yet it has sometimes taken him aback when the 'verisimilitude' of his novels based on his own autobiography have led some individuals he transformed into fictional characters to assume he was offering a picture that was true to life, as in a conventional autobiography. In his memoir (*A Fish in the Water*, pp. 335–6), he recalls the reaction of Ernesto Vargas, his own father, to *Aunt Julia and the Scriptwriter* along these lines:

> (It was a quarrel we had without seeing each other and without exchanging a single word, when we were thousands of kilometres apart, about *Aunt Julia and the Scriptwriter*, a novel in which there are autobiographical episodes in which the father of the narrator is shown acting in much the way mine did when I married Julia. Months after the book came out I was surprised to receive a curious letter from him – I was living in Cambridge, England – in which he thanked me for acknowledging in that novel that he had been severe with me but that when all was said and done he had acted as he did for my own good 'since he had always loved me.' I didn't answer his letter. I received another card from him, a violent one this time, accusing me of being resentful and of slandering him in a book, without giving him a chance to defend himself, reproaching me for not being a believer and prophesying divine punishment for me. He warned me that he would circulate this letter among my acquaintances. And as a matter of fact, in the months and years that followed, I found out that he had sent dozens and perhaps hundreds of copies of it to relatives, friends, and acquaintances of mine in Peru.)

The personal quarrel between father and son is not contingent on a literary interpretation of a novel, but on the premise that in a novel Vargas Llosa is making overt claims about an individual, which can justify value judgements of merit or blame.

At another level it is instructive to juxtapose the claims of the memoir and some literary assumptions that had informed Vargas Llosa's novels. In *Temptation of the Word: The Novels of Vargas Llosa*, Efraín Kristal discusses *Aunt Julia and the Scriptwriter* as a turning point in the novelist's literary career. It is the first novel in which Vargas Llosa examines 'the fanatic of unbending convictions', a turn that may have been brought about in part because he 'was forced to reconsider his position within the Latin American Left because he had been repudiated by the Cuban government and by many of his former leftist friends who considered him a counterrevolutionary for his role in the Padilla case'.[6] When Vargas Llosa was a committed socialist, he thought that the kind of intellectual freedom he espoused for a creative writer was consistent with the political ends of the Cuban Revolution; when he realised that the two propositions were not compatible, he turned away from socialism, and began to brand a number of leftist politicians and intellectuals as fanatics. This turn informs his literature, and it also informs his political views in the memoir. It is worth noting, however, that the narrative strategy in the memoir (alternating between his formative years and his political campaign) results in the circumvention of the period in his life in which he was personally committed to causes which later, in the 1980s, he would consider to embody fanaticism.

From the perspective of Vargas Llosa's own political turn, it is worth revisiting his father's response to the memoir. Ernesto Vargas became venomous about what he considers to be slander against him, but he was even more insistent regarding what might be perceived as a patriarchal duty to defend Julia Urquidi Illanes, Vargas Llosa's first wife. A letter he wrote is worth citing, not for its simple corroboration of Vargas Llosa's assertions, but for its insistence on a freedom of speech distinct from that of Vargas Llosa. It is ironic that just as Vargas Llosa was moving away from the left, his father should admonish him from the perspective of a conservative living in the United States, a country Vargas Llosa had considered to be an obstacle to the liberation of Latin America in his socialist period:

> I live in a country that has taught me to respect the rights of others, to speak and write, although my 'Conservative' ideas don't overlap with your way of expressing certain things, that with your talent – by my way of understanding – can gild them without stressing the vulgarity as you do, especially, in relation to a woman who was a good companion in your life as well as being your wife. But, I don't understand the present-day transformation we are undergoing. As the 'conservative' I am, I am horrified to think that my grandchildren (your children) will read 'Aunt Julia' when they are older and I don't know how they will

judge you, reading about the crazy things you did as an irresponsible 18 year old. But don't pay attention to me, since I'm a 'conservative' my astonishment is very natural and, besides, it's your business, not mine. You know what you're doing.[7]

In his letter, Ernesto Vargas makes a connection between his own adherence to the United States and to conservative family values against his perception that his son's leftist convictions are consistent with his penchant for indiscretion in family matters. His only concession is to his son's literary talent, but his praise for Vargas Llosa's ability to write well is brought to bear as proof of his ability to deceive. Ernesto Vargas may be naive about the fictional contract, but his criticism of his son is premised on a writer's ability to mislead. At this level, Vargas Llosa's father is actually offering a challenge worth considering.

A careful reader of *A Fish in the Water* is ever-mindful that Vargas Llosa has been making choices about what to include and what to exclude from his memoir, and that he is also making choices about how to present what he does include. Vargas Llosa creates what amounts to an aesthetic of pluralism that invites judgement from multiple horizons, at times irreconcilable: literary, historical, autobiographical, political, and so on. In this context, Ernesto Vargas's letter is just one of several embedded texts in the book that serve to destabilise any naive assumptions that Vargas Llosa's truth claims are categorical, since Vargas Llosa was convinced that categorical claims to truth are the basis of fanaticism and dogmatism. In the memoir, Vargas Llosa reorients the reader's attention to writing and to its necessity for the ethical health of politics, opening the door to readings that become sensitive to the tenuous lines between truth, fiction and history. Thus he illustrates the dangers of uncritical belief in dogma.

In his own practice as a literary critic, Vargas Llosa has insisted on the benefits of investigating the biography of writers to gain insights into their creative process, and into the gestation of specific works of literature:

If [a critic's] intention is to show the mechanism of the birth of a work of fiction, the process of a man beginning one day to dialectically transform certain experiences – personal, historical and cultural – in the composition of his fictional world: how could he avoid the biography of the author?[8]

As a literary critic, Vargas Llosa is interested in biography as a starting point to understand the transformations of experiences into literature; and in the move from life to fantasy, he is aligning himself with a Hispanic tradition that harks back to Cervantes. Cervantes is also a recurrent presence in *A Fish in the Water*. In fact, *Don Quixote* is one of the key embedded texts in the memoir, one that calls our attention to the potential transformation of life through an exposure to tales. For instance, Cervantes' protagonist is the referent for his recollection of the drunken diversions of Norwin, a Nicaraguan literary savant living, studying and working in Lima:

> Norwin was young, skinny, an inveterate bohemian, generous, a tireless, lecherous whoremaster and beer drinker. After the third or fourth glass he would begin to recite the first chapter of the *Quixote*, which he knew by heart. His eyes would fill with tears: 'What great prose, damn it all!'[9]

Vargas Llosa frames his allusion to the most famous Hispanic literary exemplar of the problematic relations between authors, texts and truth to explain his decision to reject the bohemian life of newspaper journalists with quixotic literary aspirations, and his decision to move to Piura to live with his Uncle Lucho in order to begin a more ordered approach to his literary vocation. The allusions to *Don Quixote* are followed by allusions to a book the young Vargas Llosa reads in his uncle's library, Jan Valtin's memoir *Out of the Night*.[10] A one-time German communist who worked as a double-spy for the Soviet Union and Nazi Germany, Valtin finally settled in the United States, notwithstanding having been imprisoned in San Quentin Penitentiary as a Soviet spy. Though Vargas Llosa suffered none of the dangers or hardships endured by Valtin, who was tortured, kidnapped and imprisoned, and whose wife was killed by the Gestapo as punishment for his ties with communism while serving as a Nazi spy, it is still possible to read *Out of the Night* as another metatextual model for *A Fish in the Water*. Both memoirs explore the ethical conundrums that ensue when a novelist committed to the left, and to the creation of ideal communities, experiences the tensions between the dogmatic adherence to political causes and individual freedom:

> Among Uncle Lucho's books, I found an autobiography, published by Diana, a Mexico City publishing house, that kept me awake for many nights and gave me a violent political jolt: *Out of the Night*, by Jan Valtin.[11]

Given that Vargas Llosa did not officially move away from the left until the 1970s, the true 'violent political jolt' that this book produced in the young Vargas Llosa might be a retrospective projection that serves to underwrite his political turn away from the left many years later. But there is another reason why Valtin's book is particularly relevant to the concerns of Vargas Llosa many years after he read it in his uncle's home: it also raises the dilemmas of a man with literary inclinations who must make choices between his political commitments and his growing sense that the freedom of a writer is incompatible with political dogma. In a key passage of the memoir, Valtin's lover is unable to persuade him to give up his political commitments to become a novelist:

'Go on writing,' she urged. 'In this way we will win freedom.'

'Freedom from what?'

'From people who hold you in their hands like a pawn.'

'Listen,' I objected. 'I belong to the Comintern.'

'You belong to yourself – and to me!'

'I cannot do it. I believe that loyalty to a chosen cause is the greatest thing in a man's life.'

Firelei came close to me. She murmured endearments. 'Let us be ourselves,' she said. 'We need not be dependent. We are fit enough to shape our own destiny. We need not rummage in secrecy and ugliness.'[12]

In this overwrought exchange, we see dramatised the conflict between Valtin's freely chosen loyalty to the party and Firelei's vision of freedom achieved through individual artistic acts. Firelei sacrifices her artistic propensities to share Valtin's commitment to the German communist party, but the autobiography reveals Valtin's disenchantment with totalitarian regimes after his intense commitment to communism.

Echoes of Firelei's voice come to represent a political, ethical and artistic trope of doubt that Patricia Llosa, Vargas Llosa's wife, voices in *A Fish in the Water*. Patricia Llosa not only represents the voice that beckons to Vargas Llosa with reminders that he is a writer, but also represents the knowledge that the adventure of politics remained irresistible:

Whenever I've been asked why I was ready to give up my vocation as a writer and enter politics I've answered: 'For a moral reason. Because circumstances placed me in a position of leadership at a critical moment in the life of my country.' But someone who knows me as well as I know myself, or perhaps even better, Patricia, doesn't see it that way. 'The moral obligation wasn't the decisive factor,' she says. 'It was the adventure, the illusion of living an experience full of excitement and risk. Of writing the great novel in real life.'[13]

Vargas Llosa's staging of this conversation with his wife amounts to a revision of the 'violent political jolt' he felt when he read Valtin in the light of his own political experiences. Vargas Llosa remembers his admiration for a man with literary talent who was willing to sacrifice his life for a political cause, and who lived a life of extraordinary adventure:

Its author had been a German Communist, in the Nazi era, and his autobiography, full of episodes of revolution, and of hideous abuses was, to me, a detonating device, something that for the first time gave me pause and made me think about justice, political action, revolution. Although, at the end of the book, Valtin severely criticised the Communist Party, which sacrificed his wife and dealt with him in the most cynical way, I remember having finished the book feeling great admiration for those lay saints who, despite the risk of being tortured, decapitated, or condemned to spend the rest of their lives in the underground cells of the Nazis, dedicated their lives to fighting for socialism.[14]

In his essay, 'The truth of lies' (*La verdad de las mentiras*, 1990[15]), Vargas Llosa argues that narrative fiction is particularly suited to offering readers the possibility of experiencing lives that are richer and more exciting than the ones they are fated to live. Valtin's is an instance of a life that rivals those of a work of fiction. In his literary essays, and in his recent Nobel Prize speech, Vargas Llosa has also argued that there is a contradiction between totalitarian regimes, and the freedom inherent to uncensored creativity. Vargas Llosa's identification with the selflessness of a man who lived a life of adventures to advance communist causes becomes, in *A Fish in the Water*, a projection of his own views about literature onto autobiography; it also ends up complicating Firelei's exhortation to Valtin to pursue his literary career. By writing – 'To go out of oneself, to be another, in however illusory a fashion, is a way of becoming less of a slave and experiencing the risks of freedom' – Vargas Llosa transforms the naive freedom proposed by Firelei.[16] The paradoxes and contradictions in Vargas Llosa's analysis are intractable: in his commitment to communism, Valtin leads the kind of life that is akin to the works of fiction that, according to Vargas Llosa, threaten the stability of totalitarian regimes; and his identification with Valtin as an adventurer is at odds with the banalities of real-life politics for which works of fiction are intended to be a compensation.

Vargas Llosa's response to Patricia's concerns reveals an awareness of his possible susceptibility to the temptations of adventure, one he associates with a risk that the individual imaginative process of writing and, thus, living many lives, *might* overshadow true care for others:

> If the decadence, the impoverishment, the terrorism, and the multiple crises of Peruvian society had not made it an almost impossible challenge to govern such a country, it would never have entered my head to accept such a task. I have always believed that writing novels has been, in my case, a way of living the many lives – the many adventures – that I would like to have had myself and therefore I can't discard the possibility that, in those dark depths where the most secret motivations of our acts are plotted, it was the temptation of adventure, rather than some sort of altruism, that induced me to enter professional politics.[17]

Vargas Llosa's rhetoric lays bare the temptation to action as a literary temptation when he suggests a blurring of the lines between life and literature, and to explain his own case, he points to 'those dark depths where the most secret motivations of our acts are plotted'.

To be sure, a similar elision occurs when he links his charmed year with Uncle Lucho, his books and his expulsion from school after the 'strike' organised at San Miguel. In this, the third mention of *Out of the Night*, Vargas Llosa gives a literary emphasis to the word 'protagonist' when he says, 'I felt like the protagonist of *Out of the Night* after he had survived the Nazis' prisons', to express the way that, for him, becoming a protagonist in history felt like becoming the protagonist of an autobiography.[18] He suggests the powers of imaginative memory's presence in the here and now to create autobiography, just as elsewhere he likens the ways that his memories of the personal experiences that inspired the realistic chapters of *Aunt Julia* weave with fictions, fantasies and truths in a way that cannot but amount to recollections fraught with fantasy; and this too, as he had conceded, 'may go by the name of autobiography'.

Vargas Llosa's play with the literary, even fictional, potential of Valtin's autobiography is not meant, I believe, to fly in the face of the personal or historical truths of Valtin's commitment to social justice, or his morally ambiguous experiences with the Nazi Gestapo or Stalin's Russia, but to point to what Vargas Llosa sees in 'The truth of lies' as an ethical betrayal of human desires in totalitarian applications:

> When a state, in its desire to control and decide everything, wrests from human beings the right to invent and believe whatever lies they please, appropriates this right and exercises it through historians and censors, a great neuralgic centre of social life is abolished. And men and women suffer a loss that impoverishes their existence, even when their basic needs are satisfied. Because real life, true life, has never been, nor will ever be, sufficient to fulfil human desires. And because, without this vital dissatisfaction that the lies of fiction both incite and assuage, there is never authentic progress.[19]

Dwelling on Valtin's book is no idle distraction for Vargas Llosa. It figures as a marker of one of the reasons why he chose to let the form of his *Fish in the Water* change course midstream, to swerve from 'real life, true life' towards 'fantasy, a demonic gift [that] is continually opening up a gulf between what we are and what we would like to be, between what we have and what we desire', in order to arrive, via invention, at its published shape of chapters, alternating between the story of the fundamental formations of a young man (interweaving the biographical foundations and means for his early novels) and that of the trials and tribulations of a mature man in the maelstrom of a presidential candidacy in the 1990 Peruvian elections.[20]

In the first English version of what was to become the book, published by the journal *Granta*, he called his political campaign 'A Fish out of Water'.[21] In the first drafts that included the alternating chapters, he had called the sections of his youth in which he develops his literary vocation 'A Fish in the Water', and the sections devoted to the political campaign 'A Fish out of Water'. When he eliminated the subheadings and called the whole book *A Fish in the Water*, it is clear that literature has trumped strict autobiography. For, in the final version, each of the alternating chapters ends with a flight towards literature in one way or another. First, Vargas Llosa describes his departure to study in Spain, owing to a scholarship that precipitated his extended stay in Europe on the heels of the eventful months of 1958, imagining and believing, as he sat next to Julia and waved goodbye to Uncle Lucho, that 'I was sure that I would at last be a writer'.[22] He then masterfully repeats the structure of the scene (with the determination of recurrence) as the final paragraph of his political adventure:

> But only a very small group of friends of Libertad and of Solidarity found out the hour of our departure and came to the plane in which Patricia and I were embarking for Europe, on the morning of June 13, 1990. When the plane took off and the infallible clouds of Lima blotted the city from sight and we were surrounded only by blue sky, the thought crossed my mind that this departure resembled the one in 1958, which had so clearly marked the end of one stage of my life and the beginning of another, in which literature came to occupy the central place.[23]

From his revised drafts now conserved at the Princeton University Library, it is clear that he crafted an autobiography that ultimately aimed its ends towards literature. There are telling amendments and deletions in the drafts that make this clear. Even as his masterful writing glosses over gaps, such as the erasure of the telling years when he was committed to causes for which his political campaign was intended to be an alternative, Vargas Llosa's temptation is to direct his voice as an incontrovertible telling, coming face to face with his commitment to writing, freedom and the freedom in writing.

NOTES

1. Mario Vargas Llosa. *El pez en el agua. Memorias*. Barcelona: Seix Barral, 1993. Mario Vargas Llosa. *A Fish in the Water: A Memoir*. Trans. Helen Lane. New York: Farrar, Straus and Giroux, 1994.
2. Mario Vargas Llosa Papers C0641, 1944–1999, bulk 1958–1995, Series VII: Additional Papers boxes, AM 1997–30, Manuscripts Division, Department of Rare Books and Special Collections, Princeton University Library.
3. Mario Vargas Llosa. *La tía Julia y el escribidor*. Barcelona: Seix Barral, 1977.
4. Mario Vargas Llosa. *El sueño del celta*. Madrid: Alfaguara, 2010.
5. Roy C. Boland. *Una rara comedia. Visión y revisión de las novelas de Mario Vargas Llosa*. New Mexico: Research University Press, 2003, p. 6. (Translation Kelly Austin.)

6. Efraín Kristal. *Temptation of the Word: The Novels of Mario Vargas Llosa*, Nashville, Tenn.: Vanderbilt University Press, 1998, pp. 98, 100.

7. Ernesto J. Vargas, 1978. Mario Vargas Llosa Papers, Box 31, Folder 5, Manuscripts Division, Department of Rare Books and Special Collections, Princeton University Library. (Translation Kelly Austin.)

8. Mario Vargas Llosa. 'Resurrección de Belcebú o la disidencia creadora'. *Contra viento y marea*. Vol. I (1962–72). Barcelona: Seix Barral, 1986, p. 279. (Translation Kelly Austin.)

9. Vargas Llosa, *A Fish in the Water*, p. 142.

10. Jan Valtin. *Out of the Night*. New York: Alliance Book Corporation, 1941.

11. Vargas Llosa, *A Fish in the Water*, p. 183.

12. Valtin, *Out of the Night*, pp. 219–21.

13. Vargas Llosa, *A Fish in the Water*, p. 41.

14. Ibid., pp. 183–4.

15. Mario Vargas Llosa. *La verdad de las mentiras. Ensayos sobre la novela moderna*. Barcelona: Seix Barral, 1990.

16. Mario Vargas Llosa. *Making Waves*. Ed. and trans. John King. New York: Farrar, Straus and Giroux, 1996, p. 325.

17. Vargas Llosa, *A Fish in the Water*, pp. 41–2.

18. 'Me sentí el protagonista de *La noche quedó atrás* luego de sobrevivir a las cárceles nazis.' Vargas Llosa, *El pez en el agua*, p. 225. (Translation Kelly Austin.)

19. Vargas Llosa, *Making Waves*, p. 329.

20. Ibid., p. 329.

21. Mario Vargas Llosa. 'A Fish out of Water'. *Granta*, 36, summer 1991, pp. 15–76.

22. Vargas Llosa, *A Fish in the Water*, p. 467.

23. Ibid., p. 523.

13

EVELYN FISHBURN

The plays

An overview

It is not widely known that Mario Vargas Llosa's literary career began with the theatre, a genre to which he is returning with increasing enthusiasm. As he has often stated in interview, 'the theatre was my first love', a love described picturesquely as 'an ascesis, a slimming cure'.[1]

'La huida del Inca' ('The flight of the Inca'), a play in three acts, prologue and epilogue written at the age of 15 when still at school, marked his debut as a writer. It placed second in a national competition for schools run by the Ministry of Education, and was performed to great acclaim on 17 July 1952 in the Teatro Variedades in Piura, even being reviewed in the local press. It was never subsequently published.[2]

Apart from this teenage effort, Vargas Llosa has published eight plays: *The Young Lady from Tacna* (*La señorita de Tacna*, 1981), *Kathie and the Hippopotamus* (*Kathie y el hipopótamo*, 1983), *La Chunga* (*La Chunga*, 1986), *El loco de los balcones* ('The madman of the balconies') (1993), *Ojos bonitos, cuadros feos* ('Pretty eyes, ugly paintings') (1996), *Odiseo y Penélope* ('Odysseus and Penelope') (2007), *Al pie del Támesis* ('On the banks of the Thames') (2008) and *Las mil noches y una noche* ('The thousand nights and one night') (2009).[3]

A common thread, the interplay between reality and fiction, runs through them, as Vargas Llosa himself has mentioned in the prologue to 'On the banks of the Thames':

> In all of my plays I have been fascinated by the connections between life and fiction, by the role that the latter plays in the former, the ways in which one of them feeds on the other, the way in which the two can be confused, the ways in which one can reject the other, or the ways in which the two complement each other in the life of any individual.[4]

In Vargas Llosa's plays, fiction often inserts itself into a reality that is always found wanting, being too sordid, too petty, too frustrating. The first three plays form a cluster in their preoccupation with how and why stories come into being. In the words of the author: 'I never suspected that under this pretext I was in fact attempting to tell the story of that . . . process through which stories themselves come into being.'[5] Several of the plays ('Pretty eyes, ugly paintings', 'On the Bank of the Thames' and 'The madman of the balconies'), still dealing with the interplay between fiction and reality, show a greater involvement with topical concerns in Lima. It may be worth noting that 'The madman of the balconies' could be read as ironic self-parody: it was written at the time of Vargas Llosa's presidential campaign, and the protagonist of the play undertakes a selfless Quixotic project on behalf of his nation.

Most of his plays have already been translated into various languages, and all have been performed in various parts of the globe.[6] The critical attention to Vargas Llosa's plays, while not comparable to that of his fiction, has been growing steadily, not to mention the significant journalistic attention he has captured in the Spanish-speaking world, where he has been performing 'Odysseus and Penelope', 'The thousand nights and one night' and an unpublished play inspired by 'The truth of lies'(*La verdad de las mentiras*, 1990[7]), a collection of essays in which Vargas Llosa offers insights about some of his favourite novels.

Performance

On several occasions Vargas Llosa has referred to the theatre as the supreme literary genre, and he has even suggested that he prefers plays to novels.[8] While most critics are at pains to underline the thematic continuities between Vargas Llosa's fiction and his drama, perhaps it may be more important to focus on the differences between the two genres, which, as the author himself has pointed out, are fundamental. According to him, the play stands unique in that it fleshes out the text not only by having it spoken by real people, in front of us, on the stage, but also by being enriched by a whole range of stagecraft techniques.

A play is much more than its text: it is the potential embedded in the text, in what it suggests to the director and the actors and all those involved in its performance, on which it ultimately depends. It is the combination of the dialogue, the mise en scène and the acting. Yet most critical studies of Vargas Llosa's theatre focus predominantly on the text alone, failing to take account of its performativity. The following comments should give some indication of the way in which performance is essential to an appreciation of the plays. For instance, *The Young Lady of Tacna* depends on shifts in time and space to express the essential duality of its theme, and this is best dramatised on stage; *Kathie and the Hippopotamus* needs the changes in voice and gesture to suggest the transformation of the characters according to their own and each other's imagination; similarly, in *La Chunga*, the characters have a different appearance on stage, according to who it is that is imagining them, while 'Pretty eyes, ugly paintings' depends on the presence of paintings and easels and the background sound of music to prefigure the play's culminating moment.

Very recently, Vargas Llosa has extended his connection to the stage by performing with the Spanish actress Aitana Sánchez Gijón in a series of dramatised readings of extracts from favourite stories by Francisco Ayala, Faulkner, Rulfo, Borges and Onetti.[9] They are presented under the same title as that of his collection of essays on literature, 'The truth of lies', thereby linking the theatre to literature and emphasising their shared concern with the truth of fiction. For these performances, Vargas Llosa adapts the chosen texts and declaims them in his soft, mellifluous voice, while Sánchez Gijón enacts the character parts. Another collaboration with Sánchez Gijón resulted in 'Odysseus and Penelope' (*Odiseo y Penélope*), a play that premiered at the Merida Festival in August 2006 and was published in 2007 (as Vargas Llosa does not allow his plays to be published before they are performed). 'Odysseus and Penelope' is a 'minimalist' adaptation of Homer's *Odyssey*. In the play, Vargas Llosa gives pride of place to the encounter between Odysseus and his spouse, after he has returned to Ithaca and slain Penelope's suitors. That being said, in keeping with his other dramatic works, Vargas Llosa uses frequent flashbacks, and the same actors play multiple roles. Vargas Llosa finds a connection between his own theatrical aesthetic, which depicts multiple realities, and his understanding of early Greek culture, as he points out in the prologue to the piece: 'Two characters metamorphose ceaselessly, faithful to a vocation that seems to be the norm in early Greek culture, where all beings, human, gods and animals suffer from ontological instability.'[10] He repeated the feat with the same actress in his play inspired by the *Arabian Nights*, and this was also a more sophisticated version of the first, as the new play involves a comparable dynamic, with several tales and a circular structure. My suggestion is that all Vargas Llosa's theatre is a projection of a similar 'ontological instability', which informs both of these plays in which Vargas Llosa has chosen to perform the role of a narrator who can become a protagonist of the stories he is telling.

The Young Lady from Tacna

The Young Lady from Tacna is in some ways Vargas Llosa's most ambitious play. It has a complex structure, with two protagonists: Mamaé, a very old lady, reduced to living her life through her memories, and Belisario, her young great-nephew, trying to find inspiration for a love story in Mamaé's ruminations. It would be reductive to privilege one story over the other, seeing the play as either an exploration of Mamaé's past or, as most critics have done, of Belisario's fiction writing. I consider the stories intertwined in such a way that though each scene unpeels the preceding one, we are not left with any certainty, any intimation whether the spiralling fantasies are Mamaé's or those of the aspiring writer. The fact that, as Vargas Llosa himself tells us, the story was inspired by his own family's history (Mamaé was an elderly relative of his Bolivian family who never married, and Belisario one of his great-grandfathers and the author of a novel) only gives us the point of departure for an exploration of the fictional compensations of a life that has been severely constrained by a world of oppressive social conventions.

It is impossible to offer anything but a rough and imprecise summary of this extremely complex play, as it is told from multiple perspectives by unreliable narrators. Mamaé is a centenarian, babbling and incontinent, reliving her youth from the vantage point of old age. Long ago she had mysteriously broken off her engagement to Joaquín, a Chilean captain, but the cause for this probably lies in a conversation she had with another woman claiming to be his mistress. The recollections of a poet who writes some love verses on Mamaé's fan, and an incident when a black man dares to dance with her at a masquerade ball and is beaten for his impudence, add further layers to the intrigue. An Indian girl is also beaten at the behest of the Abuelo, and Mamaé's remembrance of this incident puts into question her relationship, real or imagined, with the Abuelo, the husband of her cousin in whose house she lives. Belisario, for his part, is trying to remember family stories heard during his childhood, and embellishes them with his own erotic fantasies. *The Young Lady from Tacna* is rich in irreconcilable ambiguities. Its experimental quality has been studied from a variety of angles, in particular as regards shifts in time (Rivera-Rodas, 1986) and place (Oviedo, 1977), while Gerdes and Holzapfel (1990) offer a varied exploration of the dramatic elements in the stories recalled and invented by both protagonists, summarising the play as a parable of the creative process.[11]

Kathie and the Hippopotamus

Kathie and the Hippopotamus is the play that most directly illustrates Vargas Llosa's views on the imaginative and compensatory role of fiction, as delineated in its much quoted prologue: 'To lie is to invent; it is to add to real life another fictitious one disguised as reality . . . Fiction is the life that wasn't, the life we'd liked to have had but didn't, the life we'd rather not have had or the one we'd like to relive, without which the life we are actually leading seems incomplete.'[12]

Kathie Kennety (significantly, not her real name) is bored with her everyday life and marriage to Johnny, a banker and a playboy. She escapes into fantasy by retiring for a couple of hours a day to a room at the top of her Lima house, which has been made up to resemble a Parisian garret. Here she dictates her memories of imagined exotic and erotic journeys to Santiago, an impecunious journalist and academic, who turns her crude clichéd prose into differently crude flowery language full of hyperbole and rhetorical affectation. A great deal of social comment underlies their personal interchange, critiquing all aspects of society represented. Santiago writes for money, with visible disdain for his middle-class employer and her pretensions, but in time he comes to realise that he, too, is dissatisfied with his life.[13] Juan and Ana complete the cast as characters who exist only in Kathie's and Santiago's separate fantasies, where they appear in a variety of roles. For instance, Juan represents Johnny, Kathie's husband, as well as the couple's somewhat sanctimonious son, while Ana, Santiago's wife, impersonates many versions of a disenchanted Adèle Foucher (the name of Victor Hugo's wife), as well as standing for Kathie's vapid and calculating daughter.

Interspersed among Kathie's memories of pretend travel adventures are memories of her dull family life, her failed marriage and her suppressed dreams and desires. Santiago perceives the lies and self-deception behind these confessions, which evoke, in turn, memories of his own failed marriage, the ill-treatment of his wife, his sham Marxism, his literary pretensions and his limitations as a lover. He so clearly is not Victor Hugo, his (and Vargas Llosa's) hero, who is so much admired for his literary genius, political vision and, not least, legendary sexual prowess.

Like the chameleonic Juan and Ana, Kathie and Santiago also assume different roles in each other's fantasies. Santiago, invoking the authority of an imagined German travel guide, recalls a description of the hippopotamus as an outwardly terrifying animal of 'inexhaustible sexual voracity and cataclysmic potency', yet incapable of hurting a fly (*Three Plays*, p. 123). This image, explaining the enigma of the title, stands as a recurrent metaphor of the impotence that underlies sexual bravado.

In a revealing scene near the end of the play, Kathie responds to her husband's boast of having had countless lovers by reciting her own very precise eight infidelities and placing a question mark over Juan's paternity; the scene escalates in violence and ends with Kathie pulling the trigger, to help her husband do what he is too cowardly to do himself. The play ends two hours after it began, with Kathie and Santiago in the attic, in their respective real and literary roles. Most critics have interpreted the murder scene as fictional, the expression of repressed fantasies, but given the theme of shifting ambiguity that runs through this play, and most of Vargas Llosa's theatre, another forking path could be followed: that Kathie did kill her husband and is now seeking refuge in pretending to continue to be the socialite wife of a successful businessman. The purpose of this seemingly far-fetched suggestion is not to unearth a hidden truth or replace one interpretation with another, for whether Kathie killed Juan in earnest or in desire is not the issue; what matters is the play's ongoing blurring of boundaries, the real and the imagined flowing into each other in an overall mergence of elements that would allow for such an interpretation. *Kathie and the Hippopotamus*, which starts off by suggesting a diametric opposition between real life and fantasy, ends up by showing that they are so enmeshed as to be indistinguishable. Described as a comedy and a farce on the title page, it is an original example of the theatre's potential to represent through humour the composite nature of what we understand by reality.

La Chunga

The last of the three plays written during the 1980s is *La Chunga*. Though it also has some autobiographical associations, its main source is an episode briefly mentioned in *The Green House* (*La casa verde*, 1966[14]), which is then repeated, through shared characters in other Vargas Llosa works set in the Andes, such as *Who Killed Palomino Molero?* (*¿Quién mató a Palomino Molero?*, 1986[15]) and, later, *Death in the Andes* (*Lituma en los Andes*, 1993[16]). The action takes place in Piura, in a bar presided over by the forbidding figure of Chunga. A group of four disreputable regulars, self-styled as 'The Unconquerables', are playing dice, recalling, as they have done so often in the past, the night when Meche, the lover of one of the gang, disappeared. She was sold for the night to Chunga by the Unconquerable, Josefino, who needed to raise money for his gambling debts, and has not been seen since. Only Chunga knows the truth of her whereabouts and she is not telling. The men indulge in endless speculations of exactly what happened, each projecting his own desires, dreams and frustrations into his version of events. As summed up by the author, the 'reality' revealed is not so much concerned with the ephemeral truth behind the mystery as with the deepest, innermost desires, traumas and obsessions of the Unconquerables.[17]

In its multiple shifts of time and place, and in its concern with the interplay of fiction and reality, *La Chunga* is linked to the rest of Vargas Llosa's theatrical *oeuvre*, but stands apart in the viciousness of the fantasy. Vargas Llosa's reading of Bataille's connection between evil, erotic fantasy and transgression has received critical attention.[18] Yet with the brutality and squalor of *La Chunga*, Vargas Llosa's ironic illustration of some of those ideas surpasses even the extravagances of *Kathie*. The one glimmer of genuine affection lies in the possible love between Chunga and Meche, but this brief foray into lesbianism remains undeveloped and is only one of many rumoured fabrications.

The perverse imaginings of the Unconquerables, therefore, remain hollow threats, manifestations of an empty bravura.

'The madman of the balconies'

'The madman of the balconies' best illustrates Vargas Llosa's interest in the interplay between realist topical issues and personal human drama. The central issue is the fate of Lima's famed balconies, but this is presented alongside a human drama of shattering dreams.

This work is marked by the extreme seriousness and attention to detail that characterises all of Vargas Llosa's writing. He worked on this play for some five years. Seven drafts are mentioned in the Princeton notebooks, and my own copy, on which the radio drama was based, is either the first or second version. It is dated November 1988 and has handwritten marginalia dated February 1989. Most of the amendments appear to be trivial, concerned principally with the sound and rhythm of the dialogue. But there are also more substantial changes, such as the tighter reordering of the sequence of the scenes. Two epigraphs, one on death and the other on dreams, which provided an ironic framework to the ending, were omitted in the final version, doubtless due to staging difficulties.

Historical background

Since the main focus of the play is on the role of the eponymous balconies in the cultural life of modern Lima, questioning the extent to which the rescue and restoration of Lima's balconies should be justified, it may be worth pointing out the particularly iconic character of the balconies, both as relics of former architectural splendour and as surviving representatives of essential Peruvianness. The balconies, or *balcones de cajón*, as they are called, were built throughout the centuries in, consecutively, Renaissance, Baroque, Neo-Baroque and neoclassical styles, and bear traces of Mediterranean, Middle Eastern, Moorish, Andalusian and Caribbean ancestry.

Balconies played a significant role in the life of Lima's elite families during the vice-regal period and slightly beyond, providing shelter from the summer heat as well as from persistent rain and mist. At a time when upper-class women seldom left the home, they provided a place from which the ladies of the house could see the city's street life without being seen themselves. Like all balconies, they offered the invaluable middle space necessary for courtship and romantic dalliance. They were praised for their beauty by many writers, as wide-ranging as Ricardo Palma and Paul Morand.

The future of the balconies was being fiercely debated in Lima in the 1980s. The principal issues have been meticulously and passionately set out in *Memoria y utopía de la vieja Lima* ('Memory and utopia of old Lima') one of a series of works published at that time to argue for the preservation of the historic core of Lima.[19] An interesting aspect of the debate was the question of what exactly constituted this 'historic' quality: was this, as commonly assumed, the colonial era, with its riches and splendour, or was this favouring of the colonial epoch yet another means of eradicating once more the city's pre-Columbian heritage? This last argument came from a movement known as 'la Andinización de Lima', bent on redressing the strong *criollista* drive of the previous centuries, in which the Andean, and therefore Indian heritage, had been consistently marginalised. As had been argued by Salazar Bondy in his influential 1964 essay, *Lima la horrible* ('Lima the horrible'), the mythification of the colonial capital was a means of diverting attention from the country's social and political problems. This contention is summarised by Kristal: 'Peruvian culture invented the deceitful notion of a "Colonial Arcadia" in order to conceal historical injustices and to prevent present day injustices from being fully understood.'[20]

In 'The madman of the balconies', these issues, art versus the needs of society, are placed in the wider context of Lima's present-day multiculturalism, and the city's need to provide a modern, sanitary environment. The balconies of 'The madman of the balconies' provide an excuse to air some of the above views from different perspectives, one character standing as defender of the Arcadian heritage, another speaking for the marginalised Indians, and yet another representing the notion that any nostalgic clinging to the past is an obstacle to progress. Brunelli, the main protagonist, is an amalgam of 'Bruno Roselli', the name of an actual historical character, a Florentine architect who came to Lima and there led a vociferous campaign in defence of the city's balconies. He is quoted as having compared them in iconic importance to the Eiffel Tower in Paris, the Statue of Liberty in New York and the lions in London's Trafalgar Square.

Plot and structure

The play's plot is fairly straightforward, though, as in all Vargas Llosa's theatre, its structure is not. Aldo Brunelli, the madman of the title, has emigrated from Italy and is a professor of history of art living in Lima. He is a self-appointed champion of the city's threatened balconies, and with the aid of his daughter, Ileana, he mounts a campaign to save them, acquiring as many as possible and collecting them in what is known as the 'graveyard of the balconies'. Here, they are restored by a dedicated team of enthusiasts, made up of patrician elderly ladies and other idealists. The 'enemy' in all this is Ingeniero Canepa, who spearheads a movement to modernise Lima in order to create a progressive, salubrious environment. This puts the flea-ridden balconies at grave risk. Predictably, down-to-earth materialist Canepa has a son, Diego, who is seduced by the idealism of Brunelli, and by his daughter. Diego joins the well-meaning crusade and eventually marries Ileana. But not all is as simple as it appears: Ileana had been wooed some years before by Teofilo Huamani, a Marxist activist of indigenous origin, whom she turned down out of a sense of duty to her father and his dream; her marriage to Diego is a late desperate attempt to escape from what she now perceives as a hopelessly misguided Quixotic mission. Her accusations bring Brunelli face to face with his defeat and his response is desperate: he pours petrol over his beloved, martyred balconies. Many are burned, but he survives. Ileana invites her father to live with her and Diego, but on condition that he abandon all talk of balconies.

'The madman of the balconies' opens and closes with Brunelli perched on his balcony, about to commit suicide, and consists of flashbacks of his life as he remembers it with an increasing sense of self-exploration, every memory triggering an earlier one. Its interest, clearly, extends beyond the architectural and sociopolitical: although it makes its principal characters spokespersons for certain beliefs, and may appear to be little more than a thesis drama, the play is very much about the multilayered nature of every human situation and the complexity of all human relationships. Within the circular framework, a number of binaries operate, particularly in terms of the leading male characters. Brunelli and Canepa are possible mirror images in that they each fight for their opposing beliefs, but do not form an exact parallel in that Canepa is drawn to his opponent's fervour and integrity, while Brunelli is drawn to Canepa only reluctantly, towards the end. Both can be seen, however, as avatars of the author, Vargas Llosa. Brunelli, a man obsessed by his *demonios*, or demons, represents the visionary, which corresponds to how the author usually describes himself in his creative drive; Canepa is linked in his materialist drive for progress to the Vargas Llosa of the 1960s; while Huamani, who speaks for the need for moral commitment in the face of economic misery and social injustice, can be seen as echoing the author's Sartrean phase in favour of committed art.[21] These multiple confrontations are a means of undermining any one heroic stance, and suggesting, as always with Vargas Llosa, the many truths that lie behind 'The Truth'.

Because of the topicality of the debates aired by the various characters, 'The madman of the balconies' is usually considered as belonging almost entirely to the realist mode. But this is to disregard the transcendent quality of the play, the way in which it builds on the factual inspiration for its plot and adds to it the human dilemma of a man in thrall to his fantasies. Most tellingly, when Brunelli is about to die, he confesses to himself that his dream was a self-centred delusion, and accepts his awareness of the sacrifice he was exacting from his daughter and those around him; however, when he miraculously survives, he returns to his old dream and becomes the balconies' crusader once more.

'The madman of the balconies' is a wordy play: it abounds in long speeches expressing a number of ideas. Yet, though an 'issue play', it avoids the didacticism associated with the genre in that it is basically non-judgemental. Surprisingly in an author noted for the richness of the dialogues in his novels, apart from Brunelli's flowery idealisations of colonial Lima, most of the dialogue here is straightforward and rather unexceptional, which adds to the realism of the play. However, the point is not to make the play a copy of real life, but to heighten the difference: 'Theatre isn't life, but make-believe . . .' (*Three Plays*, p. 82). The spoken exchanges and long diatribes in the play occur in the mind and memory of the protagonist, and this must be taken into serious consideration in their delivery. What this means is that their 'realism' should be attenuated by the poetico-magical context of memory.

This much was understood by all those who were involved in its successful performance at the Gate Theatre during November 1993. I was fortunate in being able to speak to the director and to some of the leading actors and to glean their professional insights.

Peter Eyre, who played the idealist professor, made him into a beguiling and naturally appealing character, though he thought that it was theatrically important not to be seduced by his poetic vision and the poetry of his lines. This was endorsed by Raad Rawi, who acted the role of Canepa, portraying him not negatively, as an opportunist developer, but as an eager, charismatic character, forward-looking and fuelled with vigour. The aim was to produce a sort of contrapuntal movement between two languages: Brunelli's high-blown poetic speech and Canepa's rationalist discourse. For this to happen, Canepa's down-to-earth dialogue needed to be injected with a particular kind of energy, and given a modern rhythm, in contrast to Brunelli's leisured, colonial pace. Huamani's interpretation had to combine ideological fervour and certainty with personal racial insecurity, while Ileana's had to move from devoted, submissive daughter, at one with her father's wishes, to becoming the strong, rebellious woman at the end, a determined and manipulative survivor. As scene after scene, incident after incident undermines the truth of what has gone before, the audience is drawn further in and left to ponder about the multiple versions of history, culture and personal drama witnessed.

Theatrically, the play has to inhabit different worlds. Making the most of the very reduced space of the Gate, the stage was divided between an old, decaying balcony, which was part of a building inclined to one side, on which the main character stood, preparing for his suicide, and to which he returned between scenes, and the 'graveyard of the balconies', where the enacting of his memories took place. The stage was flooded with bright yellows, blues and gold, and constant switches of colour and lighting were crucial elements in creating an other-worldly atmosphere, offsetting the topical realism. The crowd scenes were filled with a huge cast of mainly elderly ladies, parading placards. In their patrician bearing and appearance they represented the reactionary position, and were felt almost as embodiments of the threatened balconies. As if to underscore the importance of the visual, the play's radio version was not particularly successful. But the stage run was.

'The madman of the balconies' had its global debut in London at the Gate Theatre in November 1993. It was widely reviewed in the press, from the *Times Literary Supplement* to the *Tribune: Labour's Independent Weekly*. Most commentaries were favourable: Michael Billington called it 'a small master-piece, in that it relates private dreams to public reality'; Barry Ife thought the language a joy, and saw the balconies as a rich symbol, and a suitably operatic one: 'Suspended between earth and sky, the balcony is the natural home of the politician, the preacher and the lover ... part pulpit, part confessional.' Opinion differed regarding the quality of the prose and the translation, but the overall consensus was that the combination of themes on the one hand and the apposite use of theatrical effects on the other resulted in 'good drama'. Surely this is a playwright's highest ambition.

'Pretty eyes, ugly paintings'

'Pretty eyes, ugly paintings' takes place in present-day Lima and consists mainly of an uninterrupted dialogue between Zanelli, a sixty-year-old art critic, and the handsome young Rubén Zevallos, with occasional incursions into mem-ories of the latter's conversations with Alicia, his girlfriend. It is set late at night in Zanelli's flat, to which Zevallos has gained entrance by pretending an interest in the homosexual advances of the celebrated critic. But it soon becomes clear that he is there for quite another purpose: to enact his revenge for the death of his girlfriend. Alicia, a student and ardent admirer of Zanelli, had felt encouraged by the *maestro* to become a painter, but became demor-alised after his damning review of her first exhibition; she eventually committed suicide.

The setting up of the intrigue and development of the plot is Vargas Llosa's finest, with a masterful prolongation of suspense towards the end. Much of the discussion centres on the nature of art in opposition to art criticism. Artistic creativity is defined in line with some of Vargas Llosa's well-known ideas on the *demonios* that drive the writer, which are here transposed onto the painter: 'To convert our inner devils into images ... To give shape to our passion, form to our longings, colour and volume to our dreams'.[22] As opposed to this, 'No one dreams of being an art critic. One becomes one either through a process of elimination or inability' (p. 39). Vargas Llosa has discussed these issues in greater detail in his essays; what is of prime interest here is the dramatic effect of the tensions between creativity and criticism, as they are played out on the stage. Zanelli's impotence as an artist is pitched against his omnipotence as a critic: if not by the stroke of his brush, by the stroke of his pen he knows that he can make or break an artist. And he does.

The play has not received the attention it deserves for its dramatic quality and for the insight into the social and cultural mores of middle-class life in Lima, mocking its pretentious decorum and exposing its prejudices against both women and homosexuals. The sexism implicit in the title is the central issue of the play. Finding inspiration in a short story by Salinger, 'Pretty Mouth and Green my Eyes', Zanelli replaces the suggestive imagery of this poetic title with a crude formula, in which good looks are counterposed to bad art with unthinking bias. The compliment compounds the insult: as the suicidal artist complains, 'He did not write the bit about my "pretty eyes" because he thinks they are pretty. He did so for the wordplay, so that the contrasting adjectives should emphasise his contempt' (p. 51).

'Pretty eyes, ugly paintings' belongs, with *In Praise of the Stepmother* (*Elogio de la madrastra*, 1988[23]) and other novels of the 1990s, to a cluster of works in which Vargas Llosa's interest in the visual arts is given considerable prominence. This is a topic that awaits major study. While the pictorial interest of the play is manifest, its underlying link to music has so far gone unnoticed. Yet crucial to an understanding of the play is the fact that it unfolds against the backdrop of Mahler's song-symphony, *The Song of the Earth*, which is played twice and provides the timeframe for Zanelli to plead for his life. *The Song*'s sombre preoccupation with death and sadness, ending with a vision of the rejuvenation of spring, adds a dimension of timelessness and spirituality. This may be viewed as ironic, or not, of Zanelli's eventual release from the death threat. (Interestingly, 'The madman of the balconies' also ends on a similar note, in that Brunelli's expected suicide does not take place.)

'On the banks of the Thames'

Vargas Llosa's last play, 'On the banks of the Thames', like *Kathie and the Hippopotamus*, draws on a character who had first appeared in the novel *Conversation in The Cathedral*. In this case it is Chispas, the brother of Santiago Zavala. Unlike his brother, who preferred a life of frustration to a life in business, Chispas embraced capitalism with a sense of fervour. The play takes place several decades after the events of the novel. In the play, Chispas appears as a successful Peruvian, alone in a hotel room in London, when a woman (Raquel), claiming to be the sister of an old school friend (Pirulo), visits him. Oddly, Chispas has no recollection of his closest friend's sister. Chispas has not seen Pirulo since a violent incident took place between them in their adolescence. Discussing this event with Raquel becomes the starting point of a conversation exploring the consequences of two individuals' chosen paths, and the complexities surrounding issues of heterosexual, homosexual and transgender identity. Surprising revelations and plot twists – in which the line between memory and fantasy is often blurred – give nuance to a meditation on the costs of committing to authenticity, and, conversely, the costs of its betrayal. Raquel, who was true to her sense of self, is a portrayal of a painful road to self-discovery. Chispas, who repressed his sexual identity, is a compelling portrayal of a frustrated life, and frustration, as some of Vargas Llosa's early critics have pointed out, is one of his major themes, even though it has had many different manifestations in the *oeuvre*.

To close this reflection on his plays, it is worth noting that 'Pretty eyes, ugly paintings' is a compelling exploration of artistic frustration at the hand of destructive criticism. Could this be an indirect reflection on Vargas Llosa's feelings as a playwright? For while many of his plays have been enthusiastically received when staged, they are too often evaluated as a novelist's 'texts', without due consideration given to their rich literary and dramatic potential.[24]

NOTES

1. Carlos Espinosa Domínguez. '"Para mí el teatro es un ascesis, una cura de adelgazamiento'. Entrevista a Mario Vargas Llosa'. *Latin American Theatre Review*, 20(1), fall 1986, pp. 57–60. (Translation Evelyn Fishburn.) See also relevant chapters on theatre in *Antípodas. Special Issue Mario Vargas Llosa*, December 1988.

2. Vargas Llosa talks about his writing and directing of this play in *El pez en el agua. Memorias*. Barcelona: Seix Barral, 1993. *A Fish in the Water: A Memoir*. Trans. Helen Lane. London: Faber and Faber, 1994, pp. 186–7, 194–7.

3. Mario Vargas Llosa. *La señorita de Tacna*. Barcelona: Seix Barral, 1981. *Kathie y el hipopótamo*. Barcelona: Seix Barral, 1983. *La Chunga*. Barcelona: Seix Barral, 1986. *El loco de los balcones*. Barcelona: Seix Barral, 1993. *Ojos bonitos, cuadros feos*. Lima: Peisa, 1996. *Odiseo y Penélope*. Barcelona: Galaxia Gutenberg, 2007. *Las mil noches y una noche*. Madrid: Alfaguara, 2009. *Al pie del Támesis*. Lima: Alfaguara, 2008. To date, only *The Young Lady from Tacna*, *Kathie and the Hippopotamus* and *La Chunga* have been translated and published in English. Mario Vargas Llosa. *Three Plays*. Trans. David Graham-Young. London: Faber and Faber, 1990. *Katie and the Hippopotamus*, trans. E. Fishburn and B. Krichefski, was transmitted on BBC Radio 3, in October 1987, and *Mad for the Love of Old Balconies*, trans. E. Fishburn and B. Krichefski, on BBC Radio 3, on 23 October 1989. It was repeated on 5 November 1989 as part of the BBC World

Service Drama. An excerpt of 'On the banks of the Thames', translated by Romy Sutherland, appeared in *The Drawbridge*, 15, winter 2009, pp. 14–15.

4. Vargas Llosa, *Al pie del Támesis*, pp. 24–5. (Translation Evelyn Fishburn.)

5. Vargas Llosa, *Three Plays*, p. 7.

6. Vargas Llosa's web page includes detailed information on this. See under the heading of 'Cronología', edited by Rosario M. N. de Bedoya, 30 May 2006 (www.mvargasllosa.com/biblio.htm).

7. Mario Vargas Llosa. *La verdad de las mentiras. Ensayos sobre la novela moderna.* Barcelona: Seix Barral, 1990.

8. See Jesús M. Santos. 'Vargas Llosa. 'El teatro fue mi primer amor'. *Antípodas*, 1, December 1988, pp. 118–20.

9. I am indebted to Dr Mara García for drawing my attention to these performances.

10. 'Mario Vargas Llosa será actor'. *Clarín*, Sección Espectáculos, 2 August 2006 (http://old.clarin.com/diario/2006/08/02/espectaculos/c-00301.htm), accessed 1 July 2011. (Translation Evelyn Fishburn.)

11. Oscar Rivera-Rodas. 'El código temporal en *La señorita de Tacna. Latin American Theatre Review*, 19(2), spring 1986, pp. 5–16. Jose Miguel Oviedo. *Mario Vargas Llosa. La invención de una realidad.* Barcelona: Seix Barral, 1977. Dick Gerdes. 'Melodrama and Reality in the Plays of Mario Vargas Llosa'. *Latin American Theatre Review*, 24(1), fall 1990, pp. 17–28.

12. Vargas Llosa, *Three Plays*, p. 81.

13. Santiago may be considered a reinvention of the protagonist of *Conversation in The Cathedral* (*Conversación en La Catedral*. Barcelona: Seix Barral, 1969) with the same name, to the extent that the two characters appear to share the same past, even if they are driven by different concerns.

14. Mario Vargas Llosa. *La casa verde*. Barcelona: Seix Barral, 1966.

15. Mario Vargas Llosa. *¿Quién mató a Palomino Molero?* Barcelona: Seix Barral, 1986.

16. Mario Vargas Llosa. *Lituma en los Andes*. Barcelona: Planeta, 1993.

17. *Antípodas*, p. 132.

18. Efraín Kristal. *Temptation of the Word: The Novels of Mario Vargas Llosa.* Nashville, Tenn.: Vanderbilt University Press, 1998, pp. 115–17.

19. César Pacheco Vélez (ed.). *Memoria y utopía de la vieja Lima*. Lima: Universidad del Pacífico, 1985. See particularly pp. 262–3, 266–8.

20. Kristal, *Temptation*, p. 10. For more information on Vargas Llosa's relationship with Salazar Bondy, see pp. 10–11.

21. See Veronica Lavenia. 'El teatro de Mario Vargas Llosa. "El loco de los balcones"'. *Rassegna Iberística* (Riber), 78, September 2003, pp. 105–11.

22. Vargas Llosa, *Ojos bonitos, cuadros feos*, p. 30. (All translations are by Evelyn Fishburn.)

23. Mario Vargas Llosa. *Elogio de la madrastra*. Barcelona: Tusquets, 1988.

24. I should like to express my appreciation to the Leverhulme Foundation for their generous support.

14

CAROLINA SITNISKY

Film and the novels

Carlos Fuentes famously noted that once the sombre complexities of Mario Vargas Llosa's second novel, *The Green House* (*La casa verde*, 1966[1]), are shed to their bare bones, they can be boiled down to one of the standard plots of the Mexican cinematic melodrama: a housemaid ends up in a house of prostitution.[2] Indeed, Vargas Llosa's narrative fiction, from his first novel through to his last, features cinematic techniques and themes; and his formal experimentation with spatial and temporal planes, flashbacks and cuts, draws significantly on cinematic montage, as well as an awareness of effective camera angles to suggest a particular point of view. Film also provides the cinematic inspiration for some of his most stunning literary moments. For instance, the opening of *Conversation in The Cathedral* (*Conversación en La Catedral*, 1969[3]), in which Santiago Zavala is searching for his dog, was probably inspired by a famous sequence from Vittorio de Sica's *Umberto D* (1952), in which a desperate Umberto pursues his dog Flike. While some other major Latin American writers, most notably Manuel Puig, have written skilful novels, which can be transformed into screenplays with ease (in some cases because the original draft was a screenplay), Vargas Llosa adapts some filmic techniques from a visual to a linguistic medium, to produce original literary effects that cannot be readily transferred back to the screen.

Cinema also features in the content of Vargas Llosa's novels, playing a crucial part in the novels themselves: in rites of socialisation and in the romances of his contemporary characters. In *The Bad Girl* (*Travesuras de la niña mala*, 2006[4]), for example, a traumatised young woman (the bad girl of the title) eventually accepts the love of Ricardo Somocurcio, whose patience is tried in every chapter of the book. In the opening chapter, Ricardo declares his love to her during a Sunday matinee show in the more expensive orchestra seats of a movie theatre in Lima. Even though she rejects his romantic overtures, she accepts several other invitations to join him at the movies, where they hold hands, but do not kiss or touch, unlike the other couples around them. As in other novels by Vargas Llosa, the narrator of *The Bad Girl* alludes to films of the period in which the novel is set, in this case the fashionable movies from the French New Wave movement (Godard, Truffaut and Louis Malle), to reflect the time period and offer a counterpoint to the lives of his major characters.

Besides inspiring a number of investigative detectives, action movies, Westerns, film noir and Hollywood classics have influenced his narrative action sequences, especially those of violent conflict. Vargas Llosa skilfully interweaves stories and dialogues, changing narrators, and incorporates distinct sources and media in a montage-like fashion. The inclusion of newspaper clippings, radio shows, the recollection of dreams, letters, reports, and so on, allows readers to envision important aspects of his narrative in filmic terms and as moving images, as, for example, in *Captain Pantoja and the Special Service (Pantaleón y las visitadoras,* 1973[5]).

Vargas Llosa's early novels relied on patterns of flashbacks and flashforwards, through which he skilfully accelerated or slowed down the tempo of his narration. The influence of cinema can also be appreciated in the way his narrative visualises what a character sees, akin to cinematic points of view. For instance, in one of the most intense moments of *The Time of the Hero (La ciudad y los perros,* 1963[6]), Alberto Fernández voices the accusation to Lieutenant Gamboa that Jaguar has murdered Ricardo Arana. The techniques Vargas Llosa employs of focusing and framing, and zooming in and out, lend themselves to the easy translation of these sequences into screenplay.

Captivated by his writings, directors such as Francisco Lombardi, Sebastián Alarcón, Jorge Fons, Jon Amiel and Luis Llosa have adapted several of Vargas Llosa's novels, their films enriching the reception and the interpretation of his *oeuvre.* Two general observations can be made regarding the choices of the directors of these cinematic adaptations, which are far from simple filmic replicas of the novel. First, given that Vargas Llosa and his novels are so well known in the Spanish-speaking world, the Spanish film adaptations tend to keep the original novel title. Second, the adaptations tend to follow the basic plot-lines of Vargas Llosa's novels, but they tend not to share the ideological underpinnings that informed the original works.

Corruption and society

The mild but oppressive weather of Lima, where it is grey nine months of the year, the corruption of a military academy which claims to uphold moral values, and the indifference of the school's officials to the death of the cadet Arana ('the Slave') form the foundation of Peruvian director Francisco Lombardi's 1985 adaptation of Vargas Llosa's *The Time of the Hero.* At the opening and closing of the film, Lombardi visually represents this oppression by filming the Leoncio Prado military academy sequences in a gamut of grey tones. He also includes numerous night scenes, shot with only limited natural light to suggest a sense of foreboding. Dark interior scenes are shot with limited artificial light, when the cadets transgress the rules of the institution, while bright lighting is used when the cadets feel safe from the gaze of their superiors, as when they perform violent hazing rites to 'welcome' new cadets to the school.

Lombardi and his screenwriter, the late Peruvian poet José Watanabe, retain the novel's underlying ambiguities. Thus, the novel and the adaptation share, to some degree, the same open questions. Who killed the Slave after he denounced the transgressions of his fellow students? Who is the true villain? Who is the hero in a corrupt institution in which the transgressions of the young could be read as challenges to the authority of a corrupt social order? Nevertheless, there is a central ideological difference between the novel and the adaptation. Lombardi, who has a more apocalyptic and pessimistic view of Peru than Vargas Llosa had during his socialist period, does not overtly show the military academy as a microcosm of Peruvian society. Instead, he offers a more diffused sense of a world breaking down, as when Lieutenant Gamboa complains to his friend and co-worker, Colonel Huarina, that, in Peru, nothing seems to work as it should.

Lombardi and Watanabe also make significant changes when they transpose the literary language to a cinematographic one. The novel's narrative structure is threefold, with sequences focusing on three characters: one sequence spans their lives from adolescence to adulthood; a second narrative sequence follows the novel's protagonists through the years they are enrolled in the military academy; a third sequence focuses on the last two or three months of their schooling. Within the last, the sequence of events that lead from the theft of an exam paper from a classroom to the death of the Slave in a military exercise and the aftermath of his death is of particular significance. Lombardi gives pride of place to the third of these narrative sequences, with a limited number of flashbacks drawing on the second. The film reduces the myriad narrative voices to a first-person voice-over by a single character, Alberto Fernández, 'the Poet'. Characters such as Boa – whose interior monologues contribute to the pathos of moral indifference in the novel – disappear completely in the film. In short, Lombardi does not follow Vargas Llosa's Faulkner-like experimentation with temporal and spatial planes, or with multiple points of view, including stream of consciousness. Rather, his technique follows a more traditional Hollywood style, in which a voice-over of a protagonist frames an experience of his past narrated in a conventional chronological order. Lombardi argues that, 'From my perspective, novels that work best as film adaptations are those that tell a story and are based on very specific and concrete details and incidents. *The Time of the Hero* is one such novel ... I simplified the narrative complexity of the novel, and based the story in the present, in the actions of the characters.'[7]

It is worth noting that cinematic references abound in the original novel. Before entering the military academy, both Alberto and Jaguar were either playing soccer or attending matinees, the details of which they would discuss afterwards. Already as adolescents they would invite girls to the movies, and in the darkness of the theatre would dare to attempt their first sexual experiences. In the novel, Lieutenant Gamboa looks forward to his weekend leaves in order to see Mexican melodramatic films with his wife, the same kind of films that Carlos Fuentes referred to in explaining the basic plot structure of *The Green House*.

From the milieu of filmic references in the novel, Lombardi incorporates only one in his adaptation: Alberto's betrayal of his friend Ricardo. When Ricardo asks Alberto to let his girlfriend know that he cannot see her one weekend because he has been left unjustly consigned to school for a transgression he did not commit, Alberto takes advantage of the opportunity to invite her to see a film, a prelude to an easy seduction of a girl from a low social standing. At the cinema, while listening to English-language audio, representative of the Hollywood films that were screened in Peru in the 1950s, Alberto makes his romantic pass, which is immediately accepted by the girl. In the adaptation, as in the novel, the movie theatre and the romantic content of the film stimulate the desires of Alberto and loosen his sexual inhibitions, and those of the young woman of a lower class with whom he will not have a lasting relationship. This subplot buttresses the main theme of the film: the corruption of the military institution and the weakness of its cadets, who are also prey to betrayal and corruption.

Two other adaptations were produced from the body of literary work that Vargas Llosa produced in the 1960s: the film *Los cachorros* (1971) by the Mexican director Jorge Fons, based on the novella known in English as *The Cubs* (*Los cachorros*, 1967[8]); and *Yaguar* (1986), directed by the Chilean Sebastián Alarcón, and based on Jaguar, a similarly named character in *The Time of the Hero*. Fons, who co-wrote the screenplay of *Los cachorros* with Eduardo Luján, transfers the setting from Peru to Mexico, to tell a similar story: the coming of age of a boy whose sexual organ was mauled by a dog. In both the novel and the film, the effects of the accident are devastating to the boy, who is excluded from the possibility of a sexual life, and is humiliated and tormented by male friends and classmates, who are not aware of the reason he is unable to follow them as they discover their heterosexuality.

In the novel, Vargas Llosa includes many references to frequent movie outings that Cuéllar and his friends make, given that the cinema is, for

Vargas Llosa, the paradigmatic place in which couples come together. In the adaptation, Fons highlights the section of the novel in which Cuéllar attends movies alone, sitting in the last row, chain-smoking and spying on couples kissing. As in the novel, the film shows a traumatised Cuéllar, who, after high school graduation, becomes unhinged – acting irrationally, having car accidents, and going out to drink and gamble at night.

Fons takes Vargas Llosa's plot in a different direction from the novel. Vargas Llosa's story is about the exclusion of a young man from the reproduction of a social order, whereas the film focuses on the pressures of a castrated man in a chauvinistic society that expects signs of sexual affirmation. In the novel, Cuéllar dies in a car accident as a result of his reckless driving, though the narrator concludes the text on a lighter note, in which his peer group forgets him, relegating him to a vague memory of their collective past. In the film adaptation, Cuéllar is a young man who is sexually and perversely obsessed with his mother and who has a violent streak, expressing his sexual frustrations by committing violent acts against women. Keeping with its more violent pitch, Fons's film builds a melodramatic crescendo, in which Cuéllar is first rejected by a young woman he loves and then by his mother, who is horrified by her son's perverse attachment to her. In the film, the young man commits suicide by shooting himself in the last scene of the movie. The divergent closing scenes demonstrate the different intentions of the author and director.

The plot of *Yaguar*, filmed in 1986 by Chilean director Sebastián Alarcón during his political exile in the Soviet Union, is built around the character Jaguar from Vargas Llosa's *The Time of the Hero*. It exploits aspects of the character that are consistent with the novel as a whole: the rise of a young man who could have been a revolutionary leader, given his natural propensity to challenge a corrupt social order, his sense of discipline and his respect for strict adherence to a code of action. In the film, Alarcón's Yaguar becomes the potential instigator of a revolution in Chile, which, when the film was made, was under the dictatorship of General Augusto Pinochet.

The timeliness of the original novel, together with its revolutionary meanings, were picked up by Vargas Llosa's mentor, Salazar Bondy: 'In your novel you depict the contradictions of the underdeveloped, dissonant and deformed world that we precariously inhabit. Things will explode, are already exploding. I think therefore that the publication of your novel ought not to be too much delayed.'[9] Alarcón, enhancing the potential and implicit socialism in Vargas Llosa's Jaguar, stresses both the tensions present in a corrupt society and the possibility of change through the use of force.

Humour

Vargas Llosa closes his cycle of novels denouncing corruption in society and its institutions, with *Conversation in The Cathedral*, in which a young protagonist tries and fails to participate in a political movement that would bring revolutionary change to Peru. Wanting to distance himself from Fidel Castro and the Cuban Revolution, Vargas Llosa revisits some of his early themes in a humorous and ironic register as he strategically places the plot of his next novel, *Captain Pantoja and the Special Service*, at the end of the 1950s. In this novel, Vargas Llosa explores military corruption, fanaticism and prostitution in Peruvian society. It is also worth noting that the gestation of this novel was directly influenced by a cinematic project. Between writing the first and second drafts of the novel, Vargas Llosa was asked by Brazilian director Rui Guerra to write a screenplay inspired by Euclides da Cunha's Brazilian classic *Rebellion in the Backlands* (*Os Sertões*, 1902). Though Vargas Llosa wrote several screenplays, the film was never produced; however, the topic of a fanatically religious millenarian group led by a charismatic leader so deeply interested Vargas Llosa that he added the character of Brother Francisco and his fanatic followers into the second draft of *Captain Pantoja and the Special Service*.

Vargas Llosa's second cinematic project would take place a couple of years later, when he was hired, in 1976, by Paramount Pictures, to adapt *Captain Pantoja and the Special Service* for film. In addition to writing the screenplay, he co-directed the film with his friend José María Gutiérrez Santos, to whom he had dedicated the novel. Vargas Llosa and Gutiérrez Santos hired an international production crew for the film, including renowned actors such as the Spaniard José Sacristán in the role of Pantaleón Pantoja, the Peruvian Martha Figueroa as his wife, Pochita, and the Mexican Katy Jurado in the role of Chuchupe, as well as the French art director Jacques Renoir. For Vargas Llosa, this hands-on experience was an entertaining but unwise attempt at film adaption, as he expressed in an interview with Utero TV in 2008. Today, a copy of this film is virtually unobtainable; however, it was through the experience of shooting the film in the Dominican Republic that Vargas Llosa became fascinated by Rafael Leónidas Trujillo's thirty-year-plus dictatorship, resulting in *The Feast of the Goat* (*La fiesta del Chivo*, 2000[10]) some twenty-five years later.

Captain Pantoja and the Special Service was adapted into film for the second time in 1999, by Francisco Lombardi, this time with considerable box-office success. In line with Vargas Llosa's intentions, Lombardi and the screenwriters, Giovanna Pollarolo and Enrique Moncloa, employ a humorous tone to touch on the topic of corruption in Peru's military institution. This humorous tone is diametrically opposed to the deadly serious tone of *The Time of the Hero* – both the novel and Lombardi's film adaptation – as can be seen by comparing Lieutenant Gamboa from *The Time of the Hero* with Pantaleón Pantoja of *Captain Pantoja and the Special Service*. This direct contrast might have been Lombardi's motive in adapting these two novels. In both works, the failures of the protagonists culminate in their military demotion. Gamboa is sent to the town of Juliaca, while Pantoja is offered a post in Pomata, both towns located in inhospitable areas, far away from the attractions of Lima or any other major city. That being said, while Gamboa's failure underscores the deep-seated corruption of a social order underwritten by corrupt military institutions, Pantoja's is the personal failure of an individual caught between his desire to fulfil the orders of his superiors and the twists and turns of his unconventional responsibilities.

Like the novel, the film adaptation of *Captain Pantoja and the Special Service* maintains humorous situations in which Pantoja's military professionalism clashes with the absurdity of his mission, which is to organise and manage a prostitution service to curtail the sexual abuses perpetrated on the local populations by Peruvian army units assigned to the Amazonian region. The film centres on Pantoja's character, leaving behind the complexities of his frailties featured in the novel, in favour of highlighting his serious side, as his obsession for efficiency ends up turning on him. A considerable amount of Vargas Llosa's humour is lost in the film, whose tone is more circumspect because Lombardi had to utilise direct action to portray what is communicated indirectly in the novel in the form of letters, reports and newspaper articles, as well as Pantoja's dreams. Lombardi explains that he was not interested in presenting a comic or farcical character. In his view, Pantoja is 'a character trapped in a world of obligations, responsibilities and prejudices. His obsessive desire to carry out his duties has serious rather than humorous consequences. We opted for this interpretation, and thus solved the difficult problem of the film's tone.'[11]

Some of the technical differences include changing the name of the prostitute known in the novel as 'the Brazilian' to 'the Colombian', perhaps to accommodate the Colombian actress who played the part in the film. Pantoja's mother, Leonor, another character who is a foil for humorous situations, does not appear in the film, and thus Pantoja and his wife Pochita travel to the Amazon jungle as a couple. Since Lombardi's adaptation does not include Brother Francisco or his followers, the main obstacle to Pantoja's objectives is not the religious movement that objects to the 'depravity' of prostitution, but a character who has a smaller role in the novel:

'el Sinchi', the infamous radio host, who discovers the prostitution service and would like it to be made available to civilians.

Like *Captain Pantoja and the Special Service*, Vargas Llosa's other novel of the 1970s, *Aunt Julia and the Scriptwriter* (*La tía Julia y el escribidor*, 1977[12]), was also written in a humorous register. It shifts its focus from social commentary to a humorous exploration of the literary creative process. The novel was adapted in 1990 by the American director Jon Amiel, with the title *Tune in Tomorrow*. Vargas Llosa sets his novel at the end of the 1950s, before the advent of television in Peru, when the exiled Cuban entertainment entrepreneur, Goar Mestre – known first for his production of radio plays and then television shows that were distributed throughout Latin America – arrived in Lima. Amiel transposes the novel from Lima to New Orleans, in the southern United States. Amiel includes scenes showing that desegregation has not yet been realised in the South, where the domestic service is mainly black and does not participate socially or economically in the same loci as the whites, much as is the case in Vargas Llosa's literary world, where indigenous peoples serve the dominant whites in Peru.

Amiel's adaptation follows Vargas Llosa's novel in the manner in which the romantic relationship between the young writer Varguitas and his Aunt Julia is mediated by cinema. In the novel, the couple go to the movies to watch the Mexican melodrama *Esposa y amante* ('Wife and lover', 1950), by director Alfonso Fernández Bustamante, which comments ironically on the type of relationship that they will come to have, first through a love affair between a young man and an older woman, and then as a married couple. In the film adaptation, Marty (the Americanised name that Amiel gives to Varguitas's counterpart, played by Keanu Reeves), suggests to his aunt that she watch the recently released *An American in Paris* (1951). Through the inclusion of this classic American film and its portrayal of Gene Kelly's character – a young man who has to work to make money and fight for his love in Paris – Amiel also introduces an analogue to the conceit of the film that galvanises the love affair between Varguitas and Julia. Like the Gene Kelly character, young Marty will have to fight for his love for Julia (played in the American film by Barbara Hershey), and then goes to Paris to become a writer, as in his mind all great writers must do. Both Varguitas in the novel and Marty in the film frequently go with their older love interest to the movie theatre, where they can enjoy time together without the criticism of their family, and where they fantasise about life as if they were part of a movie.

The film is faithful to the novel's structure, which alternates realistic and imaginative registers. The realistic episodes tell the story of Varguitas's life as an aspiring writer and of his encounter with the eccentric Pedro Camacho (Carmichael, played by Peter Falk, in the film), a writer of radio plays.

The imaginative register corresponds to narratives inspired by Camacho's radio plays. As in the novel, the film contrasts Varguitas's difficulties writing a serious novel to Camacho's ease as he writes many radio plays. There are important differences, though, in how this opposition is presented in the two works: in the novel, Varguitas's episodes are narrated in the first person and the radio plays in third person, while in the film both are presented in a filmic equivalent of a third-person point of view. Amiel opts not to mix or complicate the radio plays as the novel does, to signal the mental breakdown of the scriptwriter: he chooses only one (perhaps the most melodramatic of his radio plays – the story in which Elaine gets pregnant by her brother and their uncle finds out) as the counterpoint to the less dramatically incestuous story of Marty and Julia, who is an aunt by marriage and not by blood, and who has recently divorced the young man's uncle.

Other differences between the novel and the film adaptation include the irrational contempt that Camacho feels for Argentines (transformed into Carmichael's Albanians), and, more importantly, the age of the characters. While Varguitas is eighteen and Julia thirty-two years old, in the film he is twenty-one and she is thirty-six years old. This variation allows Marty to get married without his parents' approval, whereas in the novel Varguitas falsifies documents and bribes a corrupt judge to legalise the union with his aunt. In the film, it is Pedro who organises a fake ceremony, with one of the radio-play actors as the justice of peace, tricking both Marty and Julia into believing that they are legally married.

The endings of the adaptation and the film are significantly different. In the novel, Varguitas returns to Peru as a successful and accomplished writer after eight years in Paris. He has divorced Julia and meets Camacho, who, unable to write, has been committed to a mental institution after a severe mental breakdown. Amiel, on the other hand, does not portray his scriptwriter as a pathetic figure. His Carmichael is an insane but cheeky romantic hero of sorts. In the film, Carmichael helps Marty and Julia get back together after a short breakup; he also burns down the radio station where he and Marty work, and moves to a new city with his eccentric imagination alive as ever. In the adaptation's final scene, Marty and Julia happily navigate the Seine, enacting the Hollywood story of *An American in Paris*.

The Feast of the Goat

Vargas Llosa initiated a new phase in his narrative trajectory with *The Feast of the Goat*, a novel about the corruption of a dehumanised nation under the harmful domination of a dictator. In this novel, Vargas Llosa portrays the fall of Rafael Leónidas Trujillo, the corrupt and brutal dictator of the Dominican

Republic for over three decades (1930–61), instigated by a group of his close and also amoral collaborators. The story unfolds to show the abuses and excesses of Trujillo's dictatorship, and the submission and fear of his closest collaborators. The climax of the story, the rape of an innocent girl, Urania – an allegory of the cruelty and mistreatment of the entire Dominican Republic by the dictator – is followed by the assassination of Trujillo. What distinguishes this novel from previous Vargas Llosa narratives about corrupt societies is that, in this case, there is no cathartic solution for Trujillo's collaborators: even after killing him, they cannot forgive themselves for their participation in such an amoral regime.

The film adaptation of the same title was directed in 2006 by Luis Llosa, who had previously lived in the Dominican Republic and was both fascinated and intrigued by what he calls Trujillo's myth. Llosa and his screenwriters, Zachary Sklar and Augusto Cabada (who worked with Francisco Lombardi on several films),[13] kept the adaptation's plot flowing by interweaving storylines like the novel does, all of them intersecting in 1961, the year in which Urania was sexually assaulted by Trujillo, just months before he was assassinated. The stories included in the film are: Urania's memories of her childhood and relationship with her father, senator Agustín Cabral, one of Trujillo's closest allies; the loss of Urania's innocence, when her father offers his daughter's virginity as a gift to regain the good graces of the dictator; the scheme to murder Trujillo by the men who had shared in his corruption and who felt either pangs of conscience or a sense of personal betrayal by the dictator; and the tyranny of the dictator himself.

Llosa's adaptation echoes some of the novel's techniques, by using flashbacks to introduce each of the characters involved in Trujillo's assassination, as they wait to ambush the vehicle transporting the dictator. In the film, Llosa uses flashbacks to narrate each of these men's pasts: the way in which they participated in the regime, were humiliated by the dictator and subsequently plotted his death. With regard to the structure, Llosa follows a similar chronology as the novel, with the intention, just like Vargas Llosa, of increasing the story's tension to capture the attention of readers and spectators. Another important similarity between the cinematographic adaptation and the novel is Agustín Cabral's physical paralysis as a metaphor of his moral paralysis, after sacrificing his daughter to the dictator.

The adaptation and the novel have considerably different endings. The novel shows scepticism towards the transition to democracy, especially considering that the perpetrators of Trujillo's assassination were as amoral as their leader and that the next president of the Dominican Republic was the opportunistic Joaquín Balaguer, Trujillo's close adviser. The film does not judge Balaguer. It includes photographic archival material from newspapers showing Trujillo's funeral and Balaguer's arrival to power, visual equivalents to the way in which Vargas Llosa likes to take and adapt historical elements and use them as raw material from which to build his novels.

Allusions to Vargas Llosa in other films by Lombardi

In addition to the adaptations of two of Vargas Llosa's novels, Francisco Lombardi is the film director who might be most associated with the novelist, since he has included significant references to Vargas Llosa's novels in other noteworthy films. For example, in *La boca del lobo* (1988), Lombardi examines the behaviour of the Peruvian army during the dirty war in the Andes between the Sendero Luminoso guerrillas and the Peruvian armed forces during the two last decades of the twentieth century. In this film, which was one of the first in Peru to offer a critical assessment of events of the period, the plot foreshadows the feeling of uneasiness within an army that did not know who the enemy was or where it was hidden. The story also hints at the similarities between the coercive techniques used by the terrorist group to force the indigenous population to support their cause and the techniques used by the army to pressure the indigenous communities into revealing the names of the members of Sendero Luminoso. By including a final scene in which cadet Vitín Luna dares Lieutenant Roca to a game of Russian roulette, Lombardi pays homage to Vargas Llosa's *The Green House*, the novel that he was reading at that time. Indeed, Lombardi explains that the Russian roulette scene was not based on Cimino's *The Deer Hunter* (1978):

> That film did not cross my mind. I'd been rereading *The Green House* and so that Russian roulette scene was fresh in my mind. These incidents don't get much publicity but they happen quite often in Peru, especially when two men get drunk and at least one of them is in uniform: they take out a gun and start playing Russian roulette.[14]

It could also be argued that this film was an important influence for Vargas Llosa's *Death in the Andes* (*Lituma en los Andes*, 1993[15]), a novel that portrays extensively the violence permeating Peru's Andean region, resulting from killings perpetrated by the Sendero Luminoso guerrillas. In line with Lombardi's movie, the novel also reflects on the army's difficult and, at times, impossible task of assessing whether the threats are imaginary or real.

Lombardi also adapted Alberto Fuguet's *Tinta Roja* (2000), in which he included several tributes to Vargas Llosa. For example, Lombardi kept Fuguet's choice of name for the main character as Alberto Fernández, which is also the name of the Poet in *The Time of the Hero*. Lombardi and screenwriter, Giovanna Pollarolo, also included in the adaptation additional direct references to Vargas Llosa's narrative that are not in Fuguet's novel. For example, the adaptation bases Faúndez, Fernández's boss in the crime section at the sensational newspaper *El Clamor*, on Becerrita, Vargas Llosa's real-life boss at the newspaper *La Crónica*, as mentioned in *A Fish in the Water: A Memoir* (*El pez en el agua*, 1993[16]). Another such tribute is the praise for Vargas Llosa's *Letters to a Young Novelist* (*Cartas a un joven novelista*, 1997[17]). On his first day at work, Fernández shows up with a copy of this book and Faúndez reads out loud the section of its first letter ('The man who was my papa'), which equates the literary vocation to a type of servitude. Faúndez, sizing up Fernández's personality, begins calling his new employee 'Varguitas', like the character in *Aunt Julia and the Scriptwriter*. The film viewers come to learn that it is an accurate nickname, as Fernández aspires to become a writer and live in Paris, just like Varguitas.

One can speculate whether Lombardi, Alarcón, Fons, Amiel and Luis Llosa adapted works by Mario Vargas Llosa with a sense of reciprocity, given the extent to which Vargas Llosa has paid homage to cinema in his novels, evident in the presence of endless cinematic references, the number of his characters who frequent the movies, and his use of so many narrative techniques that may have been inspired by cinematographic ones. It is striking, too, how often the lives of Vargas Llosa's characters are transcendentally changed after a movie-going experience. In adapting his novels, these directors have contributed, like Vargas Llosa, to an engaging dialogue between storytelling and the visual world of moving images.

NOTES

1. Mario Vargas Llosa. *La casa verde*. Barcelona: Seix Barral, 1966.
2. See Efraín Kristal. *Temptation of the Word: The Novels of Mario Vargas Llosa*. Nashville, Tenn.: Vanderbilt University Press, 1998, p. 50.
3. Mario Vargas Llosa. *Conversación en La Catedral*. Barcelona: Seix Barral, 1969.
4. Mario Vargas Llosa. *Travesuras de la niña mala*. Madrid: Alfaguara, 2006.
5. Mario Vargas Llosa. *Pantaleón y las visitadoras*. Barcelona: Seix Barral, 1973.
6. Mario Vargas Llosa. *La ciudad y los perros*. Barcelona: Seix Barral, 1963.
7. From an unpublished interview with Fernando Carvallo. (Translation Carolina Sitnisky.)
8. Mario Vargas Llosa. *Los cachorros. Pichula Cuéllar*. Barcelona: Editorial Lumen, 1967.
9. Kristal, *Temptation of the Word*, cites Sebastián Salazar Bondy, letter to Mario Vargas Llosa, 6 July 1962, Correspondence, Box 1, Mario Vargas Llosa Papers, Manuscripts Division, Department of Rare Books and Special Collections, Princeton University Library.
10. Mario Vargas Llosa. *La fiesta del Chivo*. Madrid: Alfaguara, 2000.
11. From an unpublished interview with Fernando Carvallo. (Translation Carolina Sitnisky.)

12. Mario Vargas Llosa. *La tía Julia y el escribidor*. Barcelona: Seix Barral, 1977.
13. Peruvian screenwriter Augusto Cabada has collaborated closely with Francisco Lombardi: together they co-wrote *Without Compassion* (1994). He also collaborated with Giovanna Pollarolo, *Fallen from Heaven* (1990). Cabada also wrote the screenplays for Lombardi's *Under the Skin* (1996) and *The Lion's Den* (1988).
14. From an unpublished interview with Fernando Carvallo. (Translation Carolina Sitnisky.)
15. Mario Vargas Llosa. *Lituma en los Andes*. Barcelona: Planeta, 1993.
16. Mario Vargas Llosa. *El pez en el agua. Memorias*. Barcelona: Seix Barral, 1993.
17. Mario Vargas Llosa. *Cartas a un joven novelista*. Barcelona: Planeta, 1997.

15

EFRAÍN KRISTAL AND JOHN KING WITH

MARIO VARGAS LLOSA

An interview

The Feast of the Goat *is a novel in which the personal and the political seem to be inextricably intertwined because you focus on the consequences of a dictatorship in the lives of its victims, years and even decades after the regime has ceased to exist. To what extent did your own feelings about Latin American dictators, and not just Trujillo, the dictator of the Dominican Republic, on which the novel is based, play a role in the conception of this novel?*

I wrote *The Feast of the Goat* not only because of Trujillo, but also because of the dictatorships of my own country, those I had experience of in Peru, the Odría dictatorship, for example, and all the various military dictatorships that we experienced in Latin America since the 1950s. In a way, all these experiences come together in the novel, *The Feast of the Goat*. That being said, the most direct experience that compelled me to write this novel was a stay in the Dominican Republic of eight months in 1975.

Trujillo had been killed many years earlier, but he was still the main topic of conversation among Dominicans of every social class. He was still looming large over the country; sometimes they still spoke of Trujillo with fear. In other cases, they told all kinds of anecdotes, stories, and I heard such incredible things that I started to investigate a little bit, to read the testimonies. My fascination grew, because I think the Trujillo dictatorship was probably the

This interview is a composite of three interviews. The first was held at the Lannan Foundation in New Mexico on 5 April 2006, and conducted in English by Efraín Kristal; the second was held at the University of Warwick's Art Centre on 20 May 2007, and was jointly conducted in English by John King and Efraín Kristal; and the last two questions are excerpted from a dialogue that took place at the Museo de la Nación in Lima on 15 December 2010, when Mario Vargas Llosa returned to Lima from Stockholm after receiving the Nobel Prize. The first is a fragment of a question asked by David Gallagher, who kindly gave his permission for its publication, and the second was asked by Efraín Kristal. William Hendel and Rosvita Rauch transcribed the texts from the English, and John King translated the last excerpt from the Spanish.

emblematic expression of a phenomenon, of a political phenomenon, that almost all Latin America experienced in the twentieth century. Trujillo had all the characteristics of the dictator. He was cruel, he was corrupt, he was ignorant, but he was all this in an extreme form, and he was also an actor. I think this histrionic aspect of the Trujillo dictatorship was the reason why Trujillo was so, let's say, popular – all over the world, because of the incredible extravaganzas that he performed during his thirty-one years in power. I think that it became, in a very sinister way, very attractive to write and to think about this man.

The novel is, I think, faithful to the basic facts of the dictatorship. But it is not a very accurate historical novel; I have taken many liberties. But on the other hand, and without any exaggeration, I was not able to put into the novel many things that did happen during those years, because I think they would have sounded unbelievable to readers. It's a case in which reality transcends art.

Many people, including Carlos Fuentes, have written essays about how you enter into a dialogue with cinematic themes in your early novels. Interestingly, since the 1980s, the references to film seem to be surreptitiously receding and references to the visual arts seem to be appearing. For example, in a novel like In Praise of the Stepmother, *you have many chapters in which you make paintings come alive. In* The Notebooks of Don Rigoberto, *you seem to focus deeply on the paintings of Egon Schiele, and of course, in* The Way to Paradise, *you address a series of paintings by Paul Gauguin. Could you tell us something about this special interest that you have in painting as an inspiration for narrative fiction?*

I still like cinema very much and I am convinced that the influence of the cinema, not only on me, but, I would say, in the modern novel, is really enormous – particularly in the organisation of time. Novels now tell stories much more rapidly than in the past because cinema has accustomed readers to these very rapid changes of time in the story and also in the point of view of the narrator. The novel now moves much more easily because of the education we have received from the way in which films tells stories. But I have always loved painting. After literature, my major enthusiasm in art is probably painting. And for many years, I had the idea to write, drawing on this artistic mode of expression: painting. I didn't want to write about a painter but to put in a novel the process of artistic creation experienced by a painter. My first attempt to do this was a small erotic novel, *In Praise of the Stepmother*, in which there are paintings which play the role of characters. It was an experiment, but after that, in *The Notebooks of Don Rigoberto*, I attempted to do something much more daring, which was to use the case of a painter that I admire very much: Egon Schiele. I wanted his paintings to become an integral part of the narrative.

And I think this is also the case in *The Way to Paradise*, in which Paul Gauguin is an important character, but Gauguin's paintings are even more important to the novel.

I am fascinated by the way paintings always tell stories. Painting is a story, like a film or a novel; a story that you, the spectator, has to decipher, to reconstruct with your imagination. This is what I have been trying to do in these novels.

For many years you had been talking about writing a novel inspired by the French political activist Flora Tristan. When the novel finally came out, you surprised many of us, because that was only half of the story: Gauguin was the other half. When in the process of creating a novel did you feel the necessity to include the life of Gauguin as a counterpoint to the life of Flora Tristan?

That was one of these surprises that I always have while writing a novel. I plan a story very carefully. Sometimes I work for a long time before writing – researching, taking notes – and then, when I start to write, radical and unpredictable changes take place. I suppose the reason is deeply mired in the unconscious. I think the unconscious plays an important role in the creative process.

It's true, that for many years I wanted to write a novel inspired by Flora Tristan – a nineteenth-century French feminist, of Peruvian origins – probably one of the first feminists in the political sense, not only in the intellectual sense. There were others before her, but she was the first to try to create a political organisation to defend a feminist agenda in the nineteenth century. She wrote very interesting books about herself, her struggles, and her political campaigns. But when I started to write the novel, I remembered that in all the biographies of Flora Tristan, there was always mention of her grandson, Paul Gauguin, the painter, a painter I admire very much.

So I started to read biographies of Gauguin to see if there were some links between him and Flora Tristan. And I discovered that, in spite of the fact that Gauguin never knew his grandmother, the character was very similar – the way they obsessed, the way they faced unpopularity. They had this vocation to go against the currents, to rebel against the established order, the established world. Both were revolutionaries, in an anarchistic way, because both were fierce individualists. So I decided to write a novel in which two rebels, the grandmother and the grandson, would appear fighting on different levels of experience – she in politics, in social terms, and he in artistic and aesthetic terms – a battle against everything, against the established order, facing all kinds of prejudices and attacks and frustrations and defeats, without ever being totally defeated. I like the idea of this progression on two different levels of reality: in art and in politics; in social terms, and in purely aesthetic terms. A battle that in spite of the appearances was, in its roots, the same battle: a battle for liberation, for transformation, for more freedom and more justice in the world.

One of the most extraordinary aspects of your writing is your uncanny ability to capture the human voice through writing. When one reads your works of literature, one has the sense of being able to identify even auditory tics in the way your various characters express themselves. To what extent is this something that you bring into the novel – whether in earlier or later periods of the development of the novel – and does it have something to do with your passion for theatre?

When I write stories set in Peru, I use my Peruvian Spanish, despite the fact that I have been living abroad for many years. But I lived in Peru during my childhood and youth, and the kind of Spanish that I learned is deeply rooted within myself. It is always there, so this kind of reference comes very naturally when I write Peruvian stories. It is very different when I write stories that are set in other countries; for example, I remember that was one of the major challenges I faced when I wrote *The War of the End of the World*, which is set in Bahía at the end of the nineteenth century. That's a novel in which the characters speak amongst themselves in Brazilian Portuguese and I was writing the novel in Spanish, so I tried to write in a way in which the Spanish could sound as Portuguese, as Brazilian Portuguese as possible, using words, *Lusitanianisms*. I had more or less the same problem with *The Feast of the Goat*. The Spanish that is spoken in the Dominican Republic is very different from Peruvian Spanish. It is the same Spanish, but with a lot of local nuances. I should add that I don't like folklore. I think folklore is very different from literature, so I don't want the language to become a character, a central theme of a novel. But I try to be a realist. I want the language to transmit or convey the idea of a very concrete place, so in *The Feast of the Goat* I used Dominican expressions, Dominican words.

Do you read some of those texts or dialogues out loud as you are writing the novel?

Yes, I am Flaubertian. Flaubert had this idea of the *mot juste* and he considered that the right word, the *mot juste*, was the word that was accepted by the ear as music, as perfect music. That's why he used to read his manuscripts out loud. If something sounds jarring, then the word is wrong and the idea is wrong because the word doesn't sound right. I follow Flaubert's lesson, but without believing in the *mot juste* as religiously as he did.

Over the decades you have written many literary manifestos; manifestos that, in some cases, have shaped a whole generation of Latin American writers. And yet, over the decades, the positions that you state in these manifestos have changed dramatically. How do you perceive these dramatic changes over the decades in your own views about the relationship between literature and life?

You are right. When I was young, for example, and under the very strong influence of Sartre, I believed in the idea of committed literature, that literature *should be* an artistic or aesthetic object, but also an instrument for producing changes in society and history, to open the minds, the consciousness, of readers to the big problems. At the time, for example, and probably under the influence of Sartre, I was against humour. Not in life, but in literature. I had this absurd idea that humour was incompatible with serious, committed literature. Then I changed completely. I discovered that humour was a fantastic instrument, not only to produce good literature, but also to present certain aspects of the human experience that can only be described and understood that way. That was an important change. I incorporated other kinds of experiences in literature, not only humour but, for example, eroticism. Reading Bataille may have had an effect on me. At a given moment, I started to tell stories that were related to this human experience. Eroticism is the way in which culture, and particularly the arts, enriches life; the sexual life of people and the act of love can become an artistic creation by introducing images and rituals that come from the arts and literature to this human experience. This was new in my literature. I would say also that, at a given moment, it was something that was in the cultural environment. Yes, I think that my idea of literature has changed to the extent that I have been changing. But probably, in the end, all of these changes have not transformed essentially what literature has always meant for me: a very rich way of facing, of fighting the frustration, the suffering, the disappointments that life produces in all human beings. We have one life. We have fantasies and appetites and we have desires that urge us to have a thousand lives in order to take advantage of all the fantastic possibilities that life offers. There is this enormous gap between our human condition and the possibilities that desires and fantasies open to our imagination. I think we have invented something that, in a way, makes us live different lives, to experience adventures of different existences. And I think this has always been literature for me as a writer and, of course, as a reader and has always been constant in what I have tried to do as a writer.

Another word that has been a constant throughout your career as a writer, as a literary critic, and as an analyst of what literature is about is the word 'demons'. And something I find quite striking is that in your early work, the demons were clearly a metaphor. But somehow, in your recent work, and going as far back as Death in the Andes, *the demons seem to be becoming more of a real presence.*

Human beings have a dimension of cruelty, of violence, that sometimes reaches such extremes that it makes you wonder. For a religious believer, this is much easier to explain with the Devil, with Original Sin. Well, I'm not a believer, but this is something which, in countries like Peru, or Latin American countries, appears suddenly, for example, in political circumstances. In Peru we had ten terrible years of terrorism. We used to say that Peru was a very peaceful country, with deep socio-economic problems, of course, but peaceful, because Peruvians are a very peaceful people. And then we had this monstrous violence of terrorism and counter-terrorism which resulted in almost 70,000 disappeared and killed in just ten years. We experienced the extremes, the really monstrous, vertiginous extremes of violence. How a system can produce this monstrosity of brutality, how human beings can reach these horrors is something that I think is always looming in my novels, particularly in the last ten or fifteen years.

In The Bad Girl, *your protagonist, Ricardo Somocurcio, decides to translate the Russian writer, Ivan Bunin. I was wondering how you became interested in Bunin and why he plays such an important role for Ricardo?*

When you write a novel a lot of things happen to you and it's difficult to explain why in a given moment I decided that Ricardo Somocurcio should try to translate literary works. It was something that at a given moment of the novel it seemed to me was possible and even necessary. Ricardo Somocurcio had been studying Russian, first for practical reasons, but then he becomes enthralled with Russian language, culture and literature. At that moment, I remembered the enthusiasm with which I read Ivan Bunin, in French translations in the 1960s. I was fascinated with Ivan Bunin because he is a complex personality. He wrote wonderful stories – also novels – but the short stories are totally apolitical masterworks. But he himself was very political and suffered a lot because of his political convictions. This aspect is, of course, avoided in the novel, because Ricardo Somocurcio is totally apolitical. He doesn't pay any kind of attention to politics. So that's how Ivan Bunin entered into the novel. When I write a novel this is something that happens all the time. In the process of writing the novel, memory works so intensely, giving me material all the time. Things that I had completely forgotten suddenly appear because they can be useful at that moment. And this is a natural process that always fascinates me, but it is not something that I do rationally. It's something that happens. It is the secret part of the personality which is always appearing, not at the beginning, but rather, when I am well advanced into the novel. This is probably the most thrilling aspect of writing a novel.

Ricardo Somocurcio lived in a number of the same cities in which you lived, roughly around the same time.

This is the only autobiographical material in the novel. The love story is imaginary, but is set in countries in which I have lived and during those years in which I have lived there. Peru, Lima, in the 1950s; Paris in the 1960s; London in the 1970s; and Madrid in the 1980s. I think I have been lucky to live in a period in which humanity has had the most extraordinary changes in all aspects of life. In a way, circumstances put me in places in which these changes were happening in a very intense way.

As an author who is published globally, do you think that literature necessarily loses a lot in translation, and how happy have you been with your works that have been translated?

I don't interfere with translators. If they want help in any way, of course I am ready. Sometimes they send me lists of words or expressions, or questions about tricky things in a book and, of course, I answer those queries. But I don't think a writer should try to get a perfect literal translation of what he has written because I don't think it is possible: we are dealing with different languages, different cultures, different minds, different overtones, different nuances. What is very important in a translation is the recreation in the language into which the work is translated, even if there are inaccuracies. If the spirit has been recreated, let's say in French or Italian, I am not worried about little inaccuracies or little changes. The spirit is much more important to me. It is important to read a book without feeling that it is a translation. When I read a translation in Spanish, I would like to feel that this is a book written in Spanish. That is, for me, a very good translation. This past month I have had a very interesting experience. I have been reading *The Odyssey*. Not being able to read classical Greek, I have read different translations in different languages and it is fantastic how the same original can generate translations that can be so different. Just in Spanish I have consulted six different translations, which seem like different books, different stories because of the way in which the book has been translated. And this is the same in the French and English translations I've consulted. The versions are so different. A good translator is not a mechanical instrument that converts a text into another language. No, it is someone who recreates what you have done using his language, and sometimes in a very creative way.

How did you become interested in Roger Casement, the historical character who inspired the protagonist of The Dream of the Celt?

He is a man without any trace of self-interest, without any political or professional ambition. He was extraordinarily generous. He had a set of values that were both very strict and based on solidarity. At the same time, there is the man who appears in the diaries, the mysterious Roger Casement. We do not know how much of himself he puts into these diaries, or whether they were also a fantasy, a fiction through which he attempted to fill the emptiness of his life. What he experienced and witnessed allows us to explore what a human being can become, what it is that lives in the recesses of each of us. Roger Casement never seems different from us. Throughout his entire life, we recognise ourselves in him, and at the same time we are amazed and somewhat horrified to contemplate the depths which human beings can plumb when left unchecked, when they live in a world that assures them impunity for all their actions.

How did you transform Roger Casement, the historical character, into a Mario Vargas Llosa character?

I was faced with a character who was not one but several characters in the same person. What is extraordinary about Roger Casement is that he had many very different facets. He was a British diplomat in Africa who carried out his duties very rigorously. He was often commended, he was decorated by the British government, he was awarded a knighthood as an exemplary diplomat. I think this largely explains the severity of his sentence, because up to that moment he had been an absolutely exemplary British subject. At the same time, he was a man who abhorred colonialism and became an Irish patriot, an Irish nationalist opposed to British subjugation of Ireland, and who conspired against the empire he served as a diplomat. Just here we have two completely contradictory characters at odds with each other. Every account of him states that he was a very refined man in the way he acted, in the way he spoke: he had a horror of vulgarity and never swore. When he was in all-male company and the obscenities and vulgar jokes started flowing, he would take offence and leave the group. And yet, at the same time, we have his diaries that are an homage to crudeness and vulgarity, written in a very extreme way, very coarse and obscene. How, then, to encapsulate all these contradictions in a single human being? Working on Roger Casement, I was often reminded of a famous phrase by Georges Bataille: 'a human being is an abyss where opposites meld into one'. This was certainly true of Roger Casement.

Also, what was very interesting about Roger Casement is that we do not know anything at all about important aspects of his life. There are almost no accounts, for example, of his final months in prison. He was held in complete isolation and there are no traces at all of his time there, apart from letters that were censored before they left the prison. So, what was he thinking, there in prison? What was he feeling, after having been the centre of so much deserved admiration for his campaigns for human rights, for weak and oppressed people, for having been such a brave defender of the indigenous peoples of the Congo and the Amazon? Did he feel that the sky had fallen in, aware that the press had labelled him a degenerate, a pervert? Victorian morality was still firmly in place. So, what did he feel? I had to invent those aspects. There was no historical documentation, and, of course, these were the sections of the novel that took the longest to write. The only reference available to document his final moments is an account by his executioner, Mr Ellis, a local barber who wrote his memoirs just before committing suicide. He states that of all the people who passed through his hands, the bravest and most dignified was Roger Casement. This short sentence was what I worked with to imagine what those final months must have been like, and also his behaviour when faced with that most definitive test: the walk up to the gallows. What fascinated me most about his character is that, in his case, we have a hero who is also human. We have come to expect exemplary heroes who are born heroes and die heroes, with an unbreakable, heroic continuity to their lives. But Roger Casement was nothing like that. He was a hero, of course; he was a man of admirable courage, of extraordinary moral conviction, who had the tenacity to live this secret double life. But he was also a weak person, whose body was sometimes at odds with values he espoused. He evidently could not contain or restrain certain behaviours, and this, I think, is what makes him a tragic hero, a hero who generates discomfort among even those Irish nationalists who would otherwise have identified with him more readily. He's a hero who makes even people who recognise his heroism feel uncomfortable and feel the need to overlook aspects of his personality so that they can respect him more. He is a character who is difficult to accept in his entirety, in his complexity, in his diversity. And I think that it was this difficult, contradictory personality – at once both so compelling and repellent – that made me think about him a great deal, and made me try to imagine him, and which led me, in some way, to invent him.

FURTHER READING

Works by Vargas Llosa are listed by date of publication; critical works are listed alphabetically.

Works by Mario Vargas Llosa in Spanish

Narrative

Los jefes. Barcelona: Editorial Rocas, 1959.
La ciudad y los perros. Barcelona: Seix Barral, 1963.
La casa verde. Barcelona: Seix Barral, 1966.
Los cachorros. Pichula Cuéllar. Barcelona: Editorial Lumen, 1967.
Conversación en La Catedral. Barcelona: Seix Barral, 1969.
Pantaleón y las visitadoras. Barcelona: Seix Barral, 1973.
La tía Julia y el escribidor. Barcelona: Seix Barral, 1977.
La guerra del fin del mundo. Barcelona: Seix Barral, 1981.
Historia de Mayta. Barcelona: Seix Barral, 1984.
¿Quién mató a Palomino Molero? Barcelona: Seix Barral, 1986.
El hablador. Barcelona: Seix Barral, 1987.
Elogio de la madrastra. Barcelona: Tusquets, 1988.
Lituma en los Andes. Barcelona: Planeta, 1993.
Los cuadernos de Don Rigoberto. Madrid: Alfaguara, 1997.
La fiesta del Chivo. Madrid: Alfaguara, 2000.
El paraíso en la otra esquina. Madrid: Alfaguara, 2003.
Travesuras de la niña mala. Madrid: Alfaguara, 2006.
Fonchito y la luna. Lima: Alfaguara Infantil, 2010.
El sueño del celta. Madrid: Alfaguara, 2010.

Drama

La señorita de Tacna. Barcelona: Seix Barral, 1981.
Kathie y el hipopótamo. Barcelona: Seix Barral, 1983.
La Chunga. Barcelona: Seix Barral, 1986.
El loco de los balcones. Barcelona: Seix Barral, 1993.
Ojos bonitos, cuadros feos. Lima: Peisa, 1996.
Teatro. Obra reunida. Madrid: Alfaguara, 2006.
Odiseo y Penélope. Barcelona: Galaxia Gutenberg, 2007.
Al pie del Támesis. Lima: Alfaguara, 2008.
Las mil noches y una noche. Madrid: Alfaguara, 2009.

Essays

Carta de batalla por Tirant lo Blanc. Barcelona: Seix Barral, 1969.
García Márquez. Historia de un deicidio. Barcelona: Seix Barral, 1971.
Historia secreta de una novela. Barcelona: Tusquets, 1971.
La orgía perpetua. Flaubert y Madame Bovary. Barcelona: Seix Barral, 1975.
Entre Sartre y Camus. Río Piedras, Puerto Rico: Huracán, 1981.
Contra viento y marea. Vol. I (1962–72). Barcelona: Seix Barral, 1986.
Contra viento y marea. Vol. II (1972–83). Barcelona: Seix Barral, 1986.
Contra viento y marea. Vol. III (1964–88). Barcelona: Seix Barral, 1990.
La verdad de las mentiras. Ensayos sobre la novela moderna. Barcelona: Seix Barral, 1990.
El pez en el agua. Memorias. Barcelona: Seix Barral, 1993.
Desafíos a la libertad. Madrid: El País, 1994.
La utopía arcaica. José María Arguedas y las ficciones del indigenismo. Mexico City: Fondo de Cultura Económica, 1996.
Cartas a un joven novelista. Barcelona: Planeta, 1997.
Bases para una interpretación de Rubén Darío (tesis universitaria, 1958) Lima: Universidad Nacional Mayor de San Marcos, 2001.
El lenguaje de la pasión. Madrid: Ediciones El País, 2001.
Diario de Irak. Madrid: Aguilar, 2003.
La tentación de lo imposible. Víctor Hugo y Los miserables. Madrid: Alfaguara, 2004.
Diccionario del amante de América Latina. Barcelona, Paidós, 2005.
Israel/Palestina. Paz o guerra santa. Madrid: Aguilar, 2006.
El viaje a la ficción. El mundo de Juan Carlos Onetti. Madrid: Alfaguara, 2008.
Sables y utopías. Visiones de América Latina. Madrid: Aguilar, 2009.
Sueño y realidad de América Latina. Lima: Seix Barral and Pontificia Universidad Católica del Perú, Fondo Editorial, 2010.

Articles

'José María Arguedas'. *El Comercio* (Lima), 4 September 1955.
'José Carlos Mariátegui'. *Cultura Peruana* (Lima), 1956, pp. 93–6.
'Crónica de un viaje a la selva'. *Cultura Peruana* (Lima), 1958, pp. 123.
'Nota sobre César Moro'. *Literatura* (Lima), 1958, p. 1.
'José María Arguedas y el indio'. *Casa de las Américas* (Havana) 4(26), 1964, pp. 139–47.
'Carta a Günter Grass'. *Vuelta* 117, August 1986, pp. 58–60.
'El Inca Garcilaso y la lengua general'. *Letras Libres* 37, January 2002, pp. 28–33.
'Una novela para el siglo XXI'. Prologue to Miguel de Cervantes Saavedra, *Don Quijote de la Mancha. Edición del IV Centenario*. Madrid: Real Academia Española. Asociación de Academias de la Lengua Española, 2004.
'Cien años de soledad. Realidad total, novela total'. *Cuadernos hispanoamericanos* 681, 2007, pp. 9–34.

Works by Mario Vargas Llosa in English translation

Narrative

The Time of the Hero. Trans. Lysander Kemp. New York: Grove Press, 1966. (*La ciudad y los perros*)

The Green House. Trans. Gregory Rabassa. New York: Harper & Row, 1968. (*La casa verde*)

Conversation in The Cathedral. Trans. Gregory Rabassa. New York: Harper & Row, 1974. (*Conversación en La Catedral*)

Captain Pantoja and the Special Service. Trans. Gregory Kolovakos and Ronald Christ. New York: Harper & Row, 1978. (*Pantaleón y las visitadoras*)

The Cubs and Other Stories. Trans. Gregory Kolovakos and Ronald Christ. New York: Harper & Row, 1979. (*Los cachorros*. Also contains 'The leaders', a translation of 'Los jefes'.)

Aunt Julia and the Scriptwriter. Trans. Helen R. Lane. New York: Farrar, Straus and Giroux, 1982. (*La tía Julia y el escribidor*)

The War of the End of the World. Trans. Helen R. Lane. New York: Avon Books, 1985. (*La guerra del fin del mundo*)

The Real Life of Alejandro Mayta. Trans. Alfred Mac Adam. New York: Farrar, Straus and Giroux, 1986. (*Historia de Mayta*)

Who Killed Palomino Molero? Trans. Alfred Mac Adam. New York: Farrar, Straus and Giroux, 1987. (*¿Quién mató a Palomino Molero?*)

The Storyteller. Trans. Helen Lane. New York: Farrar, Straus and Giroux, 1989. (*El hablador*)

In Praise of the Stepmother. Trans. Helen Lane. New York: Farrar, Straus and Giroux, 1990. (*Elogio de la madrastra*)

Death in the Andes. Trans. Edith Grossman. New York: Farrar, Straus and Giroux, 1996. (*Lituma en los Andes*)

The Notebooks of Don Rigoberto. Trans. Edith Grossman. New York: Farrar, Straus and Giroux, 1998. (*Los cuadernos de don Rigoberto*)

The Feast of the Goat. Trans. Edith Grossman. New York: Farrar, Straus and Giroux, 2001. (*La fiesta del Chivo*)

The Way to Paradise. Trans. Natasha Wimmer. New York: Farrar, Straus and Giroux, 2003. (*El paraíso en la otra esquina*)

The Bad Girl. Trans. Edith Grossman. New York: Farrar, Straus and Giroux, 2007. (*Travesuras de la niña mala*)

The Dream of the Celt. Trans. Edith Grossman. New York: Farrar, Straus and Giroux, 2012. (*El sueño del celta*)

Drama

Three Plays: The Young Lady from Tacna. Kathie and the Hippopotamus. La Chunga. Trans. David Graham-Young. London: Faber and Faber, 1990.

Essays

'Primitives and creators'. *The Times Literary Supplement* (London), 14 November 1968, pp. 1287–8.

The Perpetual Orgy: Flaubert and Madame Bovary. Trans. Helen Lane. New York: Farrar, Straus and Giroux, 1986. (*La orgía perpetua. Flaubert y* Madame Bovary)

A Writer's Reality. Ed. and intro. Myron L. Lichtblau. Syracuse University Press, 1991.

'Szyszlo in the labyrinth'. In Mario Vargas Llosa *et al.*, *Fernando de Szyszlo*. Bogotá: Ediciones Alfred Wild, 1991.

A Fish in the Water: A Memoir. Trans. Helen Lane. New York: Farrar, Straus and Giroux, 1994. (*El pez en el agua. Memorias*)

Making Waves. Ed. and trans. John King. London: Faber and Faber, 1996.

Letters to a Young Novelist. Trans. Natasha Wimmer. New York: Farrar, Straus and Giroux, 2002. (*Cartas a un joven novelista*)

The Language of Passion. Trans. Natasha Wimmer. New York: Farrar, Straus and Giroux, 2003. (*El lenguaje de la pasión*)

The Temptation of the Impossible: Victor Hugo and Les Misérables. Trans. John King. Princeton and Oxford: Princeton University Press, 2007. (*La tentación de lo imposible. Víctor Hugo y* Los miserables).

Touchstones: Essays on Literature, Art and Politics. Selected, ed. and trans. John King. London: Faber and Faber, 2007.

Wellsprings. Trans. Kristin Keenan de Cueto and John King. Cambridge, Mass.: Harvard University Press, 2008.

In Praise of Reading and Fiction: The Nobel Lecture. Trans. Edith Grossman. New York: Farrar, Straus and Giroux, 2011.

Selected criticism in English

Alonso, Carlos J. '*La tía Julia y el escribidor*: The Writing Subject's Fantasy of Empowerment'. PMLA, 106, January 1991, pp. 46–59.

Anderson, Benedict. 'El malhadado país'. In Benedict Anderson. *The Spectre of Comparisons: Nationalism, Southeast Asia and the World*. London: Verso, 1998, pp. 333–59.

Boland, Roy. *Mario Vargas Llosa: Oedipus and the 'Papa' State. A Study of Individual and Social Psychology in Mario Vargas Llosa's Novels of Peruvian Reality*. Madrid: Editorial Voz, 1990.

Booker, Keith. *Vargas Llosa among the Postmodernists*. Gainesville: University Press of Florida, 1994.

Castro, Juan E. de and Nicholas Birns, *Vargas Llosa and Latin American Politics*. New York: Palgrave Macmillan, 2010.

Castro-Klaren, Sara. *Understanding Mario Vargas Llosa*. Columbia: University of South Carolina, 1990.

Gerdes, Dick. *Mario Vargas Llosa*. Boston: Twayne Publishers, 1985.

Harss, Luis and Barbara Dohmann. *Into the Mainstream*. New York: Harper & Row, 1967.

Kristal, Efraín. *Temptation of the Word: The Novels of Mario Vargas Llosa*. Nashville, Tenn.: Vanderbilt University Press, 1998.

Martin, Gerald. 'Mario Vargas Llosa: Errant Knight of the Liberal Imagination'. In John King (ed.). *Modern Latin American Fiction*. London: Faber and Faber, 1987, pp. 205–33.

Moses, Michael Valdez. 'Vargas Llosa: Apocalyptic History and the Liberal Perspective'. In *The Novel and the Globalization of Culture*. New York and Oxford: Oxford University Press, 1995, pp. 148–92.

Muñoz, Braulio. *A Storyteller: Mario Vargas Llosa Between Civilization and Barbarism*. Lanham, Md.: Rowman & Littlefield, 2000.

Pamuk, Orhan. 'Mario Vargas Llosa and Third World Literature'. In *Other Colors: Essays and a Story*. New York: Alfred A. Knopf, 2007, pp. 168–73.

Rossman, Charles and Alan Warren Friedman (eds.). *Mario Vargas Llosa. A Collection of Critical Essays*. Austin: University of Texas Press, 1978.

Williams, Raymond Leslie. *Mario Vargas Llosa*. New York: Ungar, 1986.

Zapata, Miguel Angel. *Mario Vargas Llosa and the Persistence of Memory: Celebrating the 40th Anniversary of* La ciudad y los perros (The Time of the Hero) *and other works*. Lima: Universidad Nacional Mayor de San Marcos, and Hempstead, NY: Hofstra University, 2006.

Selected interviews in English

Boland, Roy. 'Interview: A Citizen of the World'. *Island* 58, autumn 1994, pp. 22–7.

Harss, Luis with Barbara Dohmann. 'Mario Vargas Llosa'. In *Into the Mainstream*. New York: Harper & Row, 1966.

Moran, Dominic. 'Interview with Mario Vargas Llosa'. *Hispanic Research Journal: Iberian and Latin American Studies* 7(3), September 2006, pp. 259–73.

Villanueva Chang, Jorge and Jimena Pinilla Cisneros. 'An Interview with Mario Vargas Llosa'. *World Literature Today: A Literary Quarterly of the University of Oklahoma* 76(1), winter 2002, pp. 64–9.

Selected criticism in Spanish and other languages

Angvik, Birge. *La narración como exorcismo. Mario Vargas Llosa, obras (1963–2003)*. Lima: Fondo de Cultura Económica, 2004.

Armas Marcelo, Juan Jesús. *Vargas Llosa. El vicio de escribir*. 2nd ed. Madrid: Alfaguara, 2002.

Bensoussan, Albert (ed.). *Mario Vargas Llosa*. Paris: L'Herne, 2003.

Bernucci, Leopoldo. *Historia de un malentendido. Un estudio transtextual de* La guerra del fin del mundo *de Mario Vargas Llosa*. New York: Peter Lang, 1989.

Boland, Roy. *Una rara comedia. Visión y revisión de las novelas de Mario Vargas Llosa*. New Mexico: Research University Press, 2003.

Boland, Roy and Inger Enkvist. *70 años. Estudios críticos sobre Mario Vargas Llosa*. Sydney: Antípodas, 2006.

Castro-Klaren, Sara. *Mario Vargas Llosa. Análisis introductorio*. Lima: Latinoamericana Editores, 1988.

Cornejo Polar, Antonio. *La novela peruana*. Lima: Horizonte, 1989.

Deffis de Calvo, Emilia I. and Javier Vargas de Luna. *Perú en el espejo de Vargas Llosa*. Puebla: Universidad de las Américas, 2008.

Esteban, Angel and Ana Gallego Cuiñas, *De Gabo a Mario. La estirpe del boom*. Madrid: Espasa Calpe, 2009.

Forgues, Roland. *Mario Vargas Llosa. Etica y creación*. Lima: Universidad Ricardo Palma, Editorial Universitaria, 2009.

Gargurevich, Juan. *Mario Vargas Llosa. Reportero a los quince años*. Lima: Pontificia Universidad Católica del Perú, Fondo Editorial, 2005.

Gladieu, Marie-Madeleine. *Mario Vargas Llosa*. Paris: L'Harmattan, 1989.

Granés, Carlos, *La revancha de la imaginación. Antropología de los procesos de creación. Mario Vargas Llosa y José Alejandro Restrepo*. Madrid: Consejo Superior de Investigaciones Científicas, 2008.

Harss, Luis. 'Juego de espejos en *La Casa Verde*'. In José Miguel Oviedo (ed.). *Mario Vargas Llosa*. Madrid: Taurus, 1982, pp. 143–55.

Iwasaki, Fernando (ed.). *Monográfico Mario Vargas Llosa*. In *Turia* 97–98 (Madrid), March–May 2011, pp. 151–411.

Kobylecka, Ewa. *El tiempo en la novelística de Mario Vargas Llosa*. Pontevedra: Editorial Academia del Hispanismo, 2010.

Loayza, Luis. 'Los personajes de *La Casa Verde*'. *Amaru* (Lima), 1967, p. 1.

Michaud, Stéphane. *De Flora Tristan à Mario Vargas Llosa*. Paris: Presses Sorbonne Nouvelle, 2004.

Oviedo, José Miguel. *Mario Vargas Llosa. La invención de una realidad*. Barcelona: Seix Barral, 1982.

Dossier Vargas Llosa. Lima: Taurus, 2007.

Oviedo, José Miguel (ed.). *Mario Vargas Llosa*. Madrid: Taurus, 1981.

Pacheco, José Emilio. 'Lectura de Vargas Llosa'. *Revista de la Universidad de Mexico* 22, 1968, p. 8.

Rama, Angel. '*La guerra del fin del mundo*. Una obra maestra del fanatismo artístico'. In Saúl Sosnowski and Tomás Eloy Martínez (eds.). *La crítica de la cultura en América Latina*. Caracas: Biblioteca Ayacucho, 1985, pp. 335–63.

Rodríguez Rea, Miguel Angel. *Tras las huellas de un crítico. Mario Vargas Llosa*. Lima: Pontificia Universidad Católica del Perú, 1996.

Saba, Edgara and Alonso Cueto (eds.). *Las guerras de este mundo. Sociedad, poder y ficción en la obra de Mario Vargas Llosa*. Lima: Planeta, 2008.

Salazar Bondy, Sebastián. 'Mario Vargas Llosa y un mundo de rebeldes'. *El Comercio*, 4 October, 1959.

Scheerer, Thomas M. *Mario Vargas Llosa, Leben und Werk: Eine Einführung*. Frankfurt: Suhrkamp, 1991.

Szyszlo, Fernando de, Cueto, Alonso *et al. Mario Vargas Llosa. La libertad y la vida*. Lima: Planeta and Pontificia Universidad Católica del Perú, 2008.

Tiffert Wendorff, Liliana. *Camacho c'est moi: parodia social y géneros literarios en La tía Julia y el escribidor*. Lima: Editorial San Marcos, 2006.

Tusell, Javier. *Retrato de Mario Vargas Llosa*. Barcelona: Círculo de Lectores, 1990.

Urquidi Illanes, Julia. *Lo que Varguitas no dijo*. La Paz: Khana Cruz, 1983.

Vilela Galván, Sergio and Alberto Fuguet. *El cadete Vargas Llosa. La historia oculta tras 'La ciudad y los perros'*. Santiago de Chile: Planeta, 2004.

Williams, Raymond. *Vargas Llosa. Otra historia de un deicidio*. Madrid: Taurus, 2000.

GENERAL INDEX

Alarcón, Sebastián, 200, 202, 203, 210
Allende, Isabel, 79
Amazonian region, Peru, xiv, 19, 27, 30, 31, 32, 36, 49, 52, 55, 74, 80, 82, 83, 130, 135, 141–6, 205, 220
Amiel, Jon, 200, 206–7, 210
anarchism, 67
Anderson, Perry, 8
Andes, Peru, 2, 7, 40, 88, 90–2, 93, 98–100, 138, 154, 156, 162, 190
Apollinaire, Guillaume, 109
Arabian Nights, 187
Arana, Julio, 142
Arequipa, Peru, xiii, 1, 9, 132, 167
Arguedas, José María, 95, 98, 140, 149, 161–2
Asturias, Miguel Angel, 24, 29
Ayala, Francisco, 187

Bachelet, Michelle, 157, 165
Bakhtin, Mikhail, 70, 73, 96
Balaguer, Joaquín, 121, 124, 127, 208–9
Balcells, Carmen, 149
Balzac, Honoré de, 24, 58
Barral, Carlos, 39
Barthes, Roland, 149
Bataille, Georges, 13, 102, 104, 106–10, 112, 160, 190, 216, 219
Belaúnde Terry, Fernando, xiv, xv, 40, 42, 48, 154
Benavides, Oscar R., xiii
Berlin, Isaiah, 5, 69, 153, 166
Betancourt, Rómulo, 116
Biblioteca Breve Prize, xiv
Bildungsroman, 174
Boom (of the Latin American novel), 23, 24, 25, 29, 149, 161
Borges, Jorge Luis, 4, 24, 35, 141, 147, 151, 159, 187

Botero, Fernando, 150, 164
Bretonne, Restif de la, 109
Bunin, Ivan, 138, 217
Bustamante y Rivero, José Luis, xiii

Cabada, Augusto, 211
Cabrera Infante, Guillermo, 24–5
Camus, Albert, 5, 12–13, 64–5, 153, 158
Canova, Antonio, 164
Canudos, 16, 63, 71
Carpentier, Alejo, 24, 149
Carvallo, Fernando, 210
Casa de las Américas, 152
Casement, Roger, 141–6, 147, 157, 160, 218–20
Castro, Fidel, 3, 4–5, 119, 122, 124–5, 152, 156, 204
Catholic Church, 31, 53, 76, 114, 116
Cavafy, Constantine P., 11, 148
Cervantes Prize, xvi
Cervantes, Miguel, 69–70, 105, 178–9
Chávez, Hugo, 156
Chekhov, Anton, 138, 140
chivalric novel, 3, 10, 69–70, 105, 163
Cimino, Michael, 209
Cochabamba, Bolivia, xiii, 9
Cohn, Norman, 68–9
comedy, 49–56, 61, 190
committed literature, 1, 3, 4, 130, 177, 179, 183, 193, 215–16
Complutense University, Madrid, xiv
Conrad, Joseph, 142, 147, 160
Cortázar, Julio, 23, 24, 139, 147
Crítica Española Prize, xiv
Cultura Peruana, xiii
Cunha, Euclides da, 63, 71, 204
Czechoslovakia, invasion of, 4, 152

227

INDEX OF SELECTED FICTIONAL CHARACTERS

INDEX OF SELECTED WORKS BY VARGAS LLOSA

Cambridge Companions to . . .

AUTHORS

TOPICS

Printed in Great Britain
by Amazon.co.uk, Ltd.,
Marston Gate.